BERLIN

BERLIN

CONTENTS

DISCOVER 6

EXPERIENCE 60

NEED TO KNOW 268

Left: Inside the Reichstag dome
Previous page: The monumental Berlin Cathedral
Front cover: The iconic World Clock on Alexanderplatz

DISCOVER

The Mitte district, divided by the Spree

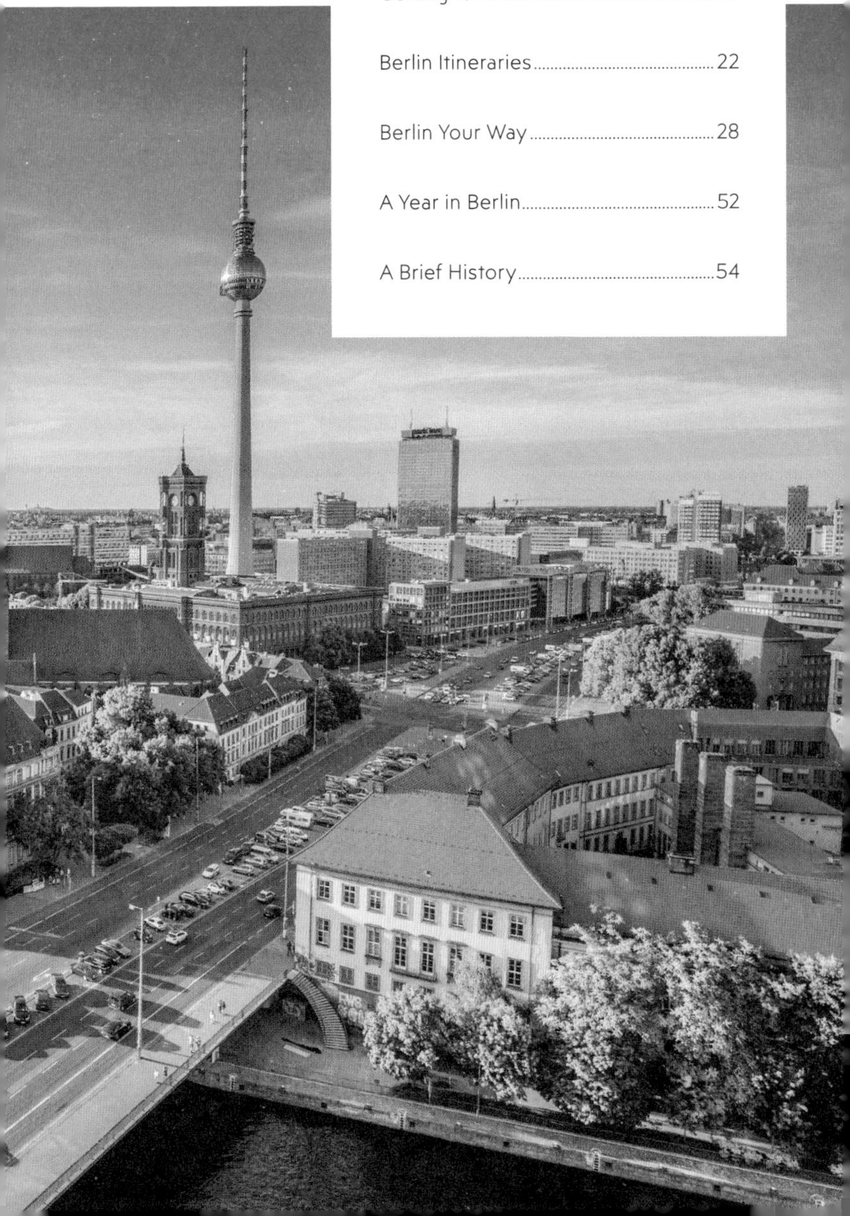

WELCOME TO
BERLIN

There's truly nowhere else like Berlin. Home to a vibrant cultural scene, distinct and diverse neighbourhoods and an intriguing but chequered history, there's enough here to fill the busiest of itineraries. Whatever your dream trip to Berlin includes, this DK travel guide makes the perfect travel companion.

1 Shoppers browsing art and antiques at the famous flea market near Tiergarten.

2 Strolling a tree-lined path in Tiergarten.

3 The Brandenburg Gate bathed by the setting sun.

The former capital of Prussia and a European stronghold, Berlin has long been a city of great significance. Its fascinating and difficult past is still very much evident today, from the disused Gestapo headquarters at the Topography of Terror to Unter den Linden, dotted with glorious Neo-Classical and Baroque buildings. This leafy boulevard is anchored in the west by the magnificent 18th-century Brandenburg Gate, an iconic symbol of reunification. Berliners celebrated the fall of the Berlin Wall here, and its presence today serves as a reminder that the city was divided into East and West for 28 years.

Perhaps an antidote to the darker chapters of its recent history, hedonism thrives here. Berlin is a natural playground for night owls, and it's almost too easy to get lost in its gritty dive bars and infamous clubs. The city charms early birds, too. Browse local flea markets for vintage treasure and swing by Urban Spree's edgy street-art galleries or lean into Berlin's quieter, greener side by following walking trails in sprawling Tiergarten or around Potsdam's regal parks. Natural beauty can also be found at sparkling lake Wannsee, the ideal location for a refreshing swim.

In a city with endless opportunities, it can be hard to know where to start. We've broken down Berlin into easily navigable chapters, with detailed itineraries, expert local knowledge, and comprehensive maps to help plan the perfect trip. Whether you're staying for the weekend or longer, this DK travel guide will ensure that you see the very best of Germany's effervescent capital. Enjoy the book, and enjoy Berlin.

REASONS TO LOVE
BERLIN

As a modern metropolis that has evolved over hundreds of years of change, Berlin is overflowing with things to see and do. Here are the highlights that no visitor should miss.

1 MARKETS

Head outside at the weekend and you'll hear the buzz of flea markets across the city, or follow the aromas of hot food and fresh fruit to one of the many Saturday food markets.

EAST SIDE GALLERY 2

History is everywhere here, but don't miss this heritage-protected stretch of the Berlin Wall *(p151)* – an anarchic collection of street art, graffiti and social commentary.

MUSEUMSINSEL 3

One of Prussia's finest legacies, Museum Island *(p82)* is a UNESCO-heritage ensemble of five museums that takes you on a cultural journey through 2,000 years of world history.

NIGHTLIFE 4

Berlin's reputation as Europe's party capital is well deserved. The city is home to some of the best techno clubs in the world, and its club scene is a huge part of the city's identity.

KAFFEE UND KUCHEN 5

Enjoy the German tradition of coffee and cake with a classic treat like apple strudel. For a more modern alternative, refuel with a barista-grade brew in a cool new coffee shop.

MUSIC

Berlin's unique energy has resulted in a diverse musical heritage. Artists from all over the world – including Iggy Pop and David Bowie – have flocked here for the creative freedom.

KU'DAMM 7

Berlin's best-known boulevard *(p206)* is lined with high-end boutiques, glamorous restaurants and historic cafés. Explore the side streets for local brands and cosy coffee shops.

8 CHEAP STREET EATS

Berlin's cheap eats are legendary. For every new restaurant opening there are several delicious doner kebab and falafel spots. Don't miss out on the city's *Currywurst*.

9 RIVERS AND LAKES

The tranquil canals and meandering rivers that crisscross the city are perfect for a peaceful stroll or a boat ride. Many more scenic stops await outside the city centre.

STREET ART 10

Berlin can sometimes feel like one giant canvas. As well as famous paintings on buildings around the city, you can visit dedicated street art galleries like Urban Spree *(p150)*.

THE REICHSTAG 11

Berlin's official parliamentary building *(p156)* has survived arson, revolution and war, and a tour through its remarkable interior is a fine way to learn about modern German history.

EXPLORE
BERLIN

This guide divides Berlin into nine colour-coded sightseeing areas, as shown on the map below. Find out more about each area on the following pages. For areas beyond the centre see p220.

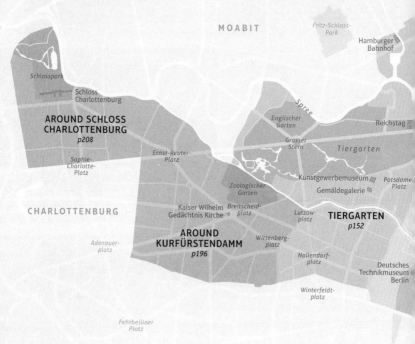

WEDDING

MOABIT

Fritz-Schloss-Park

Hamburger Bahnhof

Schlosspark

Schloss Charlottenburg

Spree

Englischer Garten

Reichstag

AROUND SCHLOSS CHARLOTTENBURG
p208

Grosser Stern

Tiergarten

Ernst-Reuter-Platz

Sophie-Charlotte-Platz

Kunstgewerbemuseum

Potsdamer Platz

Zoologischer Garten

Gemäldegalerie

CHARLOTTENBURG

Kaiser Wilhelm Gedächtnis Kirche

Breitscheid-platz

Lutzow-platz

TIERGARTEN
p152

Adenauer-platz

AROUND KURFÜRSTENDAMM
p196

Wittenberg-platz

Nollendorf-platz

Deutsches Technikmuseum Berlin

Winterfeldt-platz

Fehrbelliner Platz

WILMERSDORF

Volkspark Wilmersdorf

SCHMARGENDORF

FRIEDENAU

0 km   1
0 miles   1

N ↑

GETTING TO KNOW
BERLIN

Berlin is made up of 12 boroughs, which group together the city's 96 *Ortsteile* (localities), each one with its own character, history and highlights. The most famous sights are located in the dozen or so inner-city *Ortsteile*, but there's plenty more to see beyond the centre in Greater Berlin.

PAGE 62

AROUND UNTER DEN LINDEN

Berlin's most stately street still fulfils its role as a connecting artery between Museumsinsel and Tiergarten park. Lined with some of the city's most impressive Baroque and Neo-Classical buildings, this is the boulevard you'll want to stroll down for a first impression of Berlin: both its Prussian past and its cosmopolitan present.

Best for
Impressive architecture

Home to
Zeughaus (DHM)

Experience
Prussian-era architecture and iconic landmarks, plus coffee and cake in Café Einstein

PAGE 82

MUSEUMSINSEL

At the heart of Berlin's central Mitte district is a long island nestled in the tributaries of the winding river Spree. The UNESCO-listed museum complex on this island is one of Berlin's unique landmarks and a must-see for anyone interested in art and history. And when you're done exploring the museums, the rest of the city is only a short walk away.

Best for
Admiring unique art treasures

Home to
Neues Museum, Berliner Dom, Pergamonmuseum

Experience
Antiquities from the Middle East and European artworks from the Middle Ages to the 18th century

PAGE 102

AROUND ALEXANDERPLATZ

Berlin's most famous square is synonymous with one of the city's most iconic landmarks: the GDR-era Fernsehturm. The area is characterized by the dreary and heritage-protected Communist buildings that surround it, but it's still the beating heart of Berlin, a place where locals rush by on their morning commute or meet up with friends over the weekend.

Best for
Historic churches and bustling squares

Home to
Alexanderplatz, Marienkirche

Experience
Shopping at the Alexa Mall then heading to the Fernsehturm to check out the stunning views from the observation deck

PAGE 118

NORTH MITTE AND PRENZLAUER BERG

North of Torstrasse, Mitte begins to morph into the quieter, more residential district of Prenzlauer Berg. Characterized by its leafy, cobbled streets and refurbished *Altbaus* (19th-century tenements), it's one of the most gentrified and laid-back parts of the city. Relatively low on major sights, it offers instead a stream of pleasant cafés and restaurants, independent boutiques and cosy bars. That said, the Berlin Wall Memorial along Bernauer Strasse is a must for all history fans, and there are some interesting and unique museums scattered throughout the area.

Best for
Local bars and cafés

Home to
Gedenkstätte Berliner Mauer, Hamburger Bahnhof

Experience
The view from the area around the Wasserturm, part of a slightly elevated landscaped park that locals use for picnics and hanging out in the summer

FRIEDRICHSHAIN

PAGE 142

Once home to political anarchists, Friedrichshain has largely lost its radical left-wing image in favour of a more cosmopolitan air – especially around the central Boxhagener Platz, which is studded with buzzing cafés and restaurants, edgy bars and indie boutiques. The district is also popular for nightlife, and its Volkspark is one of the city's most popular recreational spots.

Best for
Eating out and nightlife

Home to
Karl-Marx-Allee

Experience
Urban art and nightlife in the RAW Gelände complex

TIERGARTEN

PAGE 152

At the heart of the city, Berlin's central park bursts to life with gardens, meadows and lakes threaded together with pleasant pathways. The wide boulevard Strasse des 17 Juni divides the park through the centre. Its southern fringe borders the bustling areas of Potsdamer Platz and the Kulturforum, while the northern edge runs parallel to important sights like the Reichstag and Regierungsviertel.

Best for
Museums and galleries

Home to
Reichstag, Gemäldegalerie, Potsdamer Platz

Experience
Rowing around the Neuer See in Tiergarten then a drink at one of its excellent beer gardens

$\rightarrow$

PAGE 178

KREUZBERG

One of Berlin's most dynamic districts, Kreuzberg can be divided into several unofficial "zones". The northern section can be considered part of the tourist centre, with several significant sights and museums. The eastern section, sometimes referred to as SO36, is decidedly alternative, with a buzzy nightlife and a large concentration of Turkish and Middle Eastern immigrants. In contrast, Western Kreuzberg is more gentrified, characterized by pleasant cafés, tree-lined avenues and the historical Viktoriapark.

Best for
Bars, clubs, cafés

Home to
Jüdisches Museum Berlin, Deutsches Technikmuseum Berlin

Experience
The lively bars of East Kreuzberg

PAGE 196

AROUND KURFÜRSTENDAMM

Kurfürstendamm – usually abbreviated to the more manageable "Ku'damm" – is a 3.5-km- (2.2-mile-) long boulevard beginning at bustling Breitscheidplatz, close to the historical Zoological Garden and the distinctive Kaiser Wilhelm Memorial Church. It's lined on both sides with a non-stop mix of upscale fashion boutiques and high-street stores, and punctuated throughout with cafés, hotels, restaurants and cultural venues. Its side streets are also well worth exploring.

Best for
Shops, cafés, restaurants

Home to
Kaiser Wilhelm Gedächtnis Kirche

Experience
A shopping tour, followed by coffee and cake at the iconic Romanisches Café

AROUND SCHLOSS CHARLOTTENBURG

One of Berlin's premier royal sights, the Schloss Charlottenburg palace complex is almost a small village in itself. Its ensemble of extravagant Baroque buildings includes former royal apartments, rooms brimming with antique porcelain and prestigious artworks and a mausoleum containing graves of the Hohenzollern family. The landscaped gardens are especially lovely in summer, and there are several other noteworthy museums and attractive buildings in the area.

Best for
Strolling, sightseeing

Home to
Schloss Charlottenburg

Experience
A sunset walk around the manicured palace gardens

1 Rooftop of the Reichstag.

2 The Neues Museum.

3 Riverside park with a view of the Berliner Dom.

4 The goddess of victory atop the Brandenburger Tor.

It can be hard to know where to start in a city overflowing with famous sights and world-class museums. These itineraries pick out the highlights as well as some hidden gems, so you can make the most of even a short trip to Berlin.

5 HOURS

Afternoon

Brimming with Neo-Classical architecture and artwork documenting the history of human creativity, Museumsinsel is a stately place to get a first impression of Berlin. For a taste of all the island has to offer, the Neues Museum (p86) has one of the most wide-ranging exhibitions and will provide plenty of motivation for a return visit. If you can pull yourself away from the treasures of the UNESCO-listed museums, wander over to the Humboldt Forum (p96), a replica of the former Royal Palace that overlooks the Spree. After having lunch at Bistro Lebenswelten, a relaxed café inside the museum, take a walk along Unter den Linden (p72) and admire its multitude of restored historic buildings. Be sure to look into Schinkel's Neue Wache (p69) to see Käthe Kollwitz's poignant sculpture symbolising the suffering of the Berlin people during World War II, and at Bebelplatz (p80) to see Micha Ullman's "Bibliothek", a memorial to the Nazi's 1933 book-burning. Continuing on down Unter den Linden you'll eventually end at the city's most famous icon, the Brandenburger Tor (p78), with your next stop – the Reichstag (p156) – just down the road.

Evening

Taking a tour (prebooking essential) of the magnificent Reichstag in the late afternoon means you can be on its famous domed rooftop for wonderful city views as the sun sets. The venue's Käfer restaurant offers modern and seasonal German cuisine, which you can walk off with a stroll south past the Tiergarten (p171) towards Potsdamer Platz (p162), making a stop at the impressive Holocaust Denkmal (p77).

$\rightarrow$

1 Rotating restaurant in the Fernsehturm.

2 Nikolaikirche, the oldest church in Berlin.

3 Marx and Engels.

4 DDR Museum.

1 DAY

Morning

Start with breakfast at Sphere, the rotating restaurant inside the iconic Fernsehturm *(p106)*, before heading to the viewing platform for panoramic vistas of the city. Back down at ground level, experience the everyday bustle of the city as locals crisscross Alexanderplatz, then enjoy a bit of shopping in one of the many shops that line the square. Much of the surrounding architecture, built in the 1960s by the GDR, is now heritage-listed; don't leave without admiring Walter Womacka's mosaic frieze on the Haus des Lehrers. For further insights into East German life, head to the engaging and highly interactive DDR Museum *(p110)*.

Afternoon

After the DDR Museum, walk along the riverbank past the famous statues of Marx and Engels *(p110)* towards the Nikolaiviertel *(p116)*, which, despite its medieval history and character, was actually reconstructed by the GDR; look out for the tell-tale prefabricated buildings amidst the cobbled lanes and cute houses. As well as a gorgeous Rococo façade and original staircase, the Ephraim-Palais *(p113)* offers interesting exhibitions and good lunch options nearby, such as Zur Gerichtslaube, *(Poststrasse 8)*. Located in a former medieval courthouse, the restaurant is said to be one of the oldest buildings in Berlin. Other local sights and museums worth visiting include the 18th-century Knoblauchhaus *(p112)*, the Nikolaikirche – whose foundations date back to the 13th century – and the fabulous bronze statue of St George fighting the dragon.

Evening

Drop into the Zille Museum *(p112)* to admire some of artist Heinrich Zille's collection of artworks and photographs, before heading to the Zille-Stube for hearty German fare, a beer and a welcoming atmosphere. If you still have some energy, enjoy an evening stroll around the romantic bridges, exquisite buildings and maritime atmosphere of the small but pretty Fischerinsel, one of the earliest settlement areas of Berlin.

←

1 Center am Potsdamer Platz.

2 The Gemäldegalerie.

3 The old belfry of Kaiser Wilhelm Gedächtnis Kirche.

4 Ending the evening at one of the city's traditional pubs.

2 DAYS

Day 1

Morning Start the day in style with breakfast and impressive views of the city at Panoramapunkt on the 25th floor of Kollhoff Tower (p165). From here you can explore the exciting area of Potsdamer Platz (p162), with its many museums, shops and fascinating sights, from modern art installations to original sections of the Berlin Wall outside the S-Bahn entrance – or if you have kids, enjoy a creative session at the LEGOLAND® Discovery Centre (p163). For a quick and healthy lunch, try Weilands Wellfood; for handbrewed coffee and artisan teas with homemade sandwiches, head to THE BARN Café (Alte Potsdamer Str. 5).

Afternoon After lunch, walk across to the Kulturforum (p176), West Berlin's answer to Museumsinsel. The Gemälde-galerie (p158), one of the most comprehensive museums here, is worth a couple of hours to explore. The adjacent Kunstgewerbemuseum (p166) has lots to interest design and fashion fans, while over on nearby Leipziger Platz (p164), adults and kids alike can enjoy the multimedia Spy Museum.

Evening To experience the sophisticated side of Berlin, book dinner at the Michelin-starred FACIL (p172) before attending a concert at the Philharmonie (p166). An evening stroll through the Tiergarten (p171) is a wonderful after-concert activity, or you can continue down Potsdamer Strasse (p169) for some classy cocktails at Victoria Bar.

Day 2

Morning Grab a casual breakfast at one of the hip cafés in the Bikinihaus Mall (p202), after which you can browse local fashion and design boutiques. Cross the street to explore the interiors of the unique and moving Kaiser Wilhelm Gedächtnis Kirche (p200) before hitting the nearby Ku'damm boulevard (p206) for some serious shopping.

Afternoon Head down the stylish side streets north of Ku'damm towards Savignyplatz to enjoy a delicious Italian lunch at Ristorante Aida (Knesebeckstrasse 83). Next, catch a bus or an underground train to the unmissable Charlottenburg Palace (p212), leaving enough time to explore the gorgeous palace grounds; pause in between for some restorative coffee and cake at the Orangerie.

Evening If you have some time left, explore one or more of the palace's nearby museums, which include the Berggruen (p217), the Scharf-Gerstenberg (p216) and the Käthe-Kollwitz-Museum (p216), which celebrates the life and work of this vital German artist. End your day the Berliner's way at the Brauhaus Lemke am Schloss (p214), which offers a solid menu of traditional German dishes and beers.

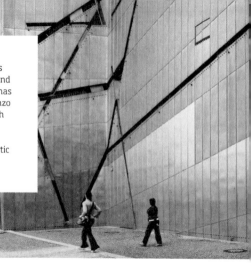

Modern and Postmodern

One of the most famous collections of modern architecture can be found at Potsdamer Platz (p162), which has skyscrapers by architects like Renzo Piano and Frank Gehry. Also worth seeking out is Daniel Libeskind's Jüdisches Museum Berlin, whose jagged, slashed façade and dramatic interior are intended to express notions of violence and absence.

→
Dramatic façade of the Jüdisches Museum Berlin

BERLIN FOR
ARCHITECTURE

Berlin's history is brought to life by an eclectic mix of architecture on display across the city. With stunning buildings and gardens designed by some of the world's most famous architects, the city is overflowing with amazing structures and spaces which make Berlin feel like an open-air art gallery.

TOP 3 GDR SIGHTS

DDR Museum
Find out what East German life was like under the watchful eye of the Stasi (p110).

East Side Gallery
The longest existing stretch of the Berlin Wall doubles as an outdoor gallery (p151), with colourful murals by 118 artists from 21 different countries.

Berlin Wall Memorial
The city's official Berlin Wall Memorial (p123) is dedicated to those killed by the Eastern border guards while trying to escape into West Berlin.

Cold War Era

The former Eastern parts of the city are peppered with blocky GDR-era architecture. The most famous and impressive ensemble is around Alexanderplatz, whose iconic Fernsehturm - along with some of the surrounding prefabricated high-rises (such as the Haus des Lehrers) - was designed by prominent East German architect Hermann Henselmann.

→
GDR-era Haus des Lehrers on Alexanderplatz

Neo-Classical Designs

For decades, Neo-Classical architecture was all the rage in Berlin, and the city centre has many striking examples of this grand and elegant style. Many can be found on Museumsinsel and Unter den Linden, which feature several designs by the prolific Karl Friedrich Schinkel. Of special note are the Konzerthaus *(p74)* on the city's handsome Gendarmenmarkt, and the Neue Wache *(p69)*, designed as a guard house for the Kronprinzenpalais and now home to a World War II memorial.

←

Neo-Classical columns decorating the Neue Wache

KARL FRIEDRICH SCHINKEL

Schinkel was one of the most renowned German architects; even today his work forms an essential element of the architectural landscape of Berlin. For many years Schinkel held a high-profile position in the Prussian Building Ministry. In Berlin and Potsdam he designed several dozen buildings, including palaces, civic buildings and churches, many of which still stand today. He also excelled at painting and even designed scenery for the opera house on Unter den Linden, among others.

A Modern Medieval Quarter

The pretty Nikolaiviertel *(p116)* is the best place to get an idea of how the city used to look, although the area is not as old as it appears. Reconstructed during the 1980s by the GDR, it features cobbled streets and the 13th-century Nikolaikirche, as well as striking examples of Rococo at the Ephraim-Palais, and Baroque at the Knoblauchhaus.

↑ Pretty cobbled streets of Nikolaiviertel

Romanticism

Visit the Alte Nationalgalerie (*p95*) to see Karl Friedrich Schinkel's *Gotischer Dom am Wasser* (1813). In the 19th century, Romanticism turned away from religious themes and instead focused on the natural world and personal expression. This painting by Schinkel is a perfect example, cleaving to the themes of Romanticism with its stormy skies and Gothic setting.

←

Karl Friedrich Schinkel's *Gotischer Dom am Wasser* (1813), Alte Nationalgalerie

BERLIN FOR
ART LOVERS

Alongside a slew of big-hitter institutions such as those on Museumsinsel, visitors to Berlin can find an endless constellation of independent galleries and private collections, showcasing the evolving history of artistic expression.

 INSIDER TIP
Berlin Welcome Card

The Berlin Welcome Card offers discounted access to many of the top museums and galleries in the city. Additionally, the card also provides unlimited access to all public transport.

Die Brücke

Die Brücke (The Bridge) was an artistic movement founded by German Expressionists, who aimed to connect the Neo-Romantic and Expressionist movements. Despite the short existence of the group (1905–13), its members produced many distinctive works in various media. Head to the Brücke Museum in Dahlem to find out more (*p246*).

Street Art

The East Side Gallery *(p151)*, a 1.3-km-(0.8-mile-) long stretch of the Berlin Wall features dozens of political pieces, including Dmitri Vrubel's disturbing depiction of Brezhnev and Honecker kissing (1990). The gallery perfectly captures the non-traditional, often rebellious nature of modern street art.

↑ East Side Gallery, a graffiti-covered stretch of the Berlin Wall

Renaissance

Religious themes were a popular source of inspiration in Renaissance art, which developed in the early 15th century. Donatello's intimate *Pazzi Madonna* (c 1425–30) was a pioneering piece in Renaissance marble relief artworks - make your way to the Bode-Museum *(p94)* on Museumsinsel to see it for yourself.

← Donatello's *Pazzi Madonna* at the Bode-Museum

New Objectivity

Neue Sachlichkeit (New Objectivity) was a reaction to Expressionism, and aimed for as much realism as possible across a variety of disciplines from architecture to painting. Founded by the likes of Otto Dix and George Grosz, the movement originated in Germany in the 1920s. See great works by these artists at the Berlinische Galerie *(Alte Jakobstrasse 124–128)*.

↑ Karl Schmidt-Rottluff exhibit at the Brücke Museum, Dahlem

→ Otto Dix's *The Poet Iwar von Lücken* (1926), Berlinische Galerie

COMMUNITY HISTORY

Berlin's LGBTQ+ legacy extends back to at least 1897, when the first gay magazine, *Der Eigene*, was published and the Scientific-Humanitarian Committee – the first organization in the world to campaign for LGBTQ+ rights – was founded by Magnus Hirschfeld. By the Weimar era *(p57)*, Berlin was known as the Gay Capital of Europe and was home to icons such as actress Marlene Dietrich. Despite the city's liberal history, same-sex marriage wasn't legalized in Germany until 2017.

Costumed participants holding signs at the 41st CSD celebration in Berlin

BERLIN FOR
LGBTQ+
CULTURE

Berlin's prominent LGBTQ+ scene sprung into life in the 19th century, and was immortalized during the Weimar era. Today, the city has the most active LGBTQ+ scene in Germany, with citywide infrastructure, regular events and a distinctive community hub in the scintillating "gaybourhood" of Schöneberg.

Remembering the past

Homosexuality was seen as a capital crime in Nazi Germany, and from 1933 to 1945, around 100,000 gay men were arrested, imprisoned or sent to concentration camps. The Memorial to Homosexuals Persecuted Under Nazism *(p173)* honours their memory. Opened in 2008, it consists of a concrete cube with a window showing two films that alternate biennially – one of two men kissing and one of two women kissing. Across the river from Tiergarten is another monument to the LGBTQ+ community: the Memorial to the First Gay Emancipation Movement. Made up of six calla lily sculptures in rainbow colours, it honours the Scientific-Humanitarian Committee.

↑ Honouring the dead at the Memorial to Homosexuals Persecuted Under Nazism

Berlin Pride

Berlin Pride – also referred to as Christopher Street Day (CSD) – comprises many offshoot events that run parallel to the main, month-long Pride festival, which usually starts at the end of May. These events include a CSD Gala, Kreuzberg Pride, Gay Night at the Zoo, Dyke March, Libertarian CSD and Radical Queer March. Other LGBTQ+ events in the city include Folsom Europe, Hustlaball, Spreewieso Berlin and the Yo!Sissy Queer Music Festival.

> 💬 INSIDER TIP
> ### MonGay Movie Nights
>
> Since 1997, the Kino International cinema (p149) has been playing films with gay and lesbian content every Monday for its MonGay series, all shown in their original version with German subtitles.

↑ Waving the rainbow flag at the Berlin Pride parade

Schöneberg

Berlin has many LGBTQ+ districts, but Schöneberg is special. Just as in the Weimar era, the vibrant centre point of the area is Nollendorfplatz. The local cafés and bars – Café Berio, Osbili, Romeo and Romeo and Prinzknecht – have long catered to the LGBTQ+ clientele that comes there. The world's first LGBTQ+ museum, the Schwules Museum, which opened in 1985, is also here, and showcases the history of the LGBTQ+ rights movement in Germany and Europe. The district also hosts regular events like Folsom Europe and major parts of Pride Week.

↑ The dome of the Nollendorfplatz U-Bahn station lit in rainbow colours

Marvellous Museums

From chatting to robots and sending notes via pneumatic tubes at the Museum for Communication, to deciphering machines and negotiating the laser maze at the Spy Museum, Berlin has plenty to offer. Kids can immerse themselves in German history by enjoying a (virtual) drive in a Trabi at the DDR Museum *(p110)* and make their own physics experiments at the Museum of Technology's Spectrum Centre.

Tin-can telephone
at the Museum für
Kommunikation

BERLIN FOR
FAMILIES

Berlin may be marketed as a youthful and entrepreneurial city, but it's also a fantastic destination for families. It offers a multitude of green spaces and waterways for relaxing between activities, inspiring and interactive museums and plenty of family-friendly restaurants and cafés.

Local Escapes

Wherever you're based in the city, you'll never be far away from one of Berlin's magnificent parks, whether it's the sprawling and central Tiergarten *(p171)*, neighbourhood parks like Volkspark Friedrichshain *(p148)*, or the historical and vast Tempelhofer Feld.

KINDERCAFÉS

Unique to Berlin, *Kindercafés* (children's cafés) were created with both children and parents in mind. They merge safe play areas with a seating area selling drinks and snacks. Many also have information boards on local events and some sell nappies and even second-hand toys and children's clothing.

↑ Ice rink by the town hall and *(inset)* a boat ride on the Spree

Outdoor Fun

Whatever the season, there is always something fun to do outdoors. In summer, enjoy a boat ride along the Spree, a stroll or picnic in one of the city's unique parks, or try your hand at some karaoke in the Mauerpark. In winter lace up your ice-skates and head to one of the many lakes dotted in and around the city, or make use of numerous sledging hills.

Family Favourites

Among the many family attractions in Berlin are two zoos, an aquarium and the legendary LEGOLAND® Discovery Centre *(p163)*. Kids will also love the fast elevator ride up the Fernsehturm *(p106)* for panoramic views of the city and a sweet treat in the revolving restaurant.

↑ Family enjoying a stroll through the Tiergarten park in central Berlin

→

Giraffe made out of Lego bricks at LEGOLAND® Discovery Centre

Global Flavours

Berlin's dining scene reflects its increasingly international population, with a range of cuisines from all around the globe. Dishes such as Japanese sashimi, Korean kimchi and Peruvian ceviche can be found at street food markets such as Markthalle IX and Prenzlauer Berg's Street Food auf Achse. Meanwhile upscale options like Ryōtei 893 and Cocolo (p192) pair contemporary cuisine with swanky interiors.

→

Cheesecake at
Cocolo Ramen
in Kreuzberg

BERLIN FOR
FOODIES

As you would expect from any cosmopolitan capital, Berlin's foodscape is deliciously diverse. Here, casual street vendors and unpretentious pubs rub shoulders with a varied and international selection of mouthwatering mid-range and Michelin-starred restaurants.

Fine Dining

Berlin has a growing number of Michelin-starred restaurants – 23 in total – making the city a top fine-dining destination for avid foodies. Particular highlights include FACIL (p172), Tim Raue, vegetarian showstopper Cookies Cream, and locavore-themed Nobelhart & Schmutzig, which focuses exclusively on ingredients from the Brandenburg region. Head over to any of them to experience some serious culinary fireworks.

←

Chic interior of
Asian-inspired
restaurant Tim Raue

MUST-TRY DISHES

Currywurst
This dish consists of chopped pork sausage and a sauce made of ketchup, Worcestershire sauce and curry powder.

Königsberger Klopse
Mince, onions, eggs, anchovies and flour are cooked in broth and served in a creamy sauce.

Eisbein
The pork knuckle is grilled or boiled and served with potatoes, peas and sauerkraut.

Unique Street Food

A trip to Berlin just wouldn't be complete without sampling the city's original street food. Every neighbourhood has stalls and kiosks selling hearty street food and scrumptious snacks like *Currywurst* (sausage mixed with ketchup and curry powder) and *Bouletten* (meatballs).

Grilled fish at the Sunday market in Mauerpark ↑

WEEKEND FOOD MARKETS

The Saturday food markets are a vital institution in Berlin, serving not only as places to buy fresh, organic produce, but also as meeting points and local hangout spots. Each neighbourhood has at least one major market; some of the best are the ones located at Kollwitzplatz, Boxhagener Platz and Wittenbergplatz.

Customers enjoying Berlin's oldest beer garden, Prater ↑

German Tradition

It may lack the abundant beer-halls of Bavaria, but Berlin certainly pulls its weight when it comes to serving up traditional German food. While the standard pub-style restaurants (*Kneipen*) such as Gaststätte Zur letzten Instanz *(p115)* remain firm favourites, there are also high-end and fusion restaurants carrying German cuisine into new territory.

Classic Beer Gardens

There's nothing quite like enjoying a chilled beer while watching the summer sun filter gently through the leaves of Berlin's copious chestnut and lime (linden) trees. Prenzlauer Berg's Prater is the city's oldest and simplest beer garden, while the Tiergarten's Café am Neuen See is one of the leafiest, with a lake you can row around, a restaurant, a self-service casual food area and a children's play area. Most beer gardens are open from late April until late September, and usually offer some kind of snacks or meals. They generally get lively between 6 and 10pm.

→ Lakeside Café am Neuen See in the Tiergarten

BERLIN FOR
BEER LOVERS

Germany's beer culture is world famous, and these days its golden, frothy Pilsners and tasty wheat and dark beers are joined by an array of craft beers made in local microbreweries, often using traditional techniques.

TOP 3 GERMAN BEER

Hefeweizen
The traditional Bavarian Weizenbier ("wheat beer"). The sweetness of the malted wheat is offset by the high carbonation and low hop bitterness.

Berliner Weissbier
A local variation of Weizenbier, it is often served in a bowl-shaped glass with a lager mixer or sweet syrups to balance out the sour flavour.

Bock
First brewed in the 14th century, this lager now has many variations. The traditional bock is dark in colour and tastes rich and sweet.

Craft Beer
Berlin's growing interest in the craft beer trend is perfectly captured in the cool aesthetic and international clientele of spots such as the Castle Pub in Mitte and Badfish in Prenzlauer Berg.

→ Customers enjoying the cool atmosphere of Kreuzberg's riverbank bars

Craft Breweries

A microbrewery with its own beer garden really takes your experience to the next level, allowing you to enjoy the brewery's home-produced beers at any time of year – whether inside on a cold winter day or out in the summer sun. Eschenbräu in Wedding *(p236)* has a tavern-like interior plus a fairly large outside terrace, and Brauhaus Südstern in Neukölln is a large pub-style space with a beer garden that backs onto a park.

←

Berliner Pilsners, made at the Berliner-Kindl-Schultheiss brewery

---

DRINK

Herman

This intimate bar has an impressive selection of beers, many from the owner's homeland of Belgium. Be warned: many of them are incredibly strong.

☎ 30 44312854
📍 Schönhauser Allee 173

Hops & Barley

A down-to-earth and friendly pub, with home-brewed beers, simple snacks and a friendly, mixed crowd.

📍 Wühlischstrasse 22/23 🌐 hopsand barley-berlin.de

↑ Trendy gastropub Salt 'n' Bone in Prenzlauer Berg

Classic Kneipen

With all the hipster bars and cafés in the city, Berlin's *Kneipen* (traditional pubs) often get overlooked, which is a shame as there are some very fine establishments that combine an excellent beer selection with warm service and a friendly, local ambience. Dating from 1913, Prenzlauer Berg's Metzer Eck is one of the oldest family-run spots in the city. Leuchtturm in Schöneberg is similarly atmospheric, attracting a mixed but mostly local clientele to its 19th-century interior: German filmmaker Wim Wenders is said to drop by from time to time.

Luxury Fashion

Kurfürstendamm is the boulevard to head to for Chanel, Louis Vuitton, Prada and Gucci. Intersecting Tauentzienstrasse has a swish Peek & Cloppenburg, several upscale stores such as Swarovski and Montblanc, and the renowned KaDeWe department store, which has a fabulous gourmet food area on the sixth floor. Friedrichstrasse's Galerie Lafayette also has a selection of upscale haute couture, including Dior and Miu Miu.

← KaDeWe, the second-largest department store in Europe

BERLIN FOR
SHOPPERS

Berlin offers the best of both worlds when it comes to retail therapy. Splash the cash at luxury fashion stores or hunt for treasure at local flea markets. Browsing the city's vintage stores is also a fantastic and sustainable way to trial new styles.

↓ Mauerpark flea market in northern Berlin

Local Markets

Most neighbourhoods offer a large market of some kind, usually food on Saturdays and a flea market on Sundays. The food markets at Kollwitzplatz (Prenzlauer Berg) and Boxhagener Platz (Friedrichshain) are especially popular, as are the Mauerpark flea market and Arkonaplatz antiques market.

Mitte's High-End Boutiques

Mitte remains the home to Berlin's most cutting-edge designers. Knitwear veteran Claudia Skoda, jewellery designer Esther Perbandt and Wibke Deertz (A D Deertz) display their designs along the district's boutique-lined side streets.

←

Suitsupply, a fashionable men's clothing store

CHRISTMAS MARKETS

Berlin fights the winter gloom with festive Christmas Markets. They're all slightly different, ranging from the intimate to the spectacular. All offer *Glühwein* (mulled wine), snacks and an assortment of gifts and entertainment.

Vintage

Vintage stores are a staple in Berlin, and there's at least one great one in most neighbourhoods. The hugely popular PICKNWEIGHT chain – where you pay by weight – has stores in several areas, and also runs Mitte's Made in Berlin and Garage in Schöneberg. Friedrichshain's Humana Kaufhaus is a one-stop shop for all ages and styles.

→

Vintage tableware *(inset)* and clothes on sale in Berlin

Culture Lovers

Mainstream galleries such as the Akademie der Künste *(p73)* have regular free entry options, while many of the independent galleries – especially those around August-strasse – are usually free. For music lovers, the Philharmonie *(p166)* and Marienkirche *(p108)* have free weekly lunchtime concerts, and Marienkirche offers regular free organ recitals. Jazz fans can enjoy cost-free, high-quality jam sessions at Mitte's B-Flat club.

$\longrightarrow$

Elyas M Barek reads the tone poem *Emil and the Detectives* at the Philharmonie

BERLIN
ON A BUDGET

Berlin is impressively affordable compared to many western European capitals, and food, beer, accommodation and cultural events can all be enjoyed on a modest budget – some even for free.

Cycling on one of the many paths ↑

On Your Bike

With more than 1,100 km (685 miles) of bike lanes criss-crossing the city, Berlin is a cyclist's paradise. Hiring a bike is an excellent way to experience the city like a local and soak in the key sights without breaking the bank. Call a Bike *(callabike.de)* offers reasonable rates *(p275)*.

> **INSIDER TIP**
> **Bus Routes**
>
> The 100, 200 and 300 buses carry passengers past major city sights such as the Fernsehturm and Brandenburger Tor – all for the price of a bus ticket. Buy a day ticket to hop on and off.

STAY

Circus Hostel
Centrally located budget boutique hotel.

📍M3 🏠Weinbergsweg 1A, North Mitte 🌐circus-berlin.de

€€€

EastSeven
Small indie hostel with a relaxed vibe.

📍N2 🏠Schwedter Strasse 7, Prenzlauer Berg 🌐eastseven.de

€€€

Historical Insights

In Berlin, centuries of fascinating history is free to explore. Iconic sights like the Brandenburg Gate and the Reichstag cost nothing to visit; nor do major wartime and GDR-era sights such as the poignant Holocaust Memorial, the Topography of Terror *(p190)*, the Berlin Wall Memorial *(p122)* and the unmissable East Side Gallery *(p151)*.

← Sun peeking through Brandenburger Tor on Pariser Platz

Park Secrets

Berlin's city parks offer not only open spaces for walks, picnics and sunbathing, but also insights into local history. Mauerpark *(p234)* contains some remnants of the Berlin Wall, while Tempelhofer Feld's former airport buildings *(p193)* have plenty of relics from the Third Reich and Cold War eras.

↑ Street entertainers at Mauerpark

Local Parks

Every Berlin neighbourhood has its own *Volkspark* (people's park), which are much loved and well used by locals. Each has its own style and character: Volkspark Friedrichshain *(p148)*, for example, has volleyball and tennis courts, GDR-era memorials and a beautiful fountain covered in fairy-tale statues.

←

Märchenbrunnen, the fairy-tale fountain in Volkspark Friedrichshain

BERLIN FOR
GREEN SPACES

Berlin has an unfair reputation for being industrial and grey, but in reality it's bursting with life and colour thanks to a variety of beautiful green spaces – not least the sprawling, sight-studded Grunewald forest in the southeast – as well as numerous waterways and abundant lakes.

TOP 3
BERLIN LAKES

Strandbad Wannsee
With a sweeping 1.2-km (0.7-mile) beach full of white sand from the Baltic, wicker chairs and 1920s architecture, this lake *(p240)* is a classic summer destination.

Müggelsee
Berlin's largest lake *(p232)* has a beach offering volleyball, a playground and a large, shallow water area that's especially good for kids and families.

Liepnitzsee
Further afield, this lake requires a bit more effort to get to, and has no facilities, but it's popular for its tranquil atmosphere and clean water.

Boats cruising along a peaceful stretch of the Spree river ↓

Vibrant Gardens

The city's gardens come into their own in spring, but can be enjoyed at any time of year. The Botanischer Garten in Dahlem *(p248)* is the big hitter, with a year-round schedule of events, and tropical greenhouses to enjoy in colder months. In the east, the Gärten der Welt offers an array of themed gardens and a Chinese tea pavilion.

$\longrightarrow$

Plants and colourful flowers *(inset)* in Dahlem's Botanischer Garten

Winding Waterways

Meandering through the city are Berlin's main rivers, the Spree and the Havel, plus a vast network of canals. In fact, Berlin has more bridges than Venice. Home to a vibrant boating scene, these waterways are also a haven for nature lovers, offering miles of riverside strolling within easy striking distance of the city centre.

Pop Concerts

Most of the big pop and rock acts pass through Berlin on their European tours and there are several exciting venues where you can catch them. The most central is the Uber Arena (formerly the Mercedes-Benz Arena) in Friedrichshain, which hosts a mix of German and international stars, while the tent-shaped Tempodrom is one of the city's most popular and idiosyncratic venues.

South African-German singer Howard Carpendale performing at the Uber Arena

BERLIN FOR
MUSIC LOVERS

Berlin's varied music scene is world famous. With everything from classical performances and pop concerts to a regular calendar of indie and alternative live acts, this city really runs the gamut. Whether you wish to dance to techno or sing the blues, you'll find every genre has a home in Berlin.

Inspiring Classical Music

For classical music connoisseurs, and anyone who wants to experience the best of Berlin, a concert at a grand, traditional venue such as the Konzerthaus (p74) will show you why Berlin is one of Europe's leading classical music destinations.

↑ The Berlin Philharmonic at Musikfest Berlin, a classical music festival

Indie Music

Berlin is a magnet for all forms of alternative culture, and music is no exception. Here you can find an array of local, national and global indie stars at cool clubs across the city, including punk favourite SO36 in Kreuzberg *(p189)*. There's also a collection of venues – Cassiopeia, Astra, Suicide Circus – at Friedrichshain's RAW Gelände complex *(p150)*.

←

Lido, a popular alternative music venue in Kreuzberg

BOWIE IN BERLIN

David Bowie spent three years (1976–9) in Schöneberg, during which time he produced albums *Low* and *Heroes* at the famous Hansa Studios *(p189)*, worked with renowned producer Brian Eno, and hung out at hotspots such as SO36 *(p189)* and the Paris Bar. A plaque at his former home *(155 Haupstrasse)* pays tribute to his time here.

Jazz

Berlin's jazz scene may not get much press, but locals can tell you it remains an absolutely integral part of the city's musical landscape. Long-standing traditional jazz venues such as A-Trane, Quasimodo and B-Flat offer up consistently high-quality line-ups of international and local players. There is also a slew of underground and alternative venues where musicians (both German and global) fuse jazz with soul, pop, rock and electronica. Jazz-themed events take place all year round, culminating in a world-renowned jazz festival – Jazzfest Berlin – each November.

↑ Jazz musicians performing at Quasimodo *(inset)* and Jazzfest Berlin

Berlin by Bike

Berlin is one of Europe's great cycling cities, with over 900 km (550 miles) of bike routes. The inner city is crisscrossed with bike lanes (*Fahrradwege*), making it ideal for sightseeing on two wheels. Outside the centre, there are marked routes that run along the Panke river, around the Tegeler See, through the Grunewald forest and even along the former Berlin Wall (*p51*). Highly recommended is the 28-km (17-mile) Wannsee route RR1, one of the longest and most scenic cycling trails in Berlin. Starting at Schlossplatz, it winds through the city's southeastern suburbs, ending at the historic Gleinicker Brücke, or the "Bridge of Spies".

BERLIN FOR
OUTDOOR
ACTIVITIES

Although Berlin is known for its vibrant cultural scene, it's also a great place to enjoy the outdoors. From fun and frivolous to downright quirky, the city offers an impressive spread of outdoor pursuits to get your adrenaline pumping.

On the Water

Berlin's lakes, such as Wannsee (*p240*) in the West and Müggelsee (*p232*) in the East, are ideal for watersports, with options to sail yachts, rent motorboats or try waterskiing. Insel der Jugend has pedalos and rowing boats for hire, while StandUpClub Berlin (*standupclub.de*) offers SUP lessons. Wannsee's Water Sports Center Berlin (*segelschule-wannsee.de*) also has various courses.

Sailing boats by the Grunewaldturm, on the scenic Wannsee

One of Germany's most famous landmarks, the majestic Brandenburg Gate

TOP 3 CYCLE RENTAL COMPANIES

Fat Tire Bike Rentals
Reserve a bike online, pick it up and off you go *(fattiretours. com/berlin)*.

Berlin on Bike
Choose from a range of themed tours, or hire a bike and explore on your own *(berlinonbike.de)*.

Berlin Take a Bike
Conveniently located on the Wall Cycle Path *(takeabike.de)*.

Hiking Trails

Strike out in pretty much any direction and within an hour you'll be in the rural environs of Brandenburg. Here, the Wuhletal hiking trail winds its way south from Eichepark to Köpenick S-Bahn station via the Wuhle river valley and various pleasant meadows and parks. The Havel Heights Trail (Havelhöhenweg) runs along the Havel from Pichelsberg through Grunewald to the Strandbad Wannsee. The Panke Hiking trail starts at Bernau in Brandenburg and ends in the city centre, taking in Alt-Lübars (the oldest village in Berlin), Schloss Tegel *(p237)* and the Lübarser Felder nature reserve, where you can see water buffaloes.

→ The beautiful canopy walkway near Beelitz, on the outskirts of Berlin

Daredevil Pursuits

Berlin is a playground for the adventurous. Options include zipping through Berlin's streets in a mini Hot Rod as part of a guided tour *(hotrod.berlin)*, gliding over the city in the iconic Die Welt helium balloon *(air-service-berlin.de)* or tackling a high-ropes course at MountMitte *(beachmitte.de)*.

→ The landmark Die Welt balloon soaring above the city

The Story of Berlin

For an overview of the city's 800-year history, head to the Berlin Story Bunker (p186). Another must-visit is the Jewish Museum (p182), which documents the integration and eventual destruction of the city's Jewish population. The Märkisches Museum (p98) is also worth a visit for its collection of local artifacts.

←

The interactive Family Album collection at the Jewish Museum

BERLIN FOR
HISTORY BUFFS

Home to Prussian palaces, Soviet architecture, monuments, and of course the infamous wall that once divided the East and West, Berlin's turbulent and fascinating history continues to draw visitors back time and time again. Nowhere else seems to offer such an insight into the events of the past.

GDR History

Traces of the GDR (German Democratic Republic) can be seen everywhere in the city. The DDR Museum (p110) offers a look at East German life, with exhibits spanning the methods of the secret police, a prison cell and a reconstructed apartment. To see the Berlin Wall, visit the East Side Gallery (p151), which features murals from 118 artists. A more historical experience can be had at the Berlin Wall Memorial (p122), which is packed with installations and stories of daring escapes and tragic deaths.

Prussian Capital

The Hohenzollerns ruled Berlin, Prussia and eventually Germany for over 500 years until the end of World War I, and transformed Berlin from a humble backwater to a cosmopolitan European capital. They created many of the city's grand sights and cultural institutions, such as Unter den Linden, Tiergarten and Schloss Charlottenburg. They also built most of Museumsinsel, the Berliner Dom, the Rotes Rathaus and the Reichstag, among others. The most famous Hohenzollern building *(p96)* is the Stadtschloss (City Palace), a reconstruction of which was opened in 2021.

→ Visitors at the Charlottenburg Palace, a Berlin landmark

THE BERLIN WALL TRAIL

Construction of the Mauerweg (Berlin Wall Trail) began in 2002 and was completed in 2006. It traces the course of the former GDR border fortifications encircling West Berlin for around 160 km (100 miles). The trail can be hiked or cycled, either in its totality, or by choosing one or more of its 14 sections. Along the way there are stretches of natural beauty, memorials to those who perished at the Wall and information points with other interesting facts. The path also runs across Mauerpark *(p234)*, which was originally part of the Berlin Wall.

↑ More than 100 graffiti paintings *(inset)* cover the East Side Gallery

A YEAR IN
BERLIN

JANUARY

△ **International Green Week** (mid-late Jan).
Food products, farming concepts and a colourful
flower hall are on show at this consumer fair.

Days of Dance Berlin (first two weeks in Jan).
At this contemporary dance festival, up-and-
coming choreographers and local dancers
perform at Sophiensaele, Sophienstrasse 18.

FEBRUARY

Mercedes-Benz Fashion Week (mid-Jan).
Berlin's premier winter fashion event is held
at various locations throughout the city.

△ **Berlinale** (mid–end Feb). Various venues join
in the third-largest film festival in the world.

MAY

Re:publica (first or second week in May).
One of the world's largest conferences on
digital culture is held at STATION Berlin.

△ **Carnival of Cultures** (Whitsun weekend,
exact date varies). For three days, the streets
of Kreuzberg come alive with song and dance
displays celebrating multicultural Berlin.

JUNE

△ **Fête de la Musique** (third Sun in Jun).
Local bands and visiting artists from across
Europe play at both indoor and outdoor
venues all over the city.

SEPTEMBER

Berlin Art Week (mid–end Sep).
International and local artists of all styles
and media are exhibited in hundreds of
galleries across the city.

△ **BMW Berlin Marathon** (third Sun in Sep).
This international event attracts thousands
of runners and brings the city's traffic to a
halt for several hours.

OCTOBER

Tag der Deutschen Einheit (3 Oct). Berlin
celebrates the reunification of Germany with
a street festival at the Brandenburg Gate.

△ **Festival of Lights** (early–mid-Oct). Dozens of
modern and historical buildings are illuminated
with magnificent light displays.

MARCH

△ **MaerzMusik** *(mid–end Mar)*. A festival for contemporary music, held at Haus der Berliner Festspiele, Schaperstrasse 24.

Festtage *(last week in Mar)*. A series of popular concerts and operas performed by world-class musicians at Staatsoper and Philharmonie.

APRIL

△ **Britzer Baumblüte** *(Apr–May)*. A month-long spring festival organized in Britz, a suburb in the south of the city famous for its beautiful gardens.

JULY

△ **Classic Open Air** *(early–mid Jul)*. Enjoy some outdoor classical music at the Konzerthaus Berlin.

Christopher Street Day *(third or fourth Sat of Jul)*. Berlin's main LGBTQ+ pride event is celebrated with a parade around the Ku'damm and many other events across the city.

AUGUST

△ **Tanz im August** *(Aug–Sep)*. Dance performances featuring companies and artists from all over the world are held across the city.

Lange Nacht der Museen *(third or fourth Sat in Aug)*. Over 100 museums stay open until midnight or later.

NOVEMBER

△ **Jazzfest Berlin** *(first week in Nov)*. Experience a world-renowned jazz festival at multiple venues across the city.

Interfilm *(mid–end Nov)*. A festival for short films that attracts cinephiles from all over the world.

DECEMBER

△ **Weihnachtsmärkte** *(throughout Dec)*. Fairs and festive Christmas gift stalls pop up all over the city to dispel the winter gloom.

Silvester *(31 Dec)*. A massive, open-air New Year's Eve party on Strasse des 17 Juni.

1

A BRIEF
HISTORY

Over the course of eight centuries, Berlin grew from fishing village to successful trading city and capital of Prussia. Having survived two world wars and over four decades of internal division, it is now the capital of one of the world's leading nations.

From Village to Prosperous Town

Berlin's written history began in the early 13th century, when the twin settlements of Berlin and Cölln grew up on opposite banks of the Spree river, around what is now the Nikolaiviertel (*p116*). Trading in fish, rye and timber, the towns formed an alliance in 1307, becoming Berlin-Cölln, a deal celebrated by the construction of a joint town hall.

The Hohenzollern Era

In 1411, Friedrich von Hohenzollern became the town's special protector, inaugurating what would become a 500-year rule for

1 A woodcut of the Stadtschloss palace. ↑

2 Friedrich Wilhelm (the Great Elector), ruler of Brandenburg-Prussia from 1640 to 1688.

3 Friedrich II (Frederick the Great) King of Prussia from 1740 to 1786.

4 August Borsig's locomotive factory.

Timeline of events

1244
First written reference to the settlement of Berlin.

1307
Signing of the treaty between Cölln and Berlin.

1415
Friedrich von Hohenzollern appointed Elector of Brandenburg.

1432
Unification of Cölln and Berlin.

1618–48
Thirty Years' War between Habsburg states and other European countries.

the House of Hohenzollern. By 1443, Elector Friedrich II had begun construction of the town's first castle, the future Stadtschloss, which became the Elector's official residence in 1451. The city grew and thrived during the 15th and 16th centuries, but was also decimated by successive epidemics of the bubonic plague and the Thirty Years' War (1618–48), which turned the whole of the Holy Roman Empire into a bloody battlefield. Friedrich Wilhelm von Hohenzollern (later known as the Great Elector; p215) ascended the Brandenburg throne in 1640, ushering in a period of unprecedented growth.

Beginnings of the Modern City

Despite Napoleon's defeat of Prussia in 1806 and a subsequent two-year occupation of the city, Berlin grew exponentially throughout the 18th and 19th centuries. A slew of significant rulers, including the "Soldier-King" Friedrich Wilhelm I (1713–40) and Friedrich II (Frederick the Great, 1740–86), oversaw the city's transformation into a sophisticated cultural centre. By the early 19th century Prussia was industrialising rapidly, with August Borsig opening his locomotive factory in Berlin in 1837.

> **PEACE OF WESTPHALIA**
>
> After four years of negotiations, the German states, France and Sweden signed the Peace of Westphalia treaties, ending the Thirty Years' War. Germany lost territory, but a new political system emerged, with German princes enjoying complete political independence under a weakened emperor and pope.

1685
Edict of Potsdam allows large numbers of French Huguenot refugees to settle in Berlin.

1791
Brandenburger Tor completed.

1701
Coronation of Friedrich III of Brandenburg as Friedrich I, the first king of Prussia.

1806
Beginning of the two-year French occupation of Berlin.

1806–14
Quadriga chariot atop the Brandenburger Tor is on display in Paris.

Building an Empire

Otto von Bismarck was appointed Chancellor under Wilhelm I, with a foreign policy to install Prussia in Austria's place at the head of all German-speaking states. Over the next six years, Prussia declared war on Denmark, Austria and France, acquiring and annexing various new territories. Bismarck's next move was the proclamation of a German Empire on 18 January 1871, with Berlin as its capital and King Wilhelm I as Kaiser (Emperor). Abolition of trade barriers and massive reparations paid by France after her defeat in the Franco-Prussian war (1870–71) led Berlin to enter another period of rapid industrial growth, accompanied by a population explosion (from 300,000 inhabitants in 1850 to 1.9 million by 1900).

Triumph and Disaster

The late 19th century saw an explosion of scientific invention in Berlin, including the completion of a new sewage system in 1876, which dramatically improved public health. By 1879 electric lamps lit the streets and in 1881 the first telephones were installed. A year later, the first urban train line, the S-Bahn,

↑ The first German telephone, by Siemens & Halske (1878)

Timeline of events

1844

Opening of the Berlin Zoo (Zoologischer Garten).

1870–71

Franco-Prussian War. Annexation of French territories.

1871

Unification of Germany; Berlin becomes the capital of the German Empire.

1882

Opening of the S-Bahn, the first urban train line.

was opened. Berlin's booming cultural life was headed by such notable figures as writer Theodor Fontane and artists Max Liebermann (p245) and Käthe Kollwitz (p216). As the city prospered, however, political developments throughout Europe were moving towards the stalemate of 1914. Initially, the outbreak of World War I had little effect on life in Berlin, but the subsequent famine, strikes and total German defeat led to the November Revolution in 1918, and the abdication of Kaiser Wilhelm II.

The Weimar Republic

A new constitution was signed in the town of Weimar in 1919, but throughout the subsequent "Weimar years" (1919–33) Germany struggled with political and economic instability. In Berlin, urban reform dramatically increased the size of the city, and the population swelled to 3.8 million. The city fell on hard times due to rising unemployment and hyperinflation, but despite this Berlin became the centre of a lively cultural scene. Leading figures included Max Reinhardt (p126) and Bertolt Brecht, and institutions like the Berlin Philharmonic (p166) and UFA film studio (p265) gained worldwide fame.

1 Otto von Bismarck, Prussian statesman and the first Chancellor of the German Empire.

2 *The Artist's Studio*, Max Liebermann, 1902.

3 Playwright and director Bertolt Brecht in his studio, with his colleague Elisabeth Hauptmann.

1897

Berlin's Institute for the Science of Sexuality is the world's first gay-rights organization to lobby for the legal rights of gay, lesbian and trans-gender people.

1914–18

World War I devastates Europe; Allied victory leads to the fall of the German Empire.

1920

The Greater Berlin Act expands the size of the city, making it the third largest in the world.

1918

November Revolution and the abdication of Kaiser Wilhelm II.

The Third Reich and World War II

The world stock market crash of 1929 and the ensuing
Depression put the German government under great pressure,
paving the way for extremist politicians and the appointment
of Adolf Hitler as Chancellor in 1933. The Reichstag fire in
February of that year was used as a pretext to arrest Communist
and liberal opponents, and, by March 1933, Hitler's Nazi
(National Socialist German Workers) Party was in control.
Hitler's invasion of Poland in 1939 signalled the start of World
War II, and in January 1942, the systematic extermination of all
Jewish Europeans began. Finally, after years of bitter warfare,
the tide began to turn against the Germans. In April 1945, more
than two million Soviet soldiers invaded Berlin, where they
found the populace starving and the city lying in ruins. Hitler
died by suicide shortly after and Germany conceded defeat.

Divided City and Reunification

At the Potsdam Conference of 1945 *(p262)*, Berlin was divided
into four sectors, occupied by Soviet, US, British and French
troops. This put the city at the centre of the Cold War (1947–91),

↑ An Allied soldier finds the
head of a broken Hitler
statue in the ruins of Berlin.

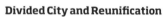

Timeline of events

1933

Hitler accedes
to power.

1939–45

World War II; much of
Berlin damaged or
destroyed during air
raids and the Battle
of Berlin.

1961

Construction of the
Berlin Wall begins,
with the installation
of barbed-wire fencing.

1963

US President John F Kennedy
proclaims "*Ich bin ein
Berliner*" ("I am a Berliner")
in a speech in Schöneberg.

between the Soviet Union and the US and NATO. Tensions increased in 1949 with the birth of two German states: the Federal Republic of Germany in the west, and the German Democratic Republic (GDR) in the east. East Berlin became the capital of the GDR, and the isolated West Berlin remained a separate enclave of western Germany in the heart of the Communist eastern state. It was eventually enclosed by the Berlin Wall for 28 years, and GDR authorities shot at any refugees attempting to cross the border. The political changes that swept across Eastern Europe in 1989 led to the fall of the Wall, and on 3 October 1990 Germany was officially reunified.

Berlin Today

Berlin's cutting-edge cultural scene attracts visitors from all over the world. People are also drawn to the city's relatively affordable rents and burgeoning opportunities in the creative and start-up business sectors. With several LGBTQ+ districts and a large population of immigrants, the city's inclusive atmosphere continues to make Berlin a model city for communities around the globe.

1 Ruins of the Reichstag after the 1933 fire. ↑

2 Adolf Hitler, Chancellor of Nazi Germany, saluting German troops.

3 Fall of the Berlin Wall.

4 A street in present-day Prenzlauer Berg.

Did You Know?

The Berlin Wall was under constant surveillance – by 1989, it was lined with 302 watchtowers.

1989

New border crossing regulations lead to the fall of the Berlin Wall on 9 November.

1990

Official reunification of Germany on 3 October, with the merging of the Federal Republic of Germany and the German Democratic Republic.

1991

Berlin becomes the capital of reunified Germany on 20 June.

2014

Germany wins the World Cup; celebration of the 25th anniversary of the fall of the Berlin Wall.

2017

The Bundestag legalizes same-sex marriage.

EXPERIENCE

D2 Bank building on Pariser Platz

AROUND UNTER DEN LINDEN

The poetic name of central Mitte's grand boulevard Unter den Linden (Under the Linden Trees) comes from the trees that line part of this avenue between the Stadtschloss city palace and the Brandenburg Gate.

The area's development began in the Baroque period with the establishment of Dorotheenstadt to the north and Friedrichstadt to the south. From the early 18th century, prestigious buildings began to appear here, and over the following two centuries Unter den Linden became one of the city's most imposing avenues. World War II bombing took a heavy toll but, despite only partial reconstruction by the East German government, the area is still home to the highest concentration of historic buildings in Berlin.

AROUND UNTER DEN LINDEN

Must See

1 Zeughaus (DHM)

Experience More

2 Maxim Gorki Theater
3 Staatsbibliothek
4 Palais am Festungsgraben
5 Humboldt Universität
6 Neue Wache
7 Reiterdenkmal Friedrichs des Grossen
8 Altes Palais
9 Pierre Boulez Saal
10 Kronprinzenpalais
11 Staatsoper Unter den Linden
12 St-Hedwigs-Kathedrale
13 Alte Bibliothek
14 Unter den Linden
15 Komische Oper
16 Französischer Dom
17 Akademie der Künste
18 Konzerthaus
19 Friedrichstadtpassagen
20 Gendarmenmarkt
21 Deutscher Dom
22 Cold War Black Box
23 Ehemaliges Regierungsviertel
24 Holocaust Denkmal
25 Asisi Panorama Berlin
26 Museum für Kommunikation
27 Admiralspalast
28 Russische Botschaft
29 Brandenburger Tor
30 Bahnhof Friedrichstrasse
31 Pariser Platz

Eat

1 Augustiner am Gendarmenmarkt

Stay

2 Clipper Boardinghouse Berlin-Gendarmenmarkt
3 Hotel Adlon

Shop

4 Annette Görtz
5 The Square Berlin East

NORTH MITTE AND PRENZLAUER BER
p118

TIERGARTEN
p152

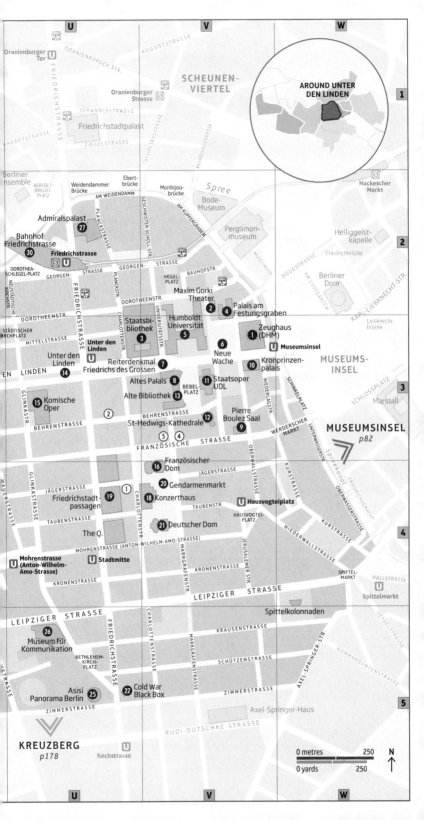

↑ The exhibition hall extension, designed by I M Pei

❶ � 🔤 🖼 🎒

ZEUGHAUS (DHM)

📍V3 🏛Unter den Linden 2 🅂Friedrichstrasse,
Museumsinsel, Hackescher 🆄Friedrichstrasse,
Museumsinsel Markt 🚌100, 300 🕙10am–6pm
daily (central building closed for renovation
until end of 2025) 🌐dhm.de

This stunning Baroque building houses the Deutsches Historisches
Museum (German History Museum), which explores the history of
Germany through a fascinating collection of art, militaria and crafts.

Located in Berlin's historic district of Mitte, the Zeughaus
was built as the armoury of the Prussian army in the 18th
century. Constructed in the Baroque style, it is a magnificent
structure; its wings surround an inner courtyard and the exterior
is decorated with Schlüter's sculptures depicting mythological
giants. Since 1952 it has housed the Deutsches Historisches Museum
(DHM), which has a permanent exhibition of over one million objects
about German history. The museum was founded in 1987 on the occasion
of the 750th anniversary of Berlin. With the reunification of Germany
in 1990, the buildings and collections of East Germany (officially the
German Democratic Republic) came into the hands of the German
Historical Museum and the collections representing the history of all
the parts of Germany moved into the Zeughaus. In 2003, a strikingly
curvaceous, glass-walled exhibition hall was added, designed by
Walter Gropius student I M Pei. Its four different levels are used for
temporary exhibitions about significant historical events.

> **Located in Berlin's historic district
> of Mitte, the Zeughaus was built as
> the armoury of the Prussian army
> in the 18th century.**

↑ *Gloria Victis*, by
Antonin Mercié, is
a moving allegory
inspired by the death
of the artist's friend

↑ The outstanding Zeughaus building,
one of the best examples of Baroque
architecture in Berlin

GALLERY GUIDE

The ground floor
houses exhibits from
1918 to the present.
The first floor con-
tains collections
dating from early
civilizations and the
Middle Ages right up
to the beginning of
the 20th century.
A subterranean
pathway links
the Zeughaus
to the temporary
shows in the
exhibition hall.

EXPERIENCE MORE

Maxim Gorki Theater

🚇 V2 🏛 Am Festungs-
graben 2 📞 20 221 15
Ⓢ Friedrichstrasse, Unter
den Linden Ⓤ Friedrich-
strasse, Museumsinsel
🚌 100, 300 🚋 M1

The Maxim Gorki theatre was
once a singing school or *Sing-
Akademie*. Berlin's oldest concert hall, it was built in 1827
by Carl Theodor Ottmer, who
based his design on drawings
by Karl Friedrich Schinkel
(*p29*). This modest Neo-
Classical building, with its
attractive façade resembling
a Greco-Roman temple, was
well known for the excellent
acoustic qualities of its
concert hall.

Many famous composer-
musicians have performed
here, including the violinist
Niccolò Paganini and pianist
Franz Liszt. In 1829, Felix
Mendelssohn-Bartholdy
conducted a performance of
the *St Matthew Passion* by
Johann Sebastian Bach here.
It was the first time that the
work had been performed in
front of an audience since the
composer's death in 1750.
Following reconstruction
after World War II, the
building became a theatre.

Staatsbibliothek

🚇 U3 🏛 Unter den Linden 8
Ⓢ Friedrichstrasse
Ⓤ Friedrichstrasse, Unter
den Linden 🚌 100, 300
🕐 9am-9pm Mon-Fri,
10am-5pm Sat 🌐 staats
bibliothek-berlin.de

The nucleus of the State
Library collection was
the library of the Great
Elector, Friedrich Wilhelm
(*p215*), founded in 1661, first
situated in the Stadtschloss
and later moved to the Alte
Bibliothek building. Its current
home was designed by Ernst
von Ihne and completed
in 1914 on the site of the
Academy of Science and
the Academy of Fine Arts.
This impressive building
was severely damaged
during World War II and
underwent extensive res-
toration. The collection,
of some three million books
and periodicals, was scattered
during the war. A collection
of priceless music manu-
scripts ended up in the
Jagiellonian Library in
Krakow, Poland.

After the war, only part of
the collection was returned
to the building in Unter den
Linden, and the rest was
held in West Berlin. Since
reunification, both collections
are once again under the
same administration.

Palais am Festungsgraben

🚇 V2 🏛 Am Festungs-
graben 1 📞 61 81 46 60
Ⓢ Friedrichstrasse
Ⓤ Museumsinsel
🚌 100, 300 🚋 M1

The Festungsgraben Palace
is one of the few structures in
this part of town that retains
its original interior décor. Built
as a small Baroque palace in
1753, it owes its present form
to major extension work,
carried out in 1864 in the style
of Karl Friedrich Schinkel, by
Heinrich Bürde and Hermann
von der Hude.

The late Neo-Classical style
of the building is reminiscent
of Schinkel's later designs. The
interior includes a magnificent
double-height marble hall in
the Neo-Renaissance style
which was modelled on the
White Room in the former
Stadtschloss (*p96*). In 1934
one ground-floor room was
turned into a music salon,
and many musical instru-
ments were brought here
from the 19th-century

WILHELM AND ALEXANDER VON HUMBOLDT

The Humboldt brothers rank among the
most distinguished Berlin citizens. Wilhelm
(1767-1835) was a lawyer and politician,
occupying various government posts.
It was on his initiative that the Berlin University
(later renamed Humboldt University) was
founded, and he conducted studies in
comparative and historical linguistics
there. Alexander, shown right (1769-1859),
a professor at the university, researched
natural science, including meteorology,
oceanography and agricultural science.

 Neo-Classical façade of the Neue Wache

house (now demolished) of wealthy merchant and manufacturer Johann Weydinger (1773–1837).

The palace is now used for private events.

5

Humboldt Universität

V3 **Unter den Linden 6** **20930** **Friedrichstrasse** **Friedrichstrasse, Museumsinsel, Unter den Linden** **100, 300**

The university building was constructed in 1753 for Prince Heinrich of Prussia, the brother of Frederick the Great. The university was founded in 1810 on the initiative of Wilhelm von Humboldt. It became the Berlin University but was renamed in von Humboldt's honour in 1949.

The overall design of the palace, with its main block and the courtyard enclosed within a pair of wings, has been extended many times. Two marble statues (1883) by Paul Otto stand at the entrance gate and represent Wilhelm von Humboldt (holding a book) and his brother Alexander, a well-known naturalist and traveller (sitting on a globe). The

entrance gate leads to the courtyard, designed by Reinhold Begas.

Many renowned scholars have worked at the university, including philosophers Fichte and Hegel, physicians Rudolf Virchow and Robert Koch, and physicists Max Planck and Albert Einstein. Among its graduates are Heinrich Heine, Karl Marx and Friedrich Engels.

After World War II, the university was in the Russian sector of the divided city and the difficulties encountered by the students of the western zone led to the establishment of a new university in 1948 – the Freie Universität *(p248)*.

6

Neue Wache

V3 **Unter den Linden 4** **Hackescher Markt** **Museumsinsel** **100, 300** **10am–6pm daily**

This war memorial, designed by Karl Friedrich Schinkel and built in the 1810s, is one of the finest examples of Neo-Classical architecture in Berlin. its façade is dominated by a huge Doric portico with a frieze of bas-reliefs depicting goddesses of victory. On the triangular tympanum above the pediment are allegorical representations of Battle, Victory, Flight and Defeat.

EAT

Augustiner am Gendarmenmarkt

Hearty German fare (knuckle of pork, beef goulash) can be found at this Bavarian pub, which overlooks the Gendarmenmarkt, one of Berlin's most beautiful squares.

U4 **Charlottenstrasse 55** **204 540 20**

€€€

In the 1930s, the building, originally a royal guardhouse, was turned into a monument to soldiers killed during World War I. In 1960, following its restoration, Neue Wache became the Memorial to the Victims of Fascism and Militarism. In 1993, it was again rededicated, this time to the memory of all victims of war and dictatorship.

Inside the building is a granite slab over the ashes of an unknown soldier, a resistance fighter and a concentration camp prisoner. Under the circular opening in the roof is a copy of the 20th-century sculpture *Mother with her Dead Son*, by Berlin artist Käthe Kollwitz, who lost her own son in World War I.

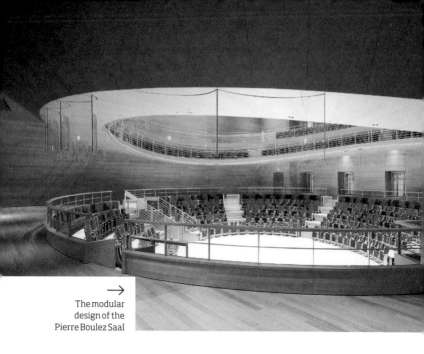

→ The modular design of the Pierre Boulez Saal

 7

Reiterdenkmal Friedrichs des Grossen

V3 Unter den Linden
Museumsinsel, Unter den Linden 100, 300

This equestrian statue of Frederick the Great is one of the most famous monuments in Berlin, featuring the massive, 5.6-m- (18.5-ft-) high bronze standing on the centre lane of Unter den Linden. It was designed by Christian Daniel Rauch and completed in 1851. It depicts Frederick the Great on horseback, wearing a uniform and a royal cloak. The base of the high plinth is surrounded by statues of notable military leaders, politicians, scientists and artists. The top tier of the plinth is decorated with bas-relief scenes from the life of Frederick the Great. Out of line with GDR ideology, the monument was moved to Potsdam, where it stood by the Hippodrome in Park Sanssouci (p250) until its return in 1980.

 8

Altes Palais

V3 Unter den Linden 9
Museumsinsel, Unter den Linden 100, 300

The Neo-Classical Old Palace, near the former Opernplatz (Bebelplatz), was built for the heir to the throne – Prince Wilhelm (later Kaiser Wilhelm I). The Kaiser lived here all his life. He was able to watch the changing of the guards every day from the ground-floor window on the far left.

The palace, built in the 1830s, was designed by Carl Ferdinand Langhans. Its splendid furnishings were destroyed during World War II but the palace was subsequently restored and is now used by Humboldt Universität (p69).

← Frederick the Great astride his bronze steed

> **The early Neo-Classical façade of the State Opera House is one of the most beautiful sights along Unter den Linden.**

Pierre Boulez Saal

V3 Französische Strasse 33D **U** Unter den Linden, Hausvogteiplatz **100, 147** M1, M12 **Hours vary, check website** boulezsaal.de

This concert hall opened in 2017 as part of the Barenboim-Said Akademie – an institution formed in continuation of Edward Said and Daniel Barenboim's West-Eastern Divan Orchestra to focus on music education in the humanistic tradition of the orchestra. American architect Frank Gehry has given the Pierre Boulez Saal impeccable acoustics and an intimate layout that ensures that no audience member is more than 14 m (50 ft) from the conductor. The hall hosts a diverse chamber music programme throughout the year, featuring both orchestras and soloists, with regular performances from the in-house Boulez Ensemble. There are also concerts for children.

⑩ Kronprinzenpalais

V3 Unter den Linden 3 **U** Museumsinsel **100, 300**

The striking, late Neo-Classical Crown Prince's Palace takes its name from its original inhabitants – the heirs to the royal, and later to the imperial, throne. Its form is the outcome of numerous changes made to what was originally a modest house dating from 1669. The first extensions, designed in the late Baroque style, were conducted by Philipp Gerlach in the 1730s. Between 1856 and 1857 Johann Heinrich Strack added the second floor. These extensions were rebuilt following World War II.

The palace served the royal family until the abolition of the monarchy. Under the Communist rule, it was renamed Palais Unter den Linden and reserved for official government guests. It was here, on 31 August 1990, that the pact was signed that paved the way for reunification to begin.

Next to the palace, at Unter den Linden 1, is where the Kommandantur, the official quarters of the city's garrison commander, once stood. Totally destroyed during the last days of World War II, the original façade was rebuilt in 2003 by the giant German media company Bertelsmann, as part of their Berlin headquarters. Today, the building is mainly used for staging large exhibitions.

Joined to the main palace by an overhanging passageway is the smaller Prinzessinnenpalais (Princesses' Palace), built for the daughters of Friedrich Wilhelm III. Today,

behind the Baroque façade, a modern venue called PalaisPopulaire displays the Deutsche Bank's art collection. The ground-floor café, LePopulaire, offers traditional coffee and cake with stunning view of Berlin's landmarks.

---

⑪ Staatsoper Unter den Linden

V3 Unter den Linden 7 **U** Museumsinsel, Unter den Linden **100, 300** **Hours vary, check website** staatsoper-berlin.de

The early Neo-Classical façade of the State Opera House is arguably one of the most beautiful sights along the famous Unter den Linden. It was built by Georg Wenzeslaus von Knobelsdorff in 1741–3, but has been rebuilt and restored several times: in the 1840s after a fire, after World War II and after water damage in the GDR era. The latest works, completed in 2017, resulted in magical acoustics and much more comfortable seats.

The building is the home of the Berlin State Opera and has played host to stellar singers, musicians and artists; one of its directors and conductors was Richard Strauss. Audiences can expect Baroque opera as well as new productions.

€400 m

The refurbishment cost of the Staatsoper: almost double the original estimate.

→ Lime (linden) trees on Unter den Linden

⑫ St-Hedwigs-Kathedrale

 V3 △ Bebelplatz ⑤ & Ⓤ Hausvogteiplatz, Museuminsel & Unter den Linden 🚌 100, 300 ⏱ Hours vary, check website ⓦ hedwigs-kathedrale.de

The massive church of St Hedwig, set back from the road and crowned with a copper dome, is the Catholic Cathedral of the Roman Archdiocese of Berlin. It was built to serve the Catholics of Silesia (part of present-day Poland), which became part of the Kingdom of Prussia in 1742 following defeat in the Silesian Wars of 1740–63.

The initial design, by Georg Wenzeslaus von Knobelsdorff, was similar to the Roman Pantheon. Construction began in 1747 and the cathedral was consecrated in 1773, although work continued until 1778. Later, additional work was carried out from 1886 to 1887. The cathedral was badly damaged during World War II, and rebuilt between 1952 and 1963. Major renovations between 2019 and 2024 saw the altar move directly under the dome.

The crypt holds the tombs of many bishops of Berlin. It is also the resting place of Bernhard Lichtenberg (1875–1943), a priest killed in a concentration camp and beatified as a martyr by Pope John Paul II.

---

⑬ Alte Bibliothek

 V3 △ Bebelplatz 1 Ⓒ 20 93 0 Ⓤ Unter den Linden 🚌 100, 300

The Old Library, known by locals as the *Kommode* or "chest of drawers" after its curved façade, is one of the city's most beautiful Baroque buildings. It was designed by Georg Christian Unger and built around 1775 to house the royal library collection. Unger based his design on an unrealized plan for an extension to the Hofburg complex in Vienna by Josef Emanuel Fischer von Erlach some 50 years earlier. The concave façade of the building is accentuated by the insertion of three breaks, surrounded at the top by a row of massive Corinthian pilasters. The building now houses the law faculty of Humboldt University.

⑭ Unter den Linden

 U3 ⑤ Brandenburger Tor Ⓤ Brandenburger Tor, Unter den Linden 🚌 100, 300

One of the most famous streets in Berlin, Unter den Linden starts at Schlossplatz and runs down to the Brandenburg Gate *(p78)* and Pariser Platz. It was once the route to the royal hunting grounds that were later transformed into the Tiergarten *(p171)*. In the 17th century, the street was planted with lime trees, to which it owes its name. The current trees were planted in the 1950s.

During the 18th century, Unter den Linden became the main street of the westward-growing city. It was gradually filled with prestigious buildings, many of which were restored after World War II. Today it also has several cafés and restaurants, as well as many smart shops. This street is also the venue for many interesting outdoor events; it is usually crowded with tourists and students browsing the bookstalls around the Humboldt Universität *(p69)* and the Staatsbibliothek.

Komische Oper

Q U3 **A** Behrenstrasse 55/57 **S** & **U** Brandenburger Tor **U** Unter den Linden **🚌** 100, 147, 300 **W** komische-oper-berlin.de

Looking at the modern façade of the Comic Opera theatre, it is hard to believe that it hides one of Berlin's most impressive interiors. Built in 1892, it has served as a variety theatre and as the German National Theatre, and has only housed the Komische Oper since World War II. The postwar reconstruction deprived the building of its former façades but the beautiful Viennese Neo-Baroque interior remained, full of stuccoes and gilded ornaments. Particularly interesting are the statues on the pilasters of the top balcony by Theodor Friedel. The Komische Oper is one of Berlin's three leading opera companies, presenting contemporary renditions musicals, operas and operettas. Extensive renovation has been ongoing since 2023 so performances are temporarily being held at different venues across the city. For more information, check the website.

Französischer Dom

Q V4 **A** Gendarmenmarkt 6 **U** Stadtmitte, Hausvogteiplatz **O** Hours vary, check website **W** franzoesischerdom.de

The French Cathedral stands facing its German counter-part, the Deutscher Dom *(p75)*, across the Gendarmenmarkt square. It was built for the French Huguenot community, who found refuge in Protestant Berlin following their expulsion from France after the revocation of the Edict of Nantes. The main building of the church, completed in 1705, was modelled on the Huguenot church in Charenton, France, which was destroyed in 1688.

The structure is dominated by a massive, cylindrical tower, which is encircled by Corinthian porticoes at its base. It was added around 1785, some 80 years after the church was built. In 1987, a viewing platform and large carillon were incorporated to celebrate Berlin's 750th anniversary. It also houses the Huguenot Museum, which details the history of the Huguenots in France and Brandenburg. Well-educated and highly skilled, they played a crucial part in Berlin's rise as a city of science, craft and commerce. The French language they brought with them survives to this day in many words used in the Berlin dialect.

Akademie der Künste

Q T3 **A** Pariser Platz 4 **S** & **U** Brandenburger Tor **🚌** 100, 300 **O** 10am–10pm daily **W** adk.de

The modern glass and steel façade of the Academy of Arts belies its historic and noble origins. Founded in 1696 by Prussian King Frederick I, it was one of Europe's first such institutions. Today its primary role is advising and supporting the German government in affairs of art and culture. It also houses a prestigious archive and hosts contemporary art exhibitions.

Main entrance of the Französischer Dom, built for the dispossessed French Huguenots ↓

Konzerthaus

V4 **Gendarmen-markt 2** **Stadtmitte, Hausvogteiplatz**
konzerthaus.de

A late Neo-Classical jewel, the magnificent Concert Hall, formerly known as the Schauspielhaus, is one of the greatest achievements of Berlin's best-known architect, Karl Friedrich Schinkel *(p29)*.

It was built between 1818 and 1821 around the ruins of Carl Gotthard Langhans' National Theatre, which was destroyed by fire in 1817. The original portico columns were retained. Schinkel was responsible for the architectural structure and for the interior design, down to the door handles. Following bomb damage in World War II, it was reconstructed as a concert hall with a different interior layout. The exterior was restored to its former glory. The Konzerthaus is home to the Konzerthaus-orchester (formerly the Berlin Symphony Orchestra).

The theatre façade includes a huge Ionic portico with a set of stairs that was only used by the middle classes (the upper classes entered via a separate entrance where they could leave their horse-drawn carriages). The whole building is richly decorated with sculptures alluding to drama and music: statues of musical geniuses mounted on lions and panthers, as well as figures representing the Muses and a Bacchanal procession. The façade is crowned with the sculpture of Apollo riding a chariot pulled by griffins.

In front of the theatre stands a shining white marble statue of the poet and philosopher Friedrich Schiller.

It was sculpted by Reinhold Begas, and erected in 1869. Removed by the Nazis during the 1930s, the monument was finally returned to its rightful place in 1988. Schiller's head was copied by the sculptor from a bust of the poet created in 1794 by Johann Heinrich Dannecker. The statue is mounted on a high pedestal surrounded by allegorical figures repre-senting Lyric Poetry, Drama, Philosophy and History.

Friedrichstadt-passagen

U4 **Friedrichstrasse Quartier 205, 206, 207** **Stadtmitte, Hausvogteiplatz**

This group of passages is part of a huge development of shops, offices, restaurants and apartments built along Friedrichstrasse.

Quartier 207 is the former home of Galeries Lafayette, a branch of the French department store. Although this charming building, constructed almost entirely of glass, was designed by Jean Nouvel to house a shopping complex, it is awaiting a new purpose now. The building's axis is formed by an inner courtyard, which is defined by two glass cones with their bases facing each other. The highly reflective glass panes, together with the multicoloured stands that are clustered around the structure, make an extraordinary impression on the visitor.

The next passage, Quartier 206, has offices, a private medical centre as well as some stores, It is the work of the American design team Pei Cobb Freed & Partners. The building owes its alluring, but somewhat nouveau-riche, appearance to the use of forms inspired by Art Deco architecture, including sophisticated details and expensive stone cladding.

The southernmost building in the complex, and the largest passage, is Quartier 205 – now called "The Q" – another complex of shops, designed by Oswald Mathias Ungers.

→

Quartier 206 in the Friedrichstadtpassagen

↑ The Deutscher Dom, overlooking the expansive Gendarmenmarkt

 20

Gendarmenmarkt

📍V4 🚇Stadtmitte, Hausvogteiplatz

This is one of Berlin's most beautiful squares, created at the end of the 17th century as a marketplace for the newly established Friedrichstadt. It is named after the Regiment Gens d'Armes, who stabled their horses here. Two cathedrals with magnificent towers, the Deutscher Dom and the Französischer Dom (p73), stand on each side with the Konzerthaus in the middle.

---

21 🖊️

Deutscher Dom

📍V4 🏛️Gendarmenmarkt 1 🚇Stadtmitte, Hausvogtei- platz 📞22 73 04 31 🕐May-Sep: 10am-7pm Tue-Sun; Oct-Apr: 10am- 6pm Tue-Sun

The German Cathedral at the southern end of Gendar- menmarkt, to the left of the Konzerthaus, is an old German Protestant-Reformed church built in 1708 by Giovanni Simonetti. The design was based on a five-petal shape, and in 1785 it acquired a dome-covered tower

identical to that of the French Cathedral across the square. Burned down in 1945, the church was finally rebuilt in 1993. Its exterior was pain- stakingly reconstructed, including its sculpted decorations. The interior is now modern and hosts an exhibition, *"Wege, Irrwege, Umwege"* ("Paths, Confusions, Detours"), about Germany's parliamentary democracy.

---

 22 🖊️

Cold War Black Box

📍U5 🏛️Friedrichstrasse 47 🚇Stadtmitte, Kochstrasse 🚌M29 🕐10am-6pm daily 🌐bfgg.de

Located directly across from the Haus am Checkpoint Charlie (p191), the Cold War Black Box provides a quieter, more measured look at the Cold War years. Throughout its intimate, black-walled space, it tackles big-hitter topics such as nuclear war and espionage, as well as peace and democracy.

The exhibition comprises around 500 items, including GDR-era grenades once used for practice by schoolchildren, a Geiger counter used for detect- ing and measuring radioactiv- ity in the air, and a Soviet photo gun, which was used for

reconnaissance missions. There are also several media stations with film excerpts, interviews, photos, and explorations of international connections with the Korean War and the Cuban Missile Crisis.

㉓
Ehemaliges Regierungsviertel

🗺 T5 🏛 Wilhelmstrasse, Leipziger Strasse, Voss Strasse Ⓤ Potsdamer Platz, Anton-Wilhelm-Amo-Strasse

The name means "former government district", because Wilhelmstrasse, and the area situated to the west of it up to Leipziger Platz (p164), was where the main government departments had offices from the mid-19th century until 1945. The building at Voss Strasse No. 77 was once the Reich's Chancellery and Otto von Bismarck's office, and from 1933 it served as the office of Adolf Hitler. It was from here that Hitler, his senior staff and his mistress Eva Braun withdrew to the Führerbunker, an elaborate underground complex that served as both command centre and residence.

In the spring of 1945, the square was the scene of such fierce fighting that after World War II, most of the damaged buildings had to be torn down.

Among those that survived are the former Prussian Landtag offices – the huge complex occupying the site between Leipziger and Niederkirchner Strasse. This building, designed in the Italian Renaissance style, was designed by Friedrich Schulze, and constructed between 1892 and 1904. It consists of two segments: the section on the side of Leipziger Strasse (No. 3–4) once housed the upper chamber of the National Assembly (the Herrenhaus) and is now used by the Bundesrat. The building on the side of Niederkirchner Strasse (No. 5) is the former seat of the Landtag's lower chamber, and is now the Berliner Abgeordnetenhaus (House of Representatives).

The other surviving complex is the former Ministry of Aviation, at Leipziger Strasse No. 5, built for Hermann Göring in 1936 by Ernst Sagebiel. This building is typical of the architecture of the Third Reich.

FÜHRERBUNKER

The specific location of Hitler's bunker was kept a secret for many decades to deter neo-Nazi pilgrims. Destroyed and flooded after World War II, the area now hosts an aptly unimpressive car parking area and a huddle of residential buildings. An information board installed by the nonprofit Berliner Unterwelten group (which runs fascinating tours of other bunkers and subterranean historic sites throughout the city) shows what the layout of the structure once would have been.

A small corner of the massive Holocaust Denkmal

underneath the memorial that displays the names of around 3 million Jewish Holocaust victims. There are also memorials in the nearby Tiergarten to commemorate LGBTQ+, Sinti and Roma people murdered during World War II.

Holocaust Denkmal

Q S/T4 **A** Ebertstrasse **C** 28 04 59 60 **S** & **U** Brandenburger Tor **B** 100, 300 **Q** Apr-Sep: 10am-8pm Tue-Sun; Oct-Mar: 10am-7pm Tue-Sun **Q** Mon

Designed by American architect Peter Eisenman and engineer Buro Happold, Germany's national Holocaust memorial is a striking sprawl of concrete that symbolizes the six million Jewish people and others murdered by the Nazis in concentration camps between 1933 and 1945.

Finished in 2005, it consists of a 19,000-sq-m (200,000-sq-ft) site containing 2,711 concrete slabs or "stelae" of varying heights, arranged in an austere grid pattern on a sloping field. The abstract installation is intended to disorientate, and leaves room for interpretation. For this reason, the memorial has faced criticism for the lack of information it offers on the horrific events it sets out to commemorate. There is however an information centre

25
Asisi Panorama Berlin

Q U5 **A** Friedrichstrasse 205 **S** & **U** Potsdamer Platz **U** Stadtmitte, Kochstrasse **B** M48, M29 **Q** 10am-6pm daily **W** asisi.de

Turkish-German artist Yadegar Asisi paints enormous, highly detailed panoramas known for their sense of realism. His Berlin panorama is 15 m (49 ft) high, 60 m (196 ft) wide and set inside a large cylindrical structure next to Checkpoint Charlie. It depicts a fictional day along a stretch of the Berlin Wall in the 1980s. On one side is Kreuzberg, complete with punks, run-down buildings and daily West Berlin life; on the other side, an eerily quiet Mitte, all border fortifications, no people and the TV tower looming in the distance. With a soundtrack by film composer Eric Babak, the experience is absorbing and moving.

26
Museum für Kommunikation

Q U5 **A** Leipziger Strasse 16 **U** Stadtmitte, Anton-Wilhelm-Amo-Strasse **B** 200, 265, M48 **Q** 9am-8pm Tue, 9am-5pm Wed-Fri, 10am-6pm Sat & Sun **W** mfk-berlin.de

Founded in 1872 as the Post Office Museum, the

Museum of Communication is the oldest establishment of its kind in the entire world. Soon after it was founded, it moved into the corner of the huge building constructed for the main post office. The office wings, with their modest Neo-Renaissance elevations, contrast with the grand Neo-Baroque façade. Exhibits featured here illustrate the history of postal and telecommunication services, including contemporary digital media.

↑ The Neo-Classical Russische Botschaft,
built to impress in war-ravaged 1950s Berlin

 27

Admiralspalast

U2 **Friedrichstrasse
101-102** **25 50 70 00**
S & U Friedrichstrasse

The Admiralspalast, built
in 1911, was one of the
Roaring Twenties' premier
entertainment complexes in
Berlin, and one of the many
variety and vaudeville
theatres that once lined
Friedrichstrasse. Originally
designed as an indoor
swimming pool above a
natural hot spring, it was
later transformed into an ice-
skating rink and, after heavy
damage in World War II, an
Operettentheater that staged
light musical entertainment.

In 2006, following restoration work, the theatre
reopened with a much-
discussed production of
Bertolt Brecht's *Die
Dreigroschenoper* (*The Threepenny Opera*), and now once
again serves as a vibrant
entertainment complex,
with a large stage, a café
and a nightclub. Designed
by Heinrich Schweitzer, the
beautifully restored façade
is punctuated by Doric half-
columns and inlaid with slabs
of Istrian marble. The façade
on Planckstrasse, designed
by Ernst Westphal, features
overlapping motifs.

 28

Russische Botschaft

T3 **Unter den Linden
63/65** **S & U Branden-
burger Tor** **100, 245**

The monumental white
Russian Embassy building is
an example of the Stalinist
"wedding-cake" style, or
Zuckerbäckerstil. Completed
in 1953, it was the first
postwar building erected
on Unter den Linden. It is
built on the site of a former
palace that had housed the
Russian (originally Tsarist)
embassy from 1837.

The work of Russian
architect Anatoli Strischewski,
this structure, with its strictly
symmetrical layout, resembles the old Berlin palaces
of the Neo-Classical period.
The sculptures that adorn
it, however, belong to an
altogether different era: the
gods of ancient Greece and
Rome have been replaced by
notable working-class figures.

 29

Brandenburger Tor

S3 **Pariser Platz
S & U Brandenburger
Tor** **100, 245**

The Brandenburg Gate is the
quintessential symbol of

Berlin. This magnificent
Neo-Classical structure, completed in 1795, was designed
by Carl Gotthard Langhans
and modelled on the entrance
to the Acropolis in Athens. A
pair of pavilions, once used by
guards and customs officers,
frames its powerful Doric
colonnade. The bas-reliefs
depict scenes from Greek
mythology, and the whole
structure is crowned by the
Quadriga sculpture designed
by Johann Gottfried Schadow.
The goddess of victory with
her four-horsed chariot was
originally regarded as a
symbol of peace. In 1806,
during the French occupation,
the Quadriga was dismantled
on Napoleon's orders and
taken to Paris. On its return in
1814, it was declared a symbol
of victory, and the goddess
received the staff bearing the
Prussian eagle and the iron
cross adorned with a laurel
wreath. The Brandenburg
Gate has borne witness to
many of Berlin's important
events, from military parades

Brandenburger
Tor dominating
Pariser Platz ↓

to celebrations marking the birth of the Third Reich and Hitler's ascent to power. It was here, too, that the Russian flag was raised in May 1945, and on 17 June 1953 that 25 workers demonstrating for better conditions were killed.

The gate, in East Berlin, was restored during 1956–8, after it suffered extensive damage in World War II. Until 1989 it stood watch over the divided city. It was restored again between 2000 and 2002.

Bahnhof Friedrichstrasse

Q U2 **A** Reichstagufer 17 **O** 9am–7pm Tue–Fri, 10am–6pm Sat & Sun **W** hdg.de

One of the city's most famous urban railway stations, Bahnhof Friedrichstrasse used to be the border station between East and West Berlin during the Cold War years.

It was built in 1882 to a design by Johannes Vollmer. In 1925, a roof was added, covering the hall and the platforms. The original labyrinth of passages, staircases and checkpoints no longer exists but it is possible to see a model of the station at the Stasi-Museum (p231).

The only remaining structure from the original station is the special pavilion once used as a waiting room by those waiting for emigration clearance. It earned the nickname **Tränenpalast**, the "Palace of Tears", as it is here that Berliners from different sides of the city would say goodbye to each other after a visit. Today, it is home to a small museum that looks at what the partition of Germany meant for Berliners.

Tränenpalast
O 9am–7pm Tue–Fri, 10am–6pm Sat & Sun **W** hdg.de/en/traenenpalast

Pariser Platz

Q T3 **S** & **U** Brandenburger Tor **■** 100, 245

This square, at the end of Unter den Linden, was created in 1734. Originally called Quarré, it was renamed Pariser Platz after 1814, when the Quadriga sculpture from the Brandenburg Gate was returned to Berlin from Paris.

The square, bordered on the west by the Brandenburg Gate, saw most of its buildings destroyed in 1945. Following reunification, the square was redeveloped, and twin houses designed by Josef Paul Kleihues now flank the Brandenburg Gate. On the north side of the square are the Dresdner Bank building and the French Embassy. On the south are the US Embassy, the DZ Bank head office and the Academy of Arts (p73). To the east is the rebuilt Hotel Adlon (p77), a legend in Berlin hospitality.

A SHORT WALK
AROUND BEBELPLATZ

Distance 1.5 km (1 mile) **Nearest tram station** Georgenstrasse/Am Kupfergraben **Time** 20 minutes

The section of Unter den Linden between Schlossbrücke and Friedrichstrasse is the perfect place for a walk to get an introduction to the city. There are some magnificent Baroque and Neo-Classical buildings, many of which were designed by famous architects, as well as several restored palaces that are now used as public buildings. Of particular interest is the beautiful Baroque Zeughaus (the former Arsenal), which now houses the Deutsches Historisches Museum (German History Museum).

The impressive **Reiterdenkmal Friedrichs des Grossen** *(equestrian statue of Frederick the Great, p70) dates from 1851.*

Humboldt Universität's (p69) *courtyard entrance is framed by two guardroom pavilions and crowned with the allegorical figures of Dawn and Dusk.*

The Neo-Baroque **Staatsbibliothek** *(State Library, p68) building was designed by Ernst von Ihne and completed in 1914. It houses a collection that dates from the 17th century.*

UNIVERSITÄTSSTRASSE

CHARLOTTENSTRASSE

UNTER DEN LINDEN

BEHRENSTRASSE

↑ I M Pei's modern exhibition hall at the Zeughaus (DHM)

A sleek and stylish exhibition space shows off the brands of the Volkswagen Group. There's also a shop and several dining options.

The Neo-Classical **Altes Palais** *(Old Palace, p70) was built between 1834 and 1837 for the future Kaiser Wilhelm I. It was reconstructed after World War II.*

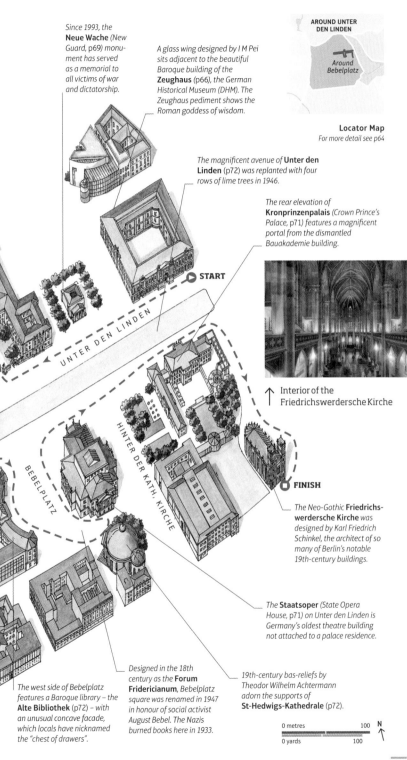

AROUND UNTER
DEN LINDEN

Around
Bebelplatz

Locator Map
For more detail see p64

Since 1993, the
Neue Wache (New
Guard, p69) monu-
ment has served
as a memorial to
all victims of war
and dictatorship.

A glass wing designed by I M Pei
sits adjacent to the beautiful
Baroque building of the
Zeughaus (p66), the German
Historical Museum (DHM). The
Zeughaus pediment shows the
Roman goddess of wisdom.

The magnificent avenue of **Unter den
Linden** (p72) was replanted with four
rows of lime trees in 1946.

The rear elevation of
Kronprinzenpalais (Crown Prince's
Palace, p71) features a magnificent
portal from the dismantled
Bauakademie building.

⯈ **START**

UNTER DEN LINDEN

HINTER DER KATH. KIRCHE

↑ Interior of the
Friedrichswerdersche Kirche

BEBELPLATZ

⬤ **FINISH**

The Neo-Gothic **Friedrichswerdersche Kirche** *was
designed by Karl Friedrich
Schinkel, the architect of so
many of Berlin's notable
19th-century buildings.*

The **Staatsoper** (State Opera
House, p71) on Unter den Linden is
Germany's oldest theatre building
not attached to a palace residence.

The west side of Bebelplatz
features a Baroque library – the
Alte Bibliothek (p72) – with
an unusual concave facade,
which locals have nicknamed
the "chest of drawers".

Designed in the 18th
century as the **Forum
Fridericianum**, Bebelplatz
square was renamed in 1947
in honour of social activist
August Bebel. The Nazis
burned books here in 1933.

19th-century bas-reliefs by
Theodor Wilhelm Achtermann
adorn the supports of
St-Hedwigs-Kathedrale (p72).

0 metres   100
0 yards   100

N ↑

MUSEUMSINSEL

The long island nestled in the tributaries of the Spree river is the cradle of Berlin's history. It was here that the settlement of Cölln was established at the beginning of the 13th century, which grew up together with its twin settlement of Berlin on the opposite bank of the Spree.

Not a trace of Gothic and Renaissance Cölln is left now: the island's character was transformed by the construction of the Brandenburg Electors' palace, which served as their residence from 1470. Over the following centuries, the palace was converted first into a royal home and later into an imperial palace – the huge Stadtschloss. Although the palace was razed to the ground in 1950, several buildings on the island's north side have survived, including the huge Berliner Dom and the impressive collection of museums that give the island its name – Museumsinsel.

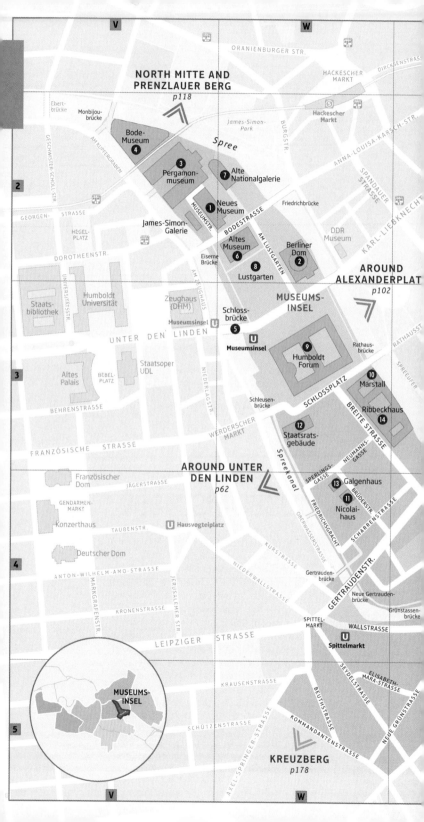

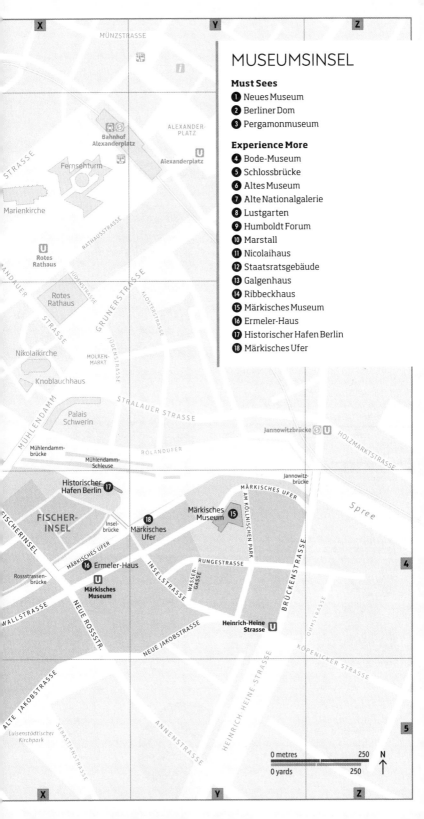

MÜNZSTRASSE

Bahnhof
Alexanderplatz

ALEXANDER-
PLATZ

U Alexanderplatz

Fernsehturm

Marienkirche

U Rotes Rathaus

Rotes
Rathaus

Nikolaikirche

Knoblauchhaus

Palais
Schwerin

Mühlendamm-
brücke

Mühlendamm-
Schleuse

STRALAUER STRASSE

ROLANDUFER

Jannowitzbrücke S U HOLZMARKTSTRASSE

MUSEUMSINSEL

Must Sees

1 Neues Museum
2 Berliner Dom
3 Pergamonmuseum

Experience More

4 Bode-Museum
5 Schlossbrücke
6 Altes Museum
7 Alte Nationalgalerie
8 Lustgarten
9 Humboldt Forum
10 Marstall
11 Nicolaihaus
12 Staatsratsgebäude
13 Galgenhaus
14 Ribbeckhaus
15 Märkisches Museum
16 Ermeler-Haus
17 Historischer Hafen Berlin
18 Märkisches Ufer

Jannowitz-
brücke

MÄRKISCHES UFER

Spree

Historischer
Hafen Berlin 17

FISCHER-
INSEL

Insel-
brücke

18
Märkisches
Ufer

Märkisches
Museum 15

AM KÖLNISCHEN PARK

16 Ermeler-Haus

MÄRKISCHES UFER

U Märkisches
Museum

Rossstrassen-
brücke

WALLSTRASSE

NEUE ROSSSTR.

INSELSTRASSE

WASSER
GASSE

RUNGESTRASSE

BRÜCKENSTRASSE

OLMSTRASSE

NEUE JAKOBSTRASSE

Heinrich-Heine
Strasse U

KÖPENICKER STRASSE

ALTE JAKOBSTRASSE

Luisenstädtischer
Kirchpark

ANNENSTRASSE

SEBASTIANSTRASSE

HEINRICH HEINE STRASSE

| 0 metres | 250 |
| 0 yards | 250 |

N ↑

NEUES MUSEUM

📍V2 🏛Bodestrasse 1-3 ⓢHackescher Markt, Friedrichstrasse ⓤMuseum-sinsel 🚌100, 300 🚋12, M1, M4, M5 🕐Jul-Aug: 9am-8pm Tue-Sat (to 6pm Sun), Sep-Jun: 10am-6pm Tue-Sun; book in advance via website 🌐smb.museum

This museum is home to an unparalleled collection of Berlin's archaeological treasures from around the world. Through its exhibits, visitors can explore human history and culture from prehistoric times to the Middle Ages.

The New Museum was built in the mid-19th century to relieve the overcrowded Altes Museum. In 1945, the building was badly damaged, but the reconstruction effort under British architect David Chipperfield – a skillful blend of conservation, restoration and creation of new spaces – was highly successful, and history remains palpable in every room.

The two main collections are the Egyptian Museum and Papyrus Collection and the Museum for Prehistory and Early History. The former showcases four millennia of ancient Egyptian and Nubian cultures, while the latter focuses on Europe and parts of Asia. Special themes and items include 19th-century wall paintings of Nordic mythological scenes, Heinrich Schliemann's collection of artifacts from Troy, the Neanderthal from Le Moustier, the Berlin Gold Hat and a bust of Nefertiti.

↑ The museum building, designed by Friedrich August Stüler

↑ The museum's architecture and décor were designed to complement the exhibits

The bust of Nefertiti is made of stucco-coated limestone

Highlights

c 1184 BCE

The "Treasure of Priam" artifacts are said to have belonged to a king of ancient Troy.

c 100–50 BCE

▽ Very little is known about the beautifully crafted Egyptian bust known as the Berlin Green Head.

c 1345 BCE

△ This bust may have served originally as a model for other portraits, and was not considered art itself.

c 200 CE

△ Bronze bracelet attributed to a Germanic tribe of eastern Germany.

Did You Know?

The museum was closed for 70 years, from 1939 to 2009.

Sarcophagi from the ↑
Egyptian Museum and
Papyrus Collection

BERLINER DOM

◎ W2 **⌂** Am Lustgarten **⑤** Hackescher Markt **🚌** 100, 300
◷ 9am–8pm daily (to 7pm in winter), noon–8pm Sun & public hols
🌐 berlinerdom.de

Standing on the east bank of the Spree, Berlin Cathedral is singled out from its neighbours on Museumsinsel, allowing visitors to fully take in this awe-inspiring city landmark.

The original Berliner Dom was completed in 1750, based on a modest Baroque design by Johann Boumann. The present Neo-Baroque structure is the work of Julius Raschdorff and dates from 1894–1905. The central copper dome is some 98 m (321 ft) high. Following severe World War II damage, the cathedral has been restored in a simplified form but still contains some original features like the pulpit and altar.

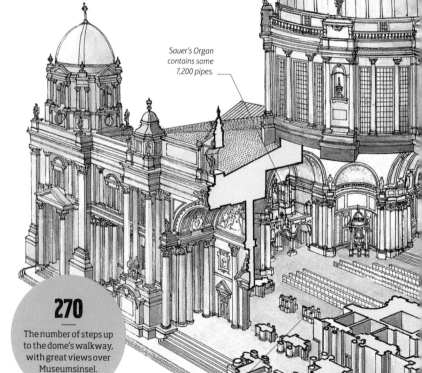

Sauer's Organ contains some 7,200 pipes.

270

The number of steps up to the dome's walkway, with great views over Museumsinsel.

Hidden beneath the floor, the Imperial Hohenzollern family crypt contains 100 richly decorated sarcophagi.

EXPERIENCE Museumsinsel

GREAT VIEW
Light Show

For ten days in October, Berlin gets a kaleidoscopic remix during the annual Festival of Lights, when famous sights like the Berliner Dom become canvases for creative light shows.

↑ The façade of the cathedral transformed by changing light and video projections during the Festival of Lights

The mosaics inside the dome contain over half a million tiles each.

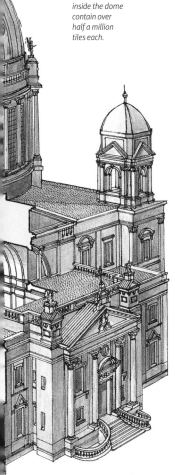

↑ The impressive Neo-Renaissance interior, featuring some extravagant furnishings and impressive decorations

DOME MOSAICS

Look up at the interior of the dome to marvel at Anton von Werner's intricate mosaics. All but destroyed during World War II, von Werner's original designs were used by Tuscan company Ferrari & Bacci to reproduce the mosaics between 1975 and 2002.

↑ The Berliner Dom, a Neo-Baroque cathedral dating back to 1750

③ 🛴 Ⓜ 🖵 🏛

PERGAMONMUSEUM

📍 V2 🏠 Am Kupfergraben 5 🚊 Hackescher Markt, Friedrichstrasse Ⓤ Museumsinsel
🚌 100, 300 🚋 12, M1 🕐 For renovations until spring 2027 🌐 smb.museum

This unique museum is home to a magnificent collection of large architectural treasures excavated by German archaeologists in the late 19th century. The exhibits are as awe-inspiring for their fabulous designs as for their grand scale.

Built between 1910 and 1930 to a design by Alfred Messel and Ludwig Hoffmann, this museum houses one of Europe's most famous collections of antiquities. The three independent collections – the Collection of Classical Antiquities (Greek and Roman), the Museum of the Ancient Near East and the Museum of Islamic Art – are the result of intensive archaeological excavations by late 19th- and early 20th-century German expeditions to the Near and Middle East. Due to extensive restoration and renovation work, this museum is completely closed to the public. The reopening is expected to happen in planned stages. The north wing, which contains the Pergamon Altar, is scheduled to reopen in 2027. Construction in the south wing will continue until 2037.

↑ The Pergamonmuseum backs onto the river Spree

→ Entrance to the James-Simon-Galerie

JAMES-SIMON-GALERIE

The Pergamonmuseum, when open to the public, can only be entered through the James-Simon-Galerie. This new entrance building, designed by David Chipperfield, and named after patron James Simon (1851–1932), serves as a central reception area for the visitors of Museumsinsel. It also has an area for temporary exhibitions and a large museum shop.

↑ The reconstructed Pergamon Altar and
a detail of one of its friezes *(inset)* from
the Antikensammlung collection

MUSEUM OF THE ANCIENT NEAR EAST

The collection on display in the Vorderasiatisches Museum (Museum of the Ancient Near East) is one of the richest in the world, due to hugely successful excavations begun by German archaeologists in the 1880s. The collection features architecture, sculpture and jewellery from Babylon, Iran and Assyria, with pieces dating as far back as the 4th century BCE.

One striking exhibit is the magnificent Ishtar Gate and the Processional Way that leads to it. These were both built during the reign of Nebuchadnezzar II (604–562 BCE) in the ancient city of Babylon. The original avenue was about 180 m (590 ft) long. Many of the bricks used in its reconstruction are new, but the lions – sacred animals of the goddess Ishtar (mistress of the sky, goddess of love and patron of the army) – are all originals. Although impressive in size, the Ishtar Gate has in fact not been reconstructed in full, and a model of the whole structure shows the scale of the original complex. Only the inner gate, framed by two towers, is on display, decorated with dragons and bulls, emblems of the Babylonian gods Marduk, patron of the city, and Adad, god of storms.

INSIDER TIP
Pergamon Panorama

A 360-degree panorama of the ancient city of Pergamon will be on show until the famous Pergamon Altar is back on display. This jaw-dropping, ultra-realistic panorama was created by artist Yadegar Asisi, who has other work on display in Berlin (p77).

→

The magnificent Ishtar Gate (6th century BCE)

COLLECTION OF CLASSICAL ANTIQUITIES

The centrepiece of the Greek and Roman antiquities collection is the huge Pergamon Altar from the acropolis of the ancient city of Pergamon in Asia Minor, which is now Bergama, Turkey. It is thought to have been built to celebrate victory in war and to have been commissioned by King Eumenes in 170 BCE. This artistic masterpiece was rediscovered in a decrepit state by German archaeologist Carl Humann, who, after long negotiations, was allowed to transport the surviving portions of the altar to Berlin. Note that the hall containing the Pergamon Altar is closed for reconstruction until 2027.

Roman architecture is represented by the striking 2nd-century CE market gate from the city of Miletus.

←

Marble statue of Athena Parthenos (Athena the Virgin)

MUSEUM OF ISLAMIC ART

The history of the Museum für Islamische Kunst (Museum of Islamic Art) began in 1904, when Wilhelm von Bode launched the collection by donating his own extensive selection of carpets. He also brought to Berlin a 45-m- (150-ft-) long section of the façade of the Mshatta Palace from the Jordanian desert. The façade, covered with exquisitely carved limestone cladding, was presented to Kaiser Wilhelm II in 1903 by Sultan Abdul Hamid of Ottoman. The palace was part of a group of defence fortresses and residential buildings dating from the Umayyad period (CE 661– 750), and probably built for the Caliph al-Walid II.

Another fascinating exhibit is a beautiful 13th-century *mihrab*, the niche in a mosque that shows the direction of Mecca. Made in the Iranian town of Kashan, renowned for its ceramics, the *mihrab* is covered in lustrous metallic glazes that make it sparkle as if studded with sapphires and gold. The collection's many vivid carpets come from as far afield as Iran, Asia Minor, Egypt and the Caucasus. Highlights include an early 15th-century carpet from Anatolia decorated with an unusual dragon and phoenix motif and, dating from the 14th century, one of the earliest Turkish carpets in existence.

Other rooms hold collections of miniature

↑ Islamic carpets on display at the Pergamonmuseum

paintings and various objects for daily use. An interesting example of provincial Ottoman architecture is an exquisitely panelled early 17th-century reception room, known as the Aleppo Zimmer, which was once part of a Christian merchant's house in the Syrian city of Aleppo.

Did You Know?

Al-Mshatta was never completed due to the assassination of the Umayyad Caliph, al-Walid II.

↑ Façade of the Mshatta Palace (744 CE)

↑ The wedge-shaped Bode-Museum on Museumsinsel

EXPERIENCE MORE

4

Bode-Museum

🔲 V2 🚉 Monbijoubrücke (Bodestrasse 1-3) ⑤ Hackescher Markt, Friedrich-strasse 🚌 100, 147, 300 🚊 12, M1, M4, M5, M6 🕐 10am–5pm Wed–Fri (to 6pm Sat & Sun) 🌐 smb.museum

The Bode-Museum building was designed in the 1890s by Ernst von Ihne to fit the wedge-shaped end of the island. The interior was designed with the help of an art historian, Wilhelm von Bode, who was the director of the Berlin state

Did You Know?

Museumsinsel was designated a UNESCO World Heritage Site in 1999.

museums at the time. The museum, which opened in 1904, displayed a rather mixed collection that included some Old Masters. Its original name, Kaiser Friedrich Museum, was changed after World War II. Following the reassembling of the Berlin collections, all of the paintings were put in the Gemäldegalerie (p158). The Egyptian art and the papyrus collection were moved to the Ägyptisches Museum (Egyptian Museum) at Charlottenburg. They are now housed at the Neues Museum (p86).

Today, the Bode-Museum is home to Skulpturensammlung, one of the largest collections of ancient sculptures in the world. Other displays include an outstanding collection of some of the world's oldest coins, from Athens in the 6th century BCE, as well as Roman, medieval and 20th-century coins. There are also sculptures by Tilman Riemenschneider, Donatello, Bernini and Canova.

5

Schlossbrücke

🔲 W3 ⑤ Hackescher Markt Ⓤ Museumsinsel 🚌 100, 300

This is one of the city's most beautiful bridges, connecting Schlossplatz with Unter den Linden (p72). It was built in 1824 to a design by Karl Friedrich Schinkel (p29), who was one of Germany's most influential architects. Statues were added to the top of the bridge's sparkling granite pillars in 1853. These figures were also created by Schinkel and made of stunning white Carrara marble. The statues depict tableaux taken from Greek mythology, for instance, Iris, Nike and Athena training and looking after their favourite young warriors.

Remember to take a close look at the wrought-iron balustrade, which is delightfully decorated with intertwined sea creatures.

Altes Museum

W2 Am Lustgarten (Bodestrasse 1-3) ⑤ Hackescher Markt Ⓤ Museumsinsel 🚌100, 300 ⓒ 10am-5pm Wed-Fri (to 6pm Sat & Sun) 🌐 smb.museum

The Old Museum building, designed by Karl Friedrich Schinkel, is a beautiful Neo-Classical structure, with a 87-m- (285-ft-) high portico supported by 18 Ionic columns. Built in 1830 for the royal collection of art and antiquities, it now houses part of Berlin's Collection of Classical Antiquities, with permanent exhibitions on the art and culture of ancient Greece and on Roman and Etruscan art and sculptures.

Alte Nationalgalerie

W2 Bodestrasse 1-3 ⑤ Hackescher Markt, Friedrichstrasse Ⓤ Museumsinsel 🚌100, 300 🚊12, M1, M4, M5 ⓒ Hours vary, check website; book in advance via website 🌐 smb.museum

The Old National Gallery was completed in 1876 to a design by Friedrich August Stüler, who took into account the sketches made by Friedrich Wilhelm IV.

↑ Adolph von Menzel's *The Artist's Bedroom* at the Alte Nationalgalerie

The building is situated on a high platform reached via a double staircase. On the top stands an equestrian statue of Friedrich Wilhelm IV, the work of Alexander Calandrelli in 1886. Details on the façade reflect the building's purpose – the tympanum features Germania as patron of art, while the top is crowned with a personification of the arts.

Originally meant to house modern art, the current gallery includes works of masters such as Adolph von Menzel, Wilhelm Leibl, Max Liebermann *(p245)* and Arnold Böcklin.

There is no shortage of sculptures either, with works by Christian Daniel Rauch, Johann Gottfried Schadow, Antonio Canova and Reinhold Begas. Another two halls display paintings from the German Romantic era, featuring Caspar David Friedrich, Karl Friedrich Schinkel and Karl Blechen.

Lustgarten

8

W2 ⑤ Hackescher Markt 🚌100, 300

The enchanting garden in front of the Altes Museum looks as though it has always been there, but in its present form it was established only in the late 1990s.

Used to grow vegetables and herbs for the Stadtschloss until the late 16th century, it became a real *Lustgarten* (pleasure garden) in the reign of the Great Elector *(p215)*. However, its statues, grottoes, fountains and vegetation were removed when Friedrich Wilhelm I (1688–1740), known for his love of military pursuits, turned the garden into an army drill ground.

Following the construction of the Altes Museum, the ground became a park, designed by Peter Joseph Lenné *(p171)*. In 1831, it was adorned with a monolithic granite bowl by Christian Gottlieb Cantian, to a design by Schinkel. The 63-tonne (70-ton) bowl, measuring nearly 7 m (23 ft) in diameter, was intended for the museum rotunda, but was too heavy to carry inside.

After 1933, the Lustgarten was paved over and turned into a parade ground, remaining as such until 1989. Its current restoration is based on Lenné's original designs.

BERLIN'S BRIDGES

Despite wartime damage, Berlin's bridges are still well worth seeing. The Spree river and the city's canals have some exemplary architecture on their banks, while many of the bridges were designed and decorated by famous architects and sculptors. There are several particularly stunning bridges as you head west from Museumsinsel.

Bridges of Museumsinsel

① Schleusenbrücke
② Jungfernbrücke
③ Gertraudenbrücke

→ The impressive Humboldt Forum overlooking the Spree

Humboldt Forum

W3 ⬛**Schlossplatz**
Ⓢ**Hackescher Markt**
Ⓤ**Museumsinsel** 🚌**100,
200, 300** ⬛**Exhibitions:
10:30am–6:30pm Wed-Mon,
events: 11am–midnight**
Ⓦ**humboldtforum.org**

The Humboldt Forum sits on the site of a gigantic residential complex known as the Stadt-schloss (City Palace). Built first as a castle in 1451, it served as the main residence of the Brandenburg Electors. Rebuilt in the style of a three-storey palace in the 16th century, it became the main seat of the Hohenzollern family for almost 500 years until the end of the monarchy. The palace partly burned down during World War II, and in 1950–51, despite protests, the building was demolished. After a lengthy debate, it was decided to rebuild the palace as a museum complex. Three of the sides of the new building, designed by Franco Stella, take inspiration from the façade of the old palace; the eastern side, how-ever, is to a more modern design. This new museum has been named after Berlin's most prominent intellectual figures: Wilhelm and Alexander von Humboldt *(p68)*. It is home to one of the largest ethno-logical collections in the world. However, there has been debate over the true owner-ship of the items it holds, many of which were acquired during Germany's colonial era. The museum is attempting a new approach when dealing with these objects, including cooperating with artists and scholars from the artifacts' home countries, such as via the Tanzania–Germany: Shared Object Histories? project. This is an issue that affects many of Germany's museums.

10

Marstall

W3 ⬛**Schlossplatz/Breite
Strasse 36-37 Museum-
sinsel** 🚌**147, 200, 248**

The buildings of the former Royal Stables form a huge complex, occupying the area between the Spree and Breite Strasse, south of Schlossplatz. The wing on the side of Breite Strasse is a fragment of the old structure built in 1669. It was designed by Michael Matthias Smids and is the only surviving early Baroque building in Berlin. The wings running along Schlossplatz and the Spree river were built much later, in 1901, but are reminiscent of the Berlin Baroque style – probably because von Ihne modelled them on designs by Jean de Bodt from 1700.

Once the imperial home of more than 300 horses, the building now houses

---

> **DECOLONIZING BERLIN'S MUSEUMS**
>
> Many of the Museumsinsel's institutions showcase artifacts from Germany's colonial past, including the Pergamonmuseum, the Ethnological Museum and the Humboldt Forum. Following controversy in recent years about how European museums should treat pieces acquired under colonialism, several museums have returned meaningful African objects stolen or bought during colonial times. In 2020, the German government agreed on a digital strategy to publish an online data-base of museum objects acquired in a colonial context.

the Hanns Eisler Academy of Music and also hosts a branch of the Berlin City Library.

⑪ Nicolaihaus

⬥ W4 🏠 Brüderstrasse 13 📞 20 45 81 63 Ⓤ Spittelmarkt 🚌 147, 265, 248

Built around 1670, the Nicolaihaus is a fine example of Baroque architecture, with its original, magnificent oak staircase still in place. The house owes its fame, however, to its time as the home and bookshop of the publisher, writer and critic Christoph Friedrich Nicolai (1733–1811). One of the outstanding personalities of the Berlin Enlightenment, Nicolai was a supporter of such notable cultural figures as the Jewish philosopher Moses Mendelssohn *(p130)* and the playwright Gotthold Ephraim Lessing. Other regular artistic visitors included Johann Gottfried Schadow, Karl Wilhelm Ramler and Daniel Chodowiecki, all commemorated with a wall plaque. Today, the building houses the offices of the German Association of Protected Buildings, and is open to the public only by appointment.

⑫ Staatsratsgebäude

⬥ W3 🏠 Schlossplatz 1 Ⓢ & Ⓤ Alexanderplatz 🚌 100, 147, 200, M48

The former Staatsratsgebäude, an administrative building that was once the seat of the highest state government council of East Germany, was constructed in 1964. While it was once surrounded by other buildings from the GDR-era, they have since been demolished. The Staatsratsgebäude features the remaining original sculptures, including the magnificent atlantes by the famous Dresden sculptor Balthasar Permoser. Their inclusion, however, was not due to their artistic merit, but rather to their propaganda value: it was from the balcony of the portal that Karl Liebknecht proclaimed the birth of the Socialist Republic. Today, the building is home to the Hertie School, which prepares its students for positions in government and civil society.

⑬ Galgenhaus

⬥ W4 🏠 Brüderstrasse 10 📞 206 13 29 13 Ⓤ Spittelmarkt 🚌 147, 265, 248 🕐 10am–6pm Mon–Sat

The Gallows House, so named for a local legend in which an innocent woman was hanged, was originally built as the presbytery of the lost church of St Peter. Redesigned in the Neo-Classical style around 1805, the front portal and one room on the ground floor are all that remain of the original Baroque structure. The new building is, however, a delight: perfectly symmetrical, it resembles nothing so much as a dolls' house made life-size.

Today, the building houses the commercial Keweing Gallery, which acquired it in 2013. Before opening, the

gallery undertook a major restoration of the building, which shows off the surviving original interior features.

⑭ Ribbeckhaus

⬥ W3 🏠 Breite Strasse 35 Ⓤ Spittelmarkt 🚌 147, 248, M48

Four identical gables crown central Berlin's only surviving Renaissance building, the Ribbeck House. It was built around 1624 for Hans Georg von Ribbeck, a court counsellor, who soon sold it to Anna Sophie of Brunswick. After her death in 1659, the house passed to her nephew, Elector Friedrich Wilhelm. As crown property, it later housed state administrative offices.

The façade has beautiful wrought-iron grilles on the ground-floor windows and a late Renaissance portal, bearing the date and coat of arms of the von Ribbecks. This was replaced in 1960 with a copy, but apart from that, the house is a remarkable example of architectural survival from the city's history.

↑ Renaissance portal of the Ribbeckhaus

The stately exterior of the Märkisches Museum in Köllnischen Park ↑

1841

The year Prussian King Friedrich Wilhelm IV dedicated Museumsinsel to art and science.

15 ⊗

Märkisches Museum

📍Y4 🏠Am Köllnischen Park 5 🚇&Ⓤ Jannowitz-brücke Ⓤ Märkisches Museum, Heinrich-Heine-Strasse 🚌147, 248, 265 🔒For renovation until 2028 🌐stadtmuseum.de

This architectural pastiche is a complex of red-brick buildings that most resembles a medie-val monastery. It was built between 1901 and 1908 to house a collection relating to the history of Berlin and the March of Brandenburg, from the time of the earliest settlers to the present. Inspired by the Brick Gothic style popular in the Branden-burg region, architect Ludwig Hoffmann included references to Wittstock Castle and to St Catherine's Church in the city of Brandenburg. In the entrance hall you'll find a statue of Roland standing guard, which is a copy of the 15th-century monument in the city of Brandenburg. The main hall features the original Gothic portal from the Berlin residence of the Margraves of Brandenburg, demolished in 1931. Also featured is one of the original horse's heads from the Schadow Quadriga, which crowns the Brandenburg Gate (p78).

A further collection in the same building is devoted to the Berlin theatre during the period 1730 to 1933, including many posters, old programmes and stage sets. One of the galleries houses some charming old-time mechanical musical instruments, which are played by musicians once a week, at 5pm on Friday.

The Märkisches Museum is a branch of the Stadtmuseum Berlin organization, and those who wish to find out more about the history of the city during the museum's ongoing renovation can visit other affiliated museums and monuments such as the Ephraim-Palais (p113). Surrounding the museum is the Köllnischer Park, which has a kennel built in 1928 to house brown bears kept as city mascots, and an unusual statue of Berlin artist Heinrich Zille (p112).

Ermeler-Haus

☑ X4 ☐ Märkisches Ufer 10 Ⓤ Märkisches Museum, Heinrich-Heine-Strasse 🚌 147, 200, 248, 265

With its harmonious Neo-Classical façade, the Ermeler House stands out as one of the most handsome villas in Berlin. This house was once the town residence of Wilhelm Ferdinand Ermeler, a wealthy merchant and shopkeeper who made his money trading in tobacco. It originally stood on Fischerinsel on the opposite bank of the river, at Breite Strasse No. 11, but in 1968 the house was dismantled and reconstructed on this new site. The house was remodelled in 1825 to Ermeler's specifications, with a decor that includes a frieze alluding to aspects of the tobacco business. Restorers have recreated much of the original façade. The Rococo furniture dates from about

---

CÖLLN

An ancient settlement in the area called Fischerinsel at the southern end of Museumsinsel, the village of Cölln with its medieval church has now been razed almost to the ground. Until 1939, however, this working-class area with its tangle of narrow streets maintained a historical character of its own. This vanished completely in the 1960s, when most of the buildings were replaced with tower blocks. A few historical houses, including the Ermeler-Haus, were reconstructed elsewhere, but the atmosphere of this part of town has changed forever.

1760 and the notable 18th-century staircase has also been rebuilt.

A modern hotel has been built to the rear of the house facing Wallstrasse, using Ermeler-Haus as its kitchens, while the first-floor rooms are used for special events.

Historischer Hafen Berlin

☑ X4 ☐ Märkisches Ufer Ⓢ Jannowitzbrücke Ⓤ Märkisches Museum, Heinrich-Heine-Strasse 🚌 147, 248, 265 🕐 1–6pm Sat & Sun 🌐 historischer-hafen-berlin.de

Moored on the south shore of the island in an area called Fischerinsel, and opposite the Märkisches Ufer, are several examples of boats, barges and tugboats that operated on the Spree river at the end of the 19th century. These

---

craft constitute an open-air museum, the Historic Port of Berlin, which was once located in the Humboldt Port. One of the boats is now used as a café, while another, the *Renate Angelika*, houses a small exhibition on the history of inland waterway transport on the Spree and Havel.

Märkisches Ufer

☑ Y4 Ⓤ Märkisches Museum Ⓢ Jannowitzbrücke 🚌 147, 248, 265

Once called Neukölln am Wasser (meaning Neukölln on the water), this street, which runs alongside the Spree river, is one of the few corners of Berlin where it is still possible to see the town as it must have looked in the 18th and 19th centuries. Eight pretty houses have been meticulously conserved here. Two Neo-Baroque houses at Nos. 16 and 18, known as Otto-Nagel-Haus, used to contain a small museum displaying paintings by Otto Nagel, a great favourite with the Communist authorities. The building now houses the photo archives for the state museums of Berlin.

A number of pretty garden cafés and fashionable restaurants make this attractive area very popular with tourists.

Boats moored at the Historischer Hafen Berlin

A SHORT WALK

MUSEUMSINSEL

Distance 1km (0.5 miles) **Nearest tram
station** Georgenstr./Am Kupfergraben
Time 15 minutes

A stroll around the northern end of this
island will introduce you to some of
Berlin's most famous sights, like the
Lustgarten and the Berliner Dom (Berlin
Cathedral). It is also where you will find
some of the most important museums
in the east of the city. These include
the Bode-Museum, the Altes Museum
and the splendid Pergamonmuseum
with its collection of antiquities

*This railway bridge
is also used by the
S-Bahn.*

START

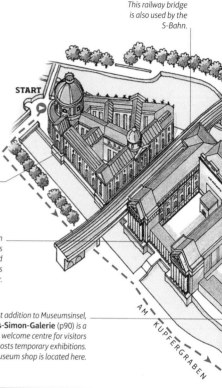

*The dome-covered rounded
corner of the **Bode-Museum**
(p94) provides a prominent
landmark at the tip of the island.*

*The **Pergamonmuseum** (p90) is known
for its reconstruction of fragments
of ancient towns such as Miletus and
Babylon, as well as the original friezes
from the Pergamon Altar.*

*The newest addition to Museumsinsel,
the **James-Simon-Galerie** (p90) is a
modern welcome centre for visitors
and also hosts temporary exhibitions.
The museum shop is located here.*

AM KUPFERGRABEN

| 0 metres | 100 | N |
| 0 yards | 100 | ↑ |

↑ The imposing façade of the Berliner Dom,
as seen from the Lustgarten

← The Lustgarten, originally used to grow food for the Stadtschloss kitchens

MUSEUMS-INSEL

Locator Map
For more detail see p84

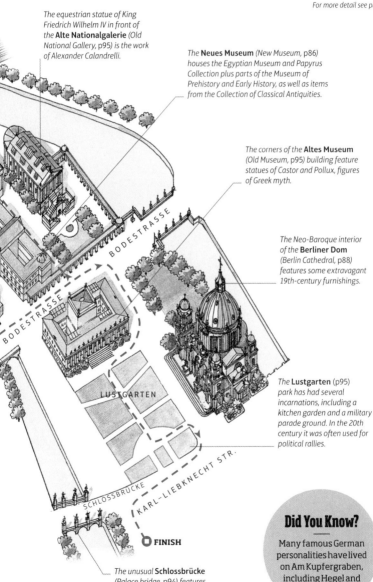

The equestrian statue of King Friedrich Wilhelm IV in front of the **Alte Nationalgalerie** *(Old National Gallery, p95)* is the work of Alexander Calandrelli.

The **Neues Museum** *(New Museum, p86)* houses the Egyptian Museum and Papyrus Collection plus parts of the Museum of Prehistory and Early History, as well as items from the Collection of Classical Antiquities.

The corners of the **Altes Museum** *(Old Museum, p95)* building feature statues of Castor and Pollux, figures of Greek myth.

The Neo-Baroque interior of the **Berliner Dom** *(Berlin Cathedral, p88)* features some extravagant 19th-century furnishings.

The **Lustgarten** *(p95)* park has had several incarnations, including a kitchen garden and a military parade ground. In the 20th century it was often used for political rallies.

BODESTRASSE

BODESTRASSE

BODESTRASSE

LUSTGARTEN

SCHLOSSBRÜCKE

KARL–LIEBKNECHT STR.

⏻ **FINISH**

The unusual **Schlossbrücke** *(Palace bridge, p94)* features statues made of stunning white Carrara marble.

Did You Know?

Many famous German personalities have lived on Am Kupfergraben, including Hegel and Angela Merkel.

Berlin-Alexanderplatz station and the Fernsehturm

AROUND ALEXANDERPLATZ

This area is the historical centre of the city, as it includes the site where the settlement of Berlin was first established in the 13th century. Traces of Berlin's earliest history can still be seen here, including the city's oldest surviving church – Marienkirche, founded in 1280 – and the reconstructed old town around the Nikolaiviertel. The area retains cosy mews and alleys, which are surrounded by postwar high-rise blocks.

The legacy of East Berlin is also particularly strong in the architecture around Alexanderplatz. The GDR regime replaced the huge apartment buildings and department stores just to the north with a square, Marx-Engels-Forum and the Fernsehturm, which can be seen from almost anywhere in the city.

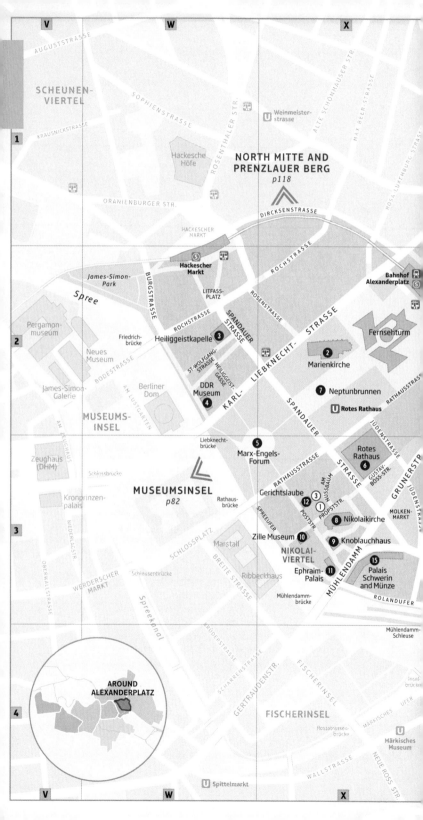

AUGUSTSTRASSE

SCHEUNEN-
VIERTEL

KRAUSNICKSTRASSE

SOPHIENSTRASSE

Hackesche
Höfe

Weinmeister-
strasse

ROSENTHALER STR.

ALTE SCHÖNHAUSER STR.

MAX BEER STRASSE

ROSA-LUXEMBURG STRASSE

**NORTH MITTE AND
PRENZLAUER BERG**
p118

ORANIENBURGER STR.

DIRCKSENSTRASSE

HACKESCHER
MARKT

Hackescher
Markt

James-Simon-
Park

Spree

BURGSTRASSE

LITFASS-
PLATZ

ROCHSTRASSE

ROSENSTRASSE

STRASSE

Bahnhof
Alexanderplatz

Pergamon-
museum

Friedrich-
brücke

ROCHSTRASSE

SPANDAUER
STRASSE

Heiliggeistkapelle **3**

Fernsehturm

Neues
Museum

ST-WOLFGANG-
STRASSE

HEILIGGEIST-
GASSE

KARL-

LIEBKNECHT-

Marienkirche **2**

James-Simon-
Galerie

Berliner
Dom

DDR
Museum **4**

AM LUSTGARTEN

SPANDAUER

Neptunbrunnen **7**

RATHAUSSTR.

MUSEUMS-
INSEL

Liebknecht-
brücke

Marx-Engels-
Forum **5**

U Rotes Rathaus

Zeughaus
(DHM)

Schlossbrücke

MUSEUMSINSEL
p82

Rathaus-
brücke

RATHAUSSTRASSE

STRASSE

Rotes
Rathaus **6**

JÜDENSTRASSE

GRUNERSTR.

Kronprinzen-
palais

NIEDERLAGSTR.

Gerichtslaube

SPREEUFER

POSTSTR.

AM
NUSSBAUM

12

3

1

PROPSTSTR.

GUSTAV-
BÖSS-STR.

JÜDENSTRASSE

MOLKEN-
MARKT

Nikolaikirche **8**

SCHLOSSPLATZ

Marstall

BREITE STRASSE

Zille Museum **10**

Knoblauchhaus **9**

WERDERSCHER
MARKT

Schleusenbrücke

Ribbeckhaus

NIKOLAI-
VIERTEL

MÜHLENDAMM

Ephraim-
Palais **11**

Palais
Schwerin
and Münze **15**

OBERWALLSTRASSE

Spreekanal

Mühlendamm-
brücke

ROLANDUFER

Mühlendamm-
Schleuse

BRÜDERSTRASSE

SCHARRENSTRASSE

GERTRAUDENSTR.

FISCHERINSEL

Insel-
brücke

**AROUND
ALEXANDERPLATZ**

FISCHERINSEL

Rossstrassen-
brücke

MÄRKISCHES UFER

U Märkisches
Museum

WALLSTRASSE

U Spittelmarkt

NEUE ROSS STR.

Must Sees
1. Alexanderplatz
2. Marienkirche

Experience More
3. Heiliggeistkapelle
4. DDR Museum
5. Marx-Engels-Forum
6. Rotes Rathaus
7. Neptunbrunnen
8. Nikolaikirche
9. Knoblauchhaus
10. Zille Museum
11. Ephraim-Palais
12. Gerichtslaube
13. Franziskaner Klosterkirche
14. Parochialkirche
15. Palais Schwerin and Münze
16. Stadtmauer

Eat
① Zum Nussbaum
② Gastätte Zur letzen Instanz

Stay
③ Nikolai Residence

FRIEDRICHSHAIN
p142

0 metres 250
0 yards 250

N

ALEXANDERPLATZ

📍Y2 Ⓢ&Ⓤ Alexanderplatz 🚌100, 200, 245, 248, 300 🚊M5, M6, M8
🕐Fernsehturm: Mar–Oct: 9am–midnight daily; Nov–Feb: 10am–midnight daily 🌐tv-turm.de

A veritable treasure-trove of Soviet architecture, Alexanderplatz is a bustling square well worth a visit for its shops and restaurants, and to get a taste of the dynamic side of Berlin the locals see every day.

Alexanderplatz, or "Alex" as it is known locally, has a long and tumultuous history, although it is difficult now to find any visible traces of the not-so-recent past. Once called Ochsenmarkt (oxen market), it was the site of a cattle and wool market. It was later renamed after Tsar Alexander I, who visited Berlin in 1805. Houses and shops sprang up along with a market hall and train station, and by the early 20th century "Alex" had become one of the city's busiest spots. In 1929, attempts were made to develop the square, though only two office buildings were added – the Alexanderhaus and the Berolinahaus. These two, both by Peter Behrens, are still standing today. World War II erased most of the square's older buildings and it is now surrounded by 1960s edifices, including the Park Inn and the Fernsehturm.

↑ The World Clock on Alexanderplatz, an iconic city landmark

Fernsehturm

The Television Tower, nicknamed Telespargel (TV asparagus) by locals, is the city's tallest structure, at 368 m (1,207 ft), and indeed is one of the tallest in Europe. One of the attractions of the tower is the revolving restaurant: a full rotation takes about half an hour, so it is possible to get a bird's-eye view of the whole city while sipping a cup of coffee. On a clear day, visibility can reach up to 40 km (25 miles).

Fernsehturm

📍X2 🏛Panoramastrasse 1A Ⓢ&Ⓤ Alexanderplatz, Rotes Rathaus 🚌100, 200, 245, 300, TXL 🚊M2, M4, M5, M6

↑ Walter Womacka's mural *Unser Leben* (*Our Life*) circling the Haus des Lehrers

> **THE FUTURE OF ALEXANDERPLATZ**
>
> The plan to breathe some contemporary life into Alexanderplatz goes back to 1993. A mix of factors has consistently thwarted those plans – as has the city's decision to protect some of the Soviet-style buildings as heritage-status structures. However, the Senate has given preliminary approval for three proposed buildings by prominent city architect Hans Kollhoff. The new high-rise buildings will have both apartments as well as several commercial establishments. Whether these plans become reality is yet to be seen, but it's the furthest the ideas have got in a quarter of a century.

↑ The iconic Berliner
Fernsehturm, the tallest
structure in Europe,
towering over the city

2

MARIENKIRCHE

☉X2 ☐Karl-Liebknecht-Strasse 8 ⑤Alexanderplatz ⑪Alexanderplatz, Rotes Rathaus ☐100, 200, 245, 248, 300 ☐M4, M5, M6 ☐10am-6pm daily ☒marienkirche-berlin.de

The church of St Mary is a tranquil, medieval oasis in the heart of Berlin. The early Gothic hall design and the lavish Baroque touches make this one of the most interesting churches in the city.

Marienkirche was first established as a parish church in the second half of the 13th century, and construction was completed early in the 14th century. The main building is a long, red-brick Gothic hall, which still contains many beautiful decorations and features dating from the mid-15th to early 18th century, such as the baptismal font (1437) and the pulpit (1703). During reconstruction works in 1380, the church was altered slightly but its overall shape changed only in the 15th century, when it acquired the front tower. In 1790, the tower was crowned with a dome designed by Carl Gotthard Langhans. The church was once hemmed in by buildings, but today it stands alone in the shadow of the Fernsehturm (Television Tower; p106).

The dome that crowns the tower includes both Baroque and Neo-Gothic elements.

→

Marienkirche, a medieval parish church

The central part of the Gothic altar, known as the retable, dating from 1510, features three unknown monks.

Totentanz, meaning "dance of death", is the name of a 22-m- (72-ft-) long Gothic wall fresco, dating from 1485.

↑ The red main hall, built in the Brick Gothic style some time in the mid- to late 13th century

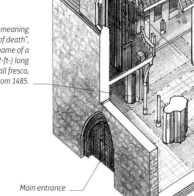

Main entrance

↑ The Baroque altar, designed by Andreas Krüger around 1762; *(inset)* sculpture detail from Andreas Schlüter's pulpit, completed in 1703

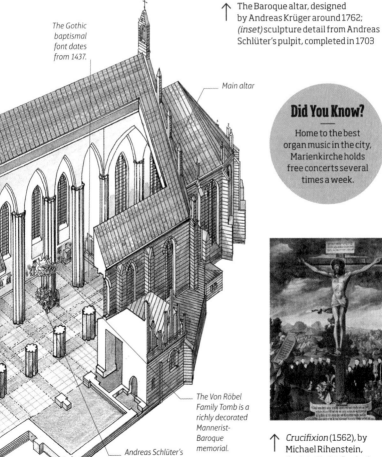

The Gothic baptismal font dates from 1437.

Main altar

The Von Röbel Family Tomb is a richly decorated Mannerist-Baroque memorial.

Andreas Schlüter's pulpit is a masterpiece carved from alabaster.

Did You Know?

Home to the best organ music in the city, Marienkirche holds free concerts several times a week.

↑ *Crucifixion* (1562), by Michael Rihenstein, depicts Christ flanked by Moses and St John the Baptist

EXPERIENCE MORE

Heiliggeistkapelle

W2 **Spandauer Strasse 1** **S** **Hackescher Markt** **100, 200, 300** **M4, M5, M6**

The Chapel of the Holy Spirit is the only surviving hospital chapel in Berlin. It was built as part of a hospital complex in the second half of the 13th century, and was rebuilt in the 15th century. The hospital was demolished in 1825, but the chapel was retained. In 1906, it was made into a newly erected College of Trade, designed by Cremer & Wolffenstein.

The chapel is a fine example of Brick Gothic construction. Its modest interior features a 15th-century star-shaped vault. The supports under the vault are decorated with half-statues of prophets and saints.

DDR Museum

W2 **Karl-Liebknecht-Strasse 1** **S** **Hackescher Markt** **U** **Museuminsel** **100, 245, 300** **10am– 8pm daily (to 10pm Sat)** **ddr-museum.de**

This hands-on museum on the Spree embankment opposite the Berliner Dom *(p88)* gives an insight into the daily lives of East Germans during the era of the DDR, and demonstrates how the secret police kept a watchful eye on the city's people. Exhibits include a replica of a typical living room and a gleaming example of the iconic Trabant car.

Marx-Engels-Forum

W3 **S** **Hackescher Markt, Alexanderplatz** **U** **Rotes Rathaus** **100, 200, 300**

This vast square, which stretches from the Neptune fountain to the Spree river in the west, was given the inappropriate name Marx-Engels-Forum. Devoid of any surroundings, the only features in this square are the statues of Karl Marx and Friedrich Engels. The statues, added in 1986, are by Ludwig Engelhart.

The square is set to be developed into a new riverside park, complete with fountains and greenery. The statues of Marx and Engels will remain the centrepiece of the redeveloped square.

Did You Know?

Karl Marx studied at Berlin's Humboldt University and became one of the renowned Young Hegelians.

The larger-than-life-size statues of Marx (seated) and Engels at the Marx-Engels-Forum

←

The tiered clock tower
of the Rotes Rathaus

 7

Neptunbrunnen

X2 Spandauer Strasse
(Rathausvorplatz)
&U Alexanderplatz, Rotes
Rathaus Hackescher
Markt 100, 200

The magnificent Neptune Fountain is a Neo-Baroque-style feature on the square outside the Rotes Rathaus. It was moved here from the former Stadtschloss (Berlin Castle) in 1969, and will return there when rebuilding of the castle is complete.

The statue of Neptune in a dynamic pose at the centre of the fountain is surrounded by four figures representing Germany's greatest rivers: the Rhine, the Vistula, the Oder and the Elbe. The naturalism of the composition and the detail, such as the beautiful bronze fishes, crayfish and fishing nets, are noteworthy.

 6

Rotes Rathaus

X3 Rathausstrasse 15
90 26 0 Alexander-platz URotes Rathaus
UKlosterstrasse 100,
200, 248 9am–6pm
Mon–Fri

This impressive structure is Berlin's main town hall; its name means simply "red town hall". Its predecessor was a much more modest building, and by the end of the 19th century it was insufficient to meet the needs of the growing metropolis.

The present building was designed by Hermann Friedrich Waesemann, and its construction was completed in 1869. The architect took his main inspiration from Italian Renaissance municipal buildings, but the tower is reminiscent of Laon cathedral in France. The walls are made from red brick and it was this,

rather than the political orientation of the mayors, that gave the town hall its name. The building has a continuous frieze known as the "stone chronicle", which was added in 1879. It features scenes and figures from the city's history and the development of its economy and science.

The Rotes Rathaus was badly damaged during World War II and, following its reconstruction (1951–8), it became the seat of the East Berlin authorities. The West Berlin magistrate was housed in the Schöneberg town hall (p241). After the reunification of Germany, the Rotes Rathaus became the centre of authority, housing the offices of the mayor, the magistrates' offices and state rooms. The forecourt sculptures were added in 1958. These are by Fritz Cremer and depict Berliners helping to rebuild the city.

STAY

Nikolai Residence
This three-star option offers accommodation right in the heart of the quaint pedestrianized Nikolaiviertel. Service is friendly and personal. The hotel is home to the Nikolais Restaurant and Bar, which serves modern Mediterranean cuisine. Visitors should note that parking can be a challenge.

X3 Am Nussbaum 5
nikolai-residence.com

€€€

 ←

The copper-clad double spires of the Nikolaikirche

  9

Knoblauchhaus

X3 Poststrasse 23 & Rotes Rathaus Klosterstrasse 200, 248 10am-6pm Tue-Sun stadtmuseum.de

A small townhouse situated on elegant Poststrasse, the Knoblauchhaus is the only Baroque building in the Nikolaiviertel that escaped damage during World War II. It was built in 1759 for the Knoblauch family, which includes the famous architect Eduard Knoblauch. His works include, among others, the Neue Synagoge (p130).

The current appearance of the building is the result of work carried out in 1835, when the façade was given a Neo-Classical look. The ground floor houses a popular wine bar, while the upper floors belong to a museum. On the first floor it is possible to see the interior of an early 19th-century middle-class home, including a beautiful Biedermeier-style room.

   10

Zille Museum

X3 Propststrasse 11 Klosterstrasse Rotes Rathaus 200, 248 11am-6pm Mon-Sat, 1-6pm Sun zille museum-berlin.de

Artist, illustrator and photographer Heinrich Zille (1858–1929) was one of Berlin's best-known personalities. Renowned for his caricatures of everyday working-class life in the city, Zille was partly responsible for Berlin's image as a loud, rebellious, snarky, poor, proud and sometimes downright unsavoury capital.

 8

Nikolaikirche

X3 Nikolaikirchplatz & Rotes Rathaus Klosterstrasse 200, 248 10am-6pm Fri-Sun stadtmuseum.de

The Nikolaikirche is the oldest sacred building of historic Berlin. The original structure erected on this site was started probably around 1230 when the town was granted its municipal rights. What remains now of this stone building is the massive base of the two-tower façade of the present church, which dates from c 1300. The presbytery was completed around 1402, but the construction of the main building went on until the mid-15th century. The result was a magnificent Gothic brick hall-church, featuring a chancel with an ambulatory and a row of low chapels. In 1877, Hermann Blankenstein, who conducted the church

restoration works, removed most of its Baroque modifications and reconstructed the front towers.

Destroyed by bombing in 1945, the Nikolaikirche was eventually rebuilt in 1987 and shows a permanent exhibit on Berlin's history. The west wall of the southern nave contains Andreas Schlüter's monument to the goldsmith Daniel Männlich and his wife, which features a gilded relief portrait of the couple above a mock doorway.

 INSIDER TIP
Free Concerts

The Nikolaikirche hosts free 30-minute classical concerts every Friday at 5pm. Under the motto "Listen - Relax - Reflect" they span works from major composers as well as chamber music, and often employ the church's own organ.

Zille's collection of sketches, drawings, lithographs, photographs and cartoons can now be found in this small but charming three-room museum, along with a film and some family pictures. It has only minimal information in English, but the gist of the artist's work is easy to appreciate. His scabrously funny portrayals of beggars, urchins, labourers and prostitutes, finding in them a zest for life that transcended the poverty of their existence, made him immensely popular with Berlin's underclass.

Nearby you can find a reconstructed (and relocated) version of one of Zille's favourite watering holes, Zum Nussbaum *(p115)*, whose characters and stories often informed his work.

> **Zille was partly responsible for Berlin's image as a loud, rebellious, snarky, poor, proud and sometimes downright unsavoury capital.**

11

Ephraim-Palais

📍 X3 🏛 Poststrasse 16
Ⓢ & Ⓤ Rotes Rathaus
Ⓤ Klosterstrasse 🚌 200, 248 🕐 10am–6pm Tue-Sun
🌐 stadtmuseum.de

The corner entrance of the Ephraim-Palais, standing at the junction of Poststrasse and Mühlendamm, used to be called *"die schönste Ecke Berlins"*, meaning "Berlin's most beautiful corner". This Baroque palace was built by Friedrich Wilhelm Dieterichs in 1766 for Nathan Veitel Heinrich Ephraim, Frederick the Great's Mint master and court jeweller. It remained in the possession of the Ephraim family until 1823, after which it changed hands several times.

During the widening of the Mühlendamm bridge in 1935 the palace was demolished, which may have been due in some part to the Jewish origin of its owner. Parts of the façade, saved from demolition, were stored in a warehouse in the western part of the city. In 1983, they were sent to East Berlin and used in the reconstruction of the palace, which was erected a few metres from its original site. One of the first-floor rooms features a restored Baroque ceiling, designed by Andreas Schlüter. The ceiling previously adorned Palais Wartenberg, which was dismantled in 1889.

The Ephraim-Palais currently houses a branch of the Stadtmuseum Berlin (Berlin City Museum). It hosts a series of temporary exhibitions and events focused on Berlin's local artistic and cultural history. The palace is also home to the Ephraim Veitel Foundation for the Promotion of Jewish Life in Germany.

→ The spiral staircase at the Ephraim-Palais with its gilded railing

12

Gerichtslaube

📍 X3 🏠 Poststrasse 28
📞 241 56 97 ⏰ & Ⓤ Rotes
Rathaus 🚌 200, 248

This small building, with its sharply angled arcades, has had a turbulent history. It was built around 1280 as part of Berlin's old town hall in Spandauer Strasse. The original building was a single-storey arcaded construction with vaults supported by a central pillar. It was open on three sides and adjoined the shorter wall of the town hall. A further storey was added in 1485 to provide a hall, to which the magnificent lattice vaults were added several decades later, in 1555.

In 1692, Johann Arnold Nering refurbished the town hall in a Baroque style but left the arcades unaltered. Then, in 1868, the whole structure was dismantled to provide space for the new town hall, the Rotes Rathaus *(p111)*. The Baroque part was lost forever, but the Gothic arcades and the first-floor hall were moved to the palace gardens in Babelsberg, where they were reassembled as a building in their own right. When the Nikolaiviertel *(p116)* was undergoing renovation, it was decided to restore the court of justice as well. The present building in Poststrasse is a copy of a part of the former town hall, erected on a different site from the original one. Inside it is a restaurant serving local cuisine.

13

Franziskaner Klosterkirche

📍 Y3 🏠 Klosterstrasse 74
Ⓤ Klosterstrasse 🚌 248

These picturesque ruins surrounded by greenery

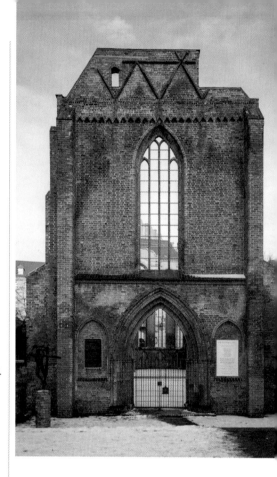

↑ Ruins of the Franziskaner Klosterkirche

are the remains of the early Gothic Franciscan Friary Church. The Franciscan friars settled in Berlin in the early 13th century. Between 1250 and 1265 they built a church and a friary, which survived almost unchanged until 1945. The church was a triple-nave basilica with an elongated presbytery, widening into a heptagonal section that was added to the structure in around 1300.

Protestants took over the church after the Reformation and the friary became a famous grammar school, whose graduates included Prussian Chancellor Otto von Bismarck.

The friary was so damaged in World War II that it was subsequently demolished, while the church was partially reconstructed in 2003–4 and is now a venue for concerts and exhibitions. The giant Corinthian capitals, emerging from the grass near the church ruins, are from a portal from the Stadtschloss (City Palace, *p96*).

1621

The year the original gin mill opened on the site of Berlin's oldest pub: Gaststätte Zur letzten Instanz.

Parochialkirche

Y3 Klosterstrasse 67
24 75 95 10 Kloster-
strasse 248 9am-
3:30pm Mon-Fri

The Parish Church was, at
one time, one of the most
beautiful Baroque churches in
Berlin. Johann Arnold Nering
prepared the initial design,
with four chapels framing a
central tower. Unfortunately,
Nering died as construction
started in 1695. The work was
continued by Martin Grünberg,
but the collapse of the nearly
completed vaults forced a
change in the design. Instead
of the intended tower over
the main structure, a vestibule
with a front tower was built.
The church was completed
in 1703, but then, in 1714,
its tower was enlarged to
accommodate a carillon.

World War II had a
devastating effect on the
Parochialkirche. The interior
was completely destroyed,
and the tower collapsed.
Following stabilization of the
main structure, the façade
was restored, with reproduced
historic elements set within a
plain interior. In 2016, a replica
of the former tower top was
mounted. It bears a new
carillon with 52 bells.

Palais Schwerin and Münze

X3 Molkenmarkt 1-3
& Rotes Rathaus
Klosterstrasse
248

These two adjoining houses
have quite different histories.
The older one, at Molkenmarkt
No. 2, is Palais Schwerin, which
was built by Jean de Bodt in
1704 for a government minister,
Otto von Schwerin. Despite
subsequent remodelling,
the palace kept its beautiful
sculpted window cornices, the
interior wooden staircase and
the magnificent cartouche
featuring the von Schwerin
family crest.

The adjoining house is the
Münze, or Mint, built in 1936.
Its façade is decorated with
a copy of the frieze that
once adorned the previous
Neo-Classical Mint building
in Werderscher Markt. The
antique style of the frieze
was designed by Friedrich
Gilly and produced in the
workshop of J G Schadow.

Stadtmauer

Y3 Waisenstrasse
& Alexanderplatz
Klosterstrasse 248

The Town Wall that once
surrounded the settlements
of Berlin and Cölln was
erected in the second half
of the 13th century. The ring
of fortifications, built from
brick and fieldstone, was
made taller in the 14th
century. Having finally lost
its military significance by
the 17th century, the wall was
almost entirely dismantled,
though some small sections
survive around Waisenstrasse,
having been incorporated
into other buildings.

Gaststätte Zur letzten
Instanz by the
Stadtmauer

EAT

Zum Nussbaum
A reconstruction of a
16th-century pub,
serving traditional
Berlin cuisine including
rollmops, meatballs and
vegetable pancakes, as
well as local beers.

X3 Am Nussbaum 3
24 23 09 5
Noon-10pm daily

€€€

Gaststätte Zur letzten Instanz
The oldest pub in Berlin
has served everyone
from Beethoven to
Angela Merkel. The
menu offers classic
German fare, including
pork knuckle and
Rinderroulade (beef
olive) in a classic
wood-panelled room.

Y3 Waisenstrasse
14-16 Noon-1am
Tue-Sat (to 10pm Sun)
Mon
zurletzteninstanz.com

€€€

A SHORT WALK
NIKOLAIVIERTEL

Distance 1 km (0.5 miles)
Nearest U-Bahn station Märkisches Museum **Time** 15 minutes

St Nicholas' Quarter, or the Nikolaiviertel, owes its name to the parish church whose spires rise above the small buildings in this part of town. The Nikolaiviertel is full of narrow alleys crammed with popular restaurants, tiny souvenir shops and small museums. The district retains the features of long-destroyed Alt-Berlin (Old Berlin) and is usually filled with tourists looking for a place to rest after a busy day of sightseeing – particularly in the summer. Almost every other house is occupied by a restaurant, inn, pub or café, so the area is quite lively until late at night.

Did You Know?

Many Berlin artists lived in the Nikolaiviertel, including Ibsen, Lessing, Kleist and Hauptmann.

The **Nikolaikirche** (p112) *is now a museum, with its original furnishings incorporated into the exhibition.*

The replica arcades and medieval courthouse of **Gerichtslaube** (p114) *now contain popular restaurants.*

0 metres 75
0 yards 75

N ↑

This statue of **St George Slaying the Dragon** *once graced a courtyard of the Stadtschloss.*

POSTSTRASSE

SPREEUFER

A Biedermeier-style room can be found on the first floor of the **Knoblauchhaus** *building (p112), which is one of the few to escape World War II damage.*

START

One noteworthy feature of the **Ephraim-Palais** (p113) *is its elegant façade. Inside, there is also an impressive spiral staircase and balustrade.*

↑ A bear, the symbol of Berlin, inside a fountain in front of Nikolaikirche

↑ The historic core of Alt-Berlin, reconstructed under the GDR

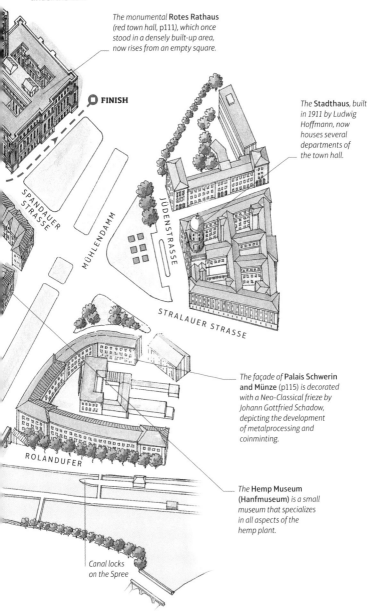

The monumental **Rotes Rathaus** *(red town hall, p111), which once stood in a densely built-up area, now rises from an empty square.*

FINISH

The **Stadthaus**, *built in 1911 by Ludwig Hoffmann, now houses several departments of the town hall.*

SPANDAUER STRASSE

MÜHLENDAMM

JÜDENSTRASSE

STRALAUER STRASSE

ROLANDUFER

The façade of **Palais Schwerin and Münze** (p115) *is decorated with a Neo-Classical frieze by Johann Gottfried Schadow, depicting the development of metalprocessing and coinminting.*

The **Hemp Museum** **(Hanfmuseum)** *is a small museum that specializes in all aspects of the hemp plant.*

Canal locks on the Spree

NORTH MITTE AND PRENZLAUER BERG

The area northwest of Alexanderplatz, formerly called Spandauer Vorstadt, is a historic district established in the Middle Ages. Some 18th-century buildings still stand here, though the area has mainly developed into a lively neighbourhood of buzzing bars, cafés and designer shops.

The southeastern part of the area is known as Scheunenviertel (Barn Quarter). In 1672, the Great Elector moved the hay barns – a fire hazard – out of the city limits. From that time it became a refuge for Jewish people fleeing Russia and Eastern Europe, and the Spandauer Vorstadt later developed into Berlin's affluent Jewish Quarter. To the north is Prenzlauer Berg, a bohemian hub in the 1990s and now, after gentrification, a beautiful and pleasant place to live and visit.

NORTH MITTE AND PRENZLAUER BERG

Must Sees
1 Gedenkstätte Berliner Mauer
2 Hamburger Bahnhof

Experience More
3 Museum für Naturkunde
4 Deutsches Theater
5 Futurium
6 Brecht-Weigel-Museum
7 Dorotheenstädtischer Friedhof
8 Friedrichstadtpalast
9 Sammlung Boros
10 Oranienburger Strasse
11 Berliner Ensemble
12 Monbijoupark
13 Hackesche Höfe
14 Neue Synagoge and Centrum Judaicum
15 Kollwitzplatz
16 Jüdischer Friedhof
17 Sophienkirche
18 Gedenkstätte Grosse Hamburger Strasse
19 Haus Schwarzenberg Museums
20 Volksbühne
21 Torstrasse
22 Sophienstrasse
23 Zionskirche
24 Alte and Neue Schönhauser Strasse
25 Prater
26 Alter Jüdischer Friedhof
27 Synagoge Rykestrasse
28 Kulturbrauerei
29 Wasserturm

Eat
① Yam Yam
② Night Kitchen
③ Rutz
④ Metzer Eck

Drink
⑤ Buck & Breck
⑥ Becketts Kopf

Stay
⑦ Circus Hotel
⑧ Ackselhaus and Blue Home

Shop
⑨ Goldhahn und Sampson
⑩ Thatchers
⑪ Saint George's English Bookshop

HEIDESTRASSE

Schiffahrtskanal

BERNAUER STR.
STRELITZER STR.

1 Gedenkstätte Berliner Mauer

ACKERSTRASSE
ANKLAM

Sophien-Friedhof

BERGSTRASSE

HABERSAATHSTRASSE

ZINNOWITZER-STRASSE

Nordbahnhof

INVALIDENSTRASSE

GARTENSTRASSE

BERGSTRASSE

SCHWARZER WEG

HESSISCHE STR.

Museum für Naturkunde **3**

Naturkundemuseum

CHAUSSEESTRASSE

SCHLEGEL-STRASSE

NOVALISSTRASSE

STRASSE

TUCHOLSKYSTR.

INVALIDENSTRASSE

Brecht-Weigel-Museum **6**

Dorotheenstädtischer Friedhof **7**

TIECK

TORSTRASSE

LINIENSTR.

Hamburger Bahnhof **2**

Sandkrug-brücke

ROBERT-KOCH-PLATZ

HANNOVERSCHE STRASSE

Oranienburger Tor

Oranienburger Strasse

Oranienburger Strasse **10**

AUGUSTST

②

Hauptbahnhof
ℹ️

Charité Universitätsmedizin Berlin

LUISENSTRASSE

Südpromde

Humboldt Universität

FRIEDRICHSTR.

Oranienburger Str.

JOHANNISSTR.

Neue Synagoge and Centrum Judaicum **14**

TUCHOLSKYSTR.

WASHINGTON-PLATZ

Futurium **5**

KAPELLE-UFER

UNTERBAUMSTR.

SCHUMANNSTR.

Deutsches Theater **4**

Sammlung Boros **9**

Friedrichstadt-palast **8**

ZIEGELSTR.

SCHEUNEN-VIERTEL

Monbijou-brücke

KARELPLATZ

REINHARDTSTR.

REINHARDTSTR.

Berliner Ensemble **11**

BERTOLT-BRECHT-PLATZ

MARIENSTRASSE

ALBRECHT-STRASSE

TIERGARTEN
p152

Bundestag

SCHIFFBAUERDAMM

LUISENSTR.

SCHIFFBAUERDAMM

Spree

Friedrich-strasse

REICHSTAGUFER

AROUND UNTER DEN LINDEN
p62

Marschallbrücke

TIERGARTEN p152
AROUND UNTER DEN LINDEN p62

L

1

2

3

4

I
J
K
L

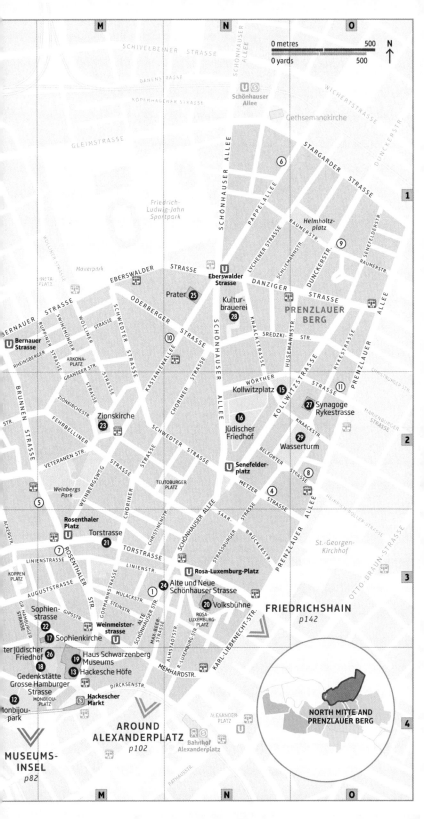

The Window of Remembrance
features photos of those who
died crossing the Wall ↑

GEDENKSTÄTTE BERLINER MAUER

📍 L2 🏠 Bernauer Strasse 119 Ⓢ Nordbahnhof Ⓤ Bernauer Strasse
🚌 M8, M10 🚋 245, 247 🕐 Hours vary, check website
🌐 berliner-mauer-gedenkstaette.de

The Berlin Wall Memorial on Bernauer Strasse is dedicated to the people who were killed by the Eastern border guards while attempting to escape into West Berlin.

Bernauer Strasse

Only small fragments of the Berlin Wall have survived. One of these, along Bernauer Strasse, is now an official place of remembrance. The location of the memorial here is poignant as the street was cut in two, resulting in people jumping to the West side from upper-floor buildings that stood right on the dividing line, while border guards were bricking up doors and windows facing west. Today, the memorial is a grim reminder of the hardship the division inflicted on the city. It includes a museum and various installations along 2 km (1 mile) of the former border.

Structure of the Berlin Wall

Initially the Berlin Wall consisted simply of rolls of barbed wire. However, these were eventually replaced by a 4-m (13-ft) wall, safeguarded by a second wall made from reinforced concrete. This second wall was topped with a thick pipe to prevent people from gripping the top with their fingers. Along the Wall ran what was known as a "death zone", an area controlled by guards with dogs. Where the border passed close to houses, the inhabitants were relocated. Along the entire length of the 55-km (96-mile) wall there were 293 watchtowers, along with 57 bunkers and, later on, alarms.

↑ The *Mauerspringer* (wall jumper) sculpture, added to the site in 2003

28

The number of years that the Berlin Wall split the city in two.

GHOST STATIONS

Hidden inside Nordbahnhof station is a fascinating public exhibition about "ghost stations": stations where trains passed through East Germany but passengers were not able to leave the train until it reached West Berlin again. These stations were dimly lit places patrolled by armed East German border guards and occasionally used for daring escapes.

2

HAMBURGER BAHNHOF

📍 J3 🏠 Invalidenstrasse 50/51 Ⓢ & Ⓤ Hauptbahnhof 🚌 120, 147, 245, M41, M85 🚋 M5, M8, M10 🕐 10am–6pm Tue–Sun (to 8pm Thu) 🌐 smb.museum

At the Museum of Contemporary Art, multimedia exhibits sit alongside exemplary pieces of modern art to help visitors understand the development of styles such as Pop Art and Expressionism.

This art museum is situated in a specially adapted Neo-Classical building that was originally constructed in 1847 as a railway station. Following extensive refurbishment by German architect Josef Paul Kleihues, it was finally opened to the public in 1996. At night, the façade is lit up by a neon light installation by American artist Dan Flavin. The museum has an ever-changing rotation of artworks by modern masters, including Beuys and Warhol, and more recent artists such as Kippenberger, Polke and Nauman. It also hosts a selection from the world-renowned Friedrich Christian Flick Collection of Art from the second half of the 20th century. Now, film, video, music and design sit alongside painting and sculpture, resulting in one of the best modern and contemporary art museums in Europe.

↑ The stark white interior of the main gallery inside the Museum of Contemporary Art, Hamburger Bahnhof

The Museum of Contemporary Art's impressive Neo-Classical ↓ façade and garden

↑ *Volk Ding Zero* (2009), a 3-m- (9-ft-) high bronze sculpture by Georg Baselitz, was inspired by African, German and Polish folk art

GALLERY GUIDE

All works on display at the Hamburger Bahnhof are temporary and exhibits shown here may not necessarily be on display. The Rieckhallen shows selected works from the Friedrich Christian Flick Collection in rotation. The main hall is used for unusual installations and occasional fashion shows.

EXPERIENCE MORE

③ Museum für Naturkunde

📍 J3 🅰 Invalidenstrasse 43
Ⓤ Naturkundemuseum
🚌 147, 245, M41, M85
🚊 M5, M8, M10 🕐 9:30am–6pm Tue–Fri, 10am–6pm Sat, Sun & public hols
🚫 Mon 🌐 museumfuer naturkunde.berlin

Berlin's Natural History Museum is one of the world's biggest, its collection numbering over 30 million exhibits. Occupying a Neo-Renaissance building completed in 1889, the museum has been operating for over a century, and despite several periods of renovation, has maintained its old-fashioned atmosphere.

The highlights of the museum include Europe's best-preserved *Tyrannosaurus rex* skeleton and the world's largest original dinosaur skeleton, which is housed in the glass-roofed courtyard. The colossal 23-m- (75-ft-) long and 12-m- (39-ft-) high *Brachiosaurus brancai* was discovered in Tanzania in 1909 by a German fossil-hunting expedition. Six other smaller reconstructed dinosaur skeletons and a replica of the fossilized remains of an *Archaeopteryx lithographica*, thought to be the prehistoric link between reptiles and birds, complete this fascinating display. The adjacent rooms feature countless colourful shells and butterflies, as well as taxidermy. Particularly popular are the dioramas – scenes of mounted animals set against the background of their natural habitat. There is also a collection of minerals and meteorites.

MAX REINHARDT (1873-1943)

This actor and director became famous as one of the 20th century's greatest theatre reformers. He worked in Berlin, first as an actor in the Deutsches Theater, and then from 1905 as its director. As well as setting up the Kammerspiele, he produced plays for the Neues Theater am Schiffbauerdamm (renamed the Berliner Ensemble) and the Schumann Circus (later to become the Friedrichstadtpalast). His experimental productions of classic and modern works brought him worldwide fame. Forced to emigrate because of his Jewish origins, he left Germany in 1933 for the United States, where he died in 1943.

↓ The Dinosaur Hall at the Museum für Naturkunde

Deutsches Theater

Q K4 **A** Schumannstrasse 13A **C** 28 44 10 **S** & **U** Friedrichstrasse **U** Oranienburger Tor **B** 147 **T** 12, M1 **W** deutschestheater.de/en

This theatre building first opened in 1850 as the Friedrich-Wilhelm Städtisches Theater, and in 1883, following reconstruction, it was renamed Deutsches Theater. It was here that Max Reinhardt began his career as an actor, before becoming director from 1905 until 1933.

Another famous figure associated with the theatre was Bertolt Brecht who, until 1933, wrote plays for it; after World War II he became the director of the Berliner Ensemble (p129), whose first venue was here at the Deutsches Theater.

Futurium

Q J4 **A** Alexanderufer 2 **U** Hauptbahnhof **B** 147, 245 **T** M5, M10 **O** 10am-6pm Wed-Mon (to 8pm Thu) **W** futurium.de

This museum gets visitors to ask the question "How do we want to live in the future?" There are three interactive exhibitions, covering the themes of nature, humans and technology. It's a big hit with families, due to its hands-on exhibits: kids of all ages can try out 3D printers or design their own city and then analyze it with respect to things like mobility, pollution and noise.

The building itself is ultra-modern, with its rectangular shape, cantilevering canopies and reflective diamond-shaped panels. As a plus-energy building, it has been awarded the gold standard in sustainability, thanks in part to its roof, which is topped with solar panels. Visitors can

reach the roof via the Skywalk, a walkway offering views of both the solar panels and the surrounding city.

Brecht-Weigel-Museum

Q K3 **A** Chausseestrasse 125 **C** 200 57 18 44 **U** Naturkundemuseum, Oranienburger Tor **B** 147, 245 **T** 12, M6 **O** 10am-3:30pm Tue & Sat, 10-11am Wed & Fri, 10am-6:30pm Thu, 11am-6pm Sun (with a tour guide)

The house where Bertolt Brecht and his wife, the actress Helene Weigel, lived and worked is now a memorial. Brecht, one of the greatest playwrights of the 20th century, was associated with Berlin from 1920, but emigrated in 1933. After the war, his left-wing views made him an attractive potential resident of the newly created German Socialist state. Lured by the promise of his own theatre, he returned to Berlin in 1948 with Weigel. He directed the Berliner Ensemble until his death, focusing mainly on productions of his own plays.

He lived in the first-floor apartment here from 1953 until he died in 1956. Weigel lived in the second-floor

 Dorotheenstädtischer Friedhof memorial to Johann Gottlieb Fichte

apartment, and after Brecht's death moved to the ground floor. She also founded an archive of Brecht's works, which is located on the second floor of the building.

Dorotheenstädtischer Friedhof

Q K3 **A** Chausseestrasse 126 **C** 461 72 79 **U** Naturkundemuseum, Oranienburger Tor **B** 142, 245, 247 **T** 12, M6, M8, **O** 8am-sunset daily

This small cemetery, established in 1763, is the final resting place of many famous Berlin citizens, including Bertolt Brecht and Helene Weigel. Many of the monuments are outstanding works of art, coming from the workshops of prominent Berlin architects, including Karl Friedrich Schinkel (p29) and Johann Gottfried Schadow, who are both buried here. A tranquil, tree-filled oasis, the cemetery is reached via a narrow path, leading from the street between the wall of the French Cemetery and the Brecht-Weigel-Museum.

DRINK

Buck & Breck

This hipster bar is cunningly disguised as an art gallery. If you can find it, and if there are seats going spare, you'll be rewarded with impeccable drinks.

Q M2 **A** Brunnenstrasse 177 **O** Hours vary, check website **W** buckandbreck.com

Becketts Kopf

Find the wrinkled visage of Mr Beckett staring from a dark window, ring the bell and enter Prenzlauer Berg's best cocktail spot.

Q N1 **A** Pappelallee 64 **O** 8pm-2am Wed-Sat **W** becketts-kopf.de

⑧
Friedrichstadtpalast

Q K4 **A** Friedrichstrasse 107 **S** Oranienburger Strasse, Friedrichstrasse **U** Oranienburger Tor **□** 147 **□** 12, M1 **W** palast.berlin

Multicoloured glass tiles and a pink, plume-shaped neon sign make up the eye-catching façade of the Friedrichstadt Palace. Built in the early 1980s, this massive theatre complex specializes in spectacular, Vegas-style shows involving gigantic casts and expensive special effects. Nearly 2,000 seats are arranged around a huge podium, used by turns as a circus arena, a swimming pool and an ice rink. A further huge stage is equipped with every technical facility. There is also a small cabaret theatre with seats for 240 spectators.

The original and much-loved Friedrichstadtpalast suffered bomb damage during World War II and was replaced with the existing version. Built as a market hall, the earlier building was later used as a circus ring. In 1918,

it became the Grosse Schauspielhaus, or Grand Playhouse, opening in 1919 with a memorable production of Aeschylus's *The Oresteia*, directed by Max Reinhardt *(p126)*. The old building was extraordinary, its central dome supported by a forest of columns and topped with Expressionist, stalactite-like decoration. An equally fantastical interior provided seating for 5,000 spectators.

⑨
Sammlung Boros

Q K4 **A** Reinhardtstrasse 20 **S** & **U** Oranienburger Tor **□** 147 **□** M1, M12 **O** 3-8pm Thu, 10am-8pm Fri-Sun **W** sammlung-boros.de

This former air-raid bunker, built by architect Karl Bonatz, is an intriguing gallery location. The bunker has a chequered history; once used as a POW prison by the Red Army, it later became a warehouse, then in the 1990s it was a popular

Michel Majerus on show at the Sammlung Boros

club. In 2003, art collector Christian Boros bought the building and converted it into a gallery space. It houses the Boros Collection of modern art. No more than 12 guests can visit at one time and advance online registration is required.

10
Oranienburger Strasse

9 K3 **S** Oranienburger Strasse, Hackescher Markt **U** Oranienburger Tor **⊞** 12, M1, M4, M5, M6

Oranienburger Strasse is home to numerous cafés, restaurants, bars and clubs. The district has traditionally been a centre for alternative culture, and was home to the famous state-sponsored Tacheles centre for the arts, which was previously occupied by artist squatters. The Tacheles centre has since closed, but its legacy lives on, with several excellent art galleries operating in this area. As you stroll around Oranienburger Strasse and

the neighbourhood, it is worth looking out for a number of interesting buildings, such as the one at Oranienburger Strasse No. 71–2, built by Christian Friedrich Becherer in 1789 for Germany's Great National Masonic Lodge.

11
Berliner Ensemble

9 K4 **A** Bertolt-Brecht-Platz 1 **C** 28 40 81 55 **S** & **U** Friedrichstrasse **⊞** 147 **⊞** 12, M1

Designed by Heinrich Seeling and completed in 1892, this theatre has seen many changes in Berlin's cultural life. First known as the Neues Theater am Schiffbauerdamm, it soon became famous for staging important premieres and for its memorable productions by Max Reinhardt. These included Shakespeare's *A Midsummer Night's Dream* in 1905, which, for the first time, used a revolving stage and real trees as part of the set. In 1928, the theatre presented the world premiere of Bertolt

Brecht's *The Threepenny Opera*. The building was destroyed during World War II and subsequently restored with a much simpler exterior, but its Neo-Baroque interior survived intact.

The theatre returned to prominence in 1954 with the arrival of the Berliner Ensemble under the directorship of Brecht and his wife, actress Helene Weigel. The move from its former home, the Deutsches Theater *(p127)*, to the new venue was celebrated by staging the world premiere of Brecht's *The Caucasian Chalk Circle*. After Brecht's death, Weigel took over the running of the theatre, maintaining its innovative tradition.

Samuel Beckett's *Endgame*, staged by the Berliner Ensemble

⓬
Monbijoupark

📍L4 🚌Oranienburger Strasse 🚊Oranienburger Strasse, Hackescher Markt 🚋M1, M4, M5, M6

Little Monbijou ("My Jewel") Park, between Oranienburger Strasse (p129) and the Spree river, was once the grounds of the Monbijou Palace. Damaged by bombing during World War II, the ruined palace was dismantled in 1960.

A rare green space in this part of the city, the well-kept park is a pleasant place to relax. It features a marble bust of the poet Adelbert von Chamisso, and there is also an open-air swimming pool for children.

⓭
Hackesche Höfe

📍M4 🚌Rosenthaler Strasse 40-41 🚊Hackescher Markt Ⓤ Weinmeisterstrasse 🚋M1, M4, M5, M6

Running from Oranienburger Strasse and Rosenthaler up as far as Sophienstrasse,

the Hackesche Höfe (Höfe means "courtyards") is a huge, early 20th-century complex that attracts more than a million visitors every year. It is made up of an intricate series of nine interconnecting courtyards surrounded by tall and beautifully proportioned buildings. The development dates from 1906, and was designed by Kurt Berendt and August Endell, both of whom were outstanding exponents of the German Secession style.

Damaged during World War II, Hackesche Höfe has been restored to its original splendour. The first court-yard is especially attractive, featuring glazed facings with geometric designs decorated in fabulous colours. A whole range of restaurants, bars, art galleries, shops and restaurants can be found here, as well as offices and apartments on the upper floors. The complex also has a small theatre, the Chamäleon, specializing in contemporary circus shows. For many Berliners the Hackesche Höfe has become something of a cult spot, and for visitors it is definitely a sight not to be missed.

↑ Triple domes of the Neue Synagoge

⓮
Neue Synagoge and Centrum Judaicum

📍L4 🚌Oranienburger Strasse 28-30 🚊Oranien-burger Strasse 🚋M1, M5 🕐Hours vary, check website 🚫Jewish hols 🌐centrum judaicum.de

The New Synagogue, by architect Eduard Knoblauch, was completed in 1866. It was the largest synagogue in Germany at the time. The design, a highly sophis-ticated response to the asymmetrical shape of the plot of land, used a narrow façade flanked by a pair of towers and crowned with a dome containing a round vestibule. Small rooms opened off the vestibule, including an anteroom and two prayer rooms – one large

---

MOSES MENDELSSOHN (1729-86)

One of the greatest German philosophers of the 18th century, Moses Mendelssohn arrived in Berlin in 1743 and was a central figure in the Jewish struggle for citizenship rights. About 50 years later, the first Jewish family was granted full civic rights; however, it was not until the Emancipation Edict of 1812 that Jewish men finally became full citizens. The grandfather of composer Felix Mendelssohn-Bartholdy, he is immortalized in the drama Nathan der Weise (Nathan the Wise) by his friend Gotthold Ephraim Lessing.

and one small. The two towers opened onto a staircase leading to the galleries, and the main hall had space for around 3,000 worshippers. An innovative use of iron in the construction of the roof and galleries put the synagogue at the forefront of 19th-century civil engineering. This structure was Berlin's largest synagogue until the night of 9–10 November 1938, when it was partially destroyed in the course of the infamous Kristallnacht (Night of Broken Glass), when thousands of synagogues, cemeteries, Jewish homes and shops were looted and burned by soldiers and Nazi supporters. It was damaged further by Allied bombing in 1943 and was finally demolished in 1958 by government authorities. Reconstruction began in 1988 and the new building was completed in 1995.

Adjoining the New Synagoge, the Centrum Judaicum (Jewish Centre) occupies the former premises of the Jewish community council, and contains a library, archives and a research centre devoted to the history and cultural heritage of the Jewish people of Berlin. The centre also uses restored rooms of the Neue Synagoge to exhibit materials relating to the local Jewish community, which includes information on the famed Jewish thinker and activist, Moses Mendelssohn.

Be aware that security is strict at both the Synagoge and the Centrum Judaicum.

> **For many Berliners the Hackesche Höfe has become something of a cult spot, and for visitors it is definitely a sight not to be missed.**

STAY

Circus Hotel
This eco-friendly hotel offers comfortable rooms, a decent in-house bar and restaurant and friendly service, all on the buzzy Rosenthaler Platz.

📍 M3
🏠 Rosenthaler Strasse 1
🌐 circus-berlin.de

€€€

Ackselhaus and Blue Home
This discreet hotel is set inside a beautifully restored 19th-century property, and has individually designed rooms and suites, plus a pleasant garden.

📍 O2
🏠 Belforter Strasse 21
🌐 ackselhaus.de

€€€

KÄTHE KOLLWITZ

One of Germany's most famous artists, Käthe Kollwitz (1867–1945) created sombre works – charcoal drawings, lithographs, woodcuts – that embraced stark but timeless themes such as poverty and death, hunger and war. During her life, Kollwitz campaigned ardently against war, and the suffering of women and children in particular. Her house at Kollwitzstrasse 56 was bombed in 1943, destroying many prints and drawings. A plaque marks the new house.

The Baroque tower of the Sophienkirche ↓

Kollwitzplatz

N2 **U** Senefelderplatz

This green square is named after the German artist Käthe Kollwitz, who once lived nearby. It was here that the socially engaged painter and sculptor observed and painted the daily hardships of the working-class people living in overcrowded tenements. One of her sculptures stands on the square, now the social hub of the district, with a Thursday organic farmers' market, cool bars, restaurants and shops that extend into the surrounding streets. Käthe Kollwitz's work can be seen at the Käthe-Kollwitz-Museum (p216).

Jüdischer Friedhof

N2 **Q** Schönhauser Allee 22–5 **C** 441 98 24 **U** Senefelderplatz **O** 8am–4pm Mon–Thu, 7:30am–1pm Fri **Q** Sat, Sun & public hols

This small Jewish Cemetery is hidden behind thick walls on Schönhauser Allee, but the serene atmosphere, with tall trees and thick undergrowth, is a welcome oasis. This Jewish "place of eternal rest" was laid out in 1827, though the oldest gravestone dates back to the 14th century. It was Berlin's second-largest Jewish cemetery after the Jüdischer Friedhof Weissensee (p235).

Among the many prominent Berliners resting here are the painter Max Liebermann (p245); Giacomo Meyerbeer, the composer and musical director of the Staatsoper Unter den Linden; and the author David Friedländer (1750–1834). The lapidarium, built in 2005, displays rescued gravestones from this and other historic Jewish cemeteries in Berlin.

Sophienkirche

M3 **Q** Grosse Hamburger Strasse 31 **C** 308 79 20 **S** Hackescher Markt **U** Weinmeisterstrasse **F** M1, M4, M5, M6 **O** 1–6pm Mon–Sat

A narrow passageway and a wrought iron gate take you through to this small Neo-Baroque church. Founded in 1712 by Queen Sophia Luisa, the wife of Friedrich I of Prussia, this was the first parish church of the newly developed Spandauer Vorstadt area, which had been growing steadily since the Middle Ages. Johann Friedrich Grael designed the tower, which was built

community. On this spot once stood a Jewish home for the elderly which, during World War II, served as a detention centre for thousands of Jewish people who were condemned to death in the camps at Auschwitz and Theresienstadt.

Until the years leading up to World War II, Grosse Hamburger Strasse was one of the main streets of Berlin's Jewish quarter. It was home to several Jewish schools, the old-people's home and the city's oldest Jewish cemetery, which was established in 1672 and in use until 1827.

At No. 27 stands a Jewish school founded in 1778 by Moses Mendelssohn (p130). Rebuilt in 1906, the building was reopened as a Jewish secondary school in 1993. The empty space once occupied by house No. 15–16, destroyed by World War II bombing, is now an installation, *The Missing House* by Christian Boltanski, with plaques recording the names and professions of the former inhabitants of the house.

Haunting figure from the Jewish memorial at Grosse Hamburger Strasse ↓

between 1729 and 1735. In 1892 the building was extended to include a presbytery, though the church still retains its original Baroque character.

A modest, rectangular structure, Sophienkirche is typical of its period, with the tower adjoining the narrower side elevation. The interior still contains a number of its original 18th-century furnishings, including the pulpit and the font.

Several gravestones dating from the 18th century have survived in the small graveyard surrounding the church.

 18

Gedenkstätte Grosse Hamburger Strasse

🚇 M4 🚇 Grosse Hamburger Strasse Ⓢ Hackescher Markt 🚊 12, M1, M4, M5, M6

An otherworldly group of figures in bronze stands on Grosse Hamburger Strasse, bearing witness to the extermination of the street's Jewish

19

Haus Schwarzenberg Museums

📍M4 🏠Rosenthaler Strasse 39 🚊Hackesher Markt Ⓤ Weinmeisterstrasse 🚌N2, N5, N42 🚊M1, M5 🌐 hausschwarzenberg.org

The Haus Schwarzenberg complex is a cool and grungy hangover from the early 1990s. Its crumbling, postwar façades are splattered with colourful street art – some by famous local artists like El Bocho and Miss Van. Its courtyard consciously eschews high-end boutiques and cafés in favour of an edgy bar, a street-art shop and gallery and the **Monsterkabinett**: a collection of moving mechanical monsters built by the owners, a nonprofit artist collective. The complex also hosts two notable, small museums that explore local resistance to the Nazis. The **Museum Blindenwerkstatt Otto Weidt** (Museum Otto Weidt's Workshop for the Blind) tells the story of Otto Weidt, a German entrepreneur who saved a number of his blind Jewish employees from the Nazis. It displays photographs and back-stories of Weidt, his family and his workers, and visitors can still see the room where Jewish families were hidden. The second museum, the engaging **Anne-Frank-Zentrum**, looks into the famous diarist's life.

Monsterkabinett
⌖ 🕐 Hours vary, check website 🌐 monsterkabinett.de

Museum Blindenwerkstatt Otto Weidt
⌖ 🕐 10am–6pm daily 🌐 museum-blindenwerkstatt.de

Anne-Frank-Zentrum
⌖ 🕐 9am–3:30pm Mon–Fri, 10am–6pm Sat & Sun 🌐 annefrank.de

Café Cinema, a legendary bohemian meeting place in Haus Schwarzenburg

 of the city's most important cultural spots, it often stages controversial performances.

 HIDDEN GEM
Secret Courtyards
Hidden away from the main street, the main door of Sophienstrasse No 21 leads into a row of lush interior courtyards that extend all the way up to Gipsstrasse.

㉑ Torstrasse

📍M3 Ⓤ Oranienburger Tor, Rosenthaler Platz, Rosa-Luxemburg-Platz
🚌142 🚊M1, M8

Formerly a customs road and Berlin's northern border around 1800, Torstrasse is now a main thoroughfare connecting Prenzlauer Allee and Friedrichstrasse. Once a largely working-class bohemian area, it has become fairly urbanized today. The 19th-century residential buildings lining the street have been gentrified to make way for cool bars, trendy cafés, gourmet restaurants, art galleries and fashion shops. "Soto", the area south of Torstrasse, has the highest concentration of independent designers and brand outfitters in the city.

㉒ Sophienstrasse

📍M3 Ⓢ Hackescher Markt
Ⓤ Weinmeisterstrasse
🚊M1, M4, M5, M6

The area around Sophienstrasse and Gipsstrasse was first settled at the end of the 17th century. In fact, Sophienstrasse was once the main street of Spandauer Vorstadt (p119). The area underwent extensive restoration during the 1980s that was designed to preserve its small-town character. Today, the narrow lanes and three-storey buildings are reminiscent of Prague's

㉒ Volksbühne

📍N3 Ⓐ Rosa-Luxemburg-Platz
☎24 06 55 Ⓤ Rosa-Luxemburg-Platz
🚌100, 142, 200 🚊M8

Founded during the early years of the 20th century, the People's Theatre owes its existence to the efforts of the 100,000 members of the Freie Volksbühne (Free People's Theatre Society). The original theatre was built in 1913, a time when the Scheunenviertel district was undergoing rapid redevelopment. During the 1920s, the theatre became famous thanks to the director Erwin Piscator (1893–1966), who later achieved great acclaim at the Metropol-Theater on Nollendorfplatz.

Destroyed during World War II, the theatre was rebuilt in the early 1950s to a design by Hans Richter. Now one

Old Town. It was one of the first parts of East Berlin in which renovation was chosen in preference to large-scale demolition and redevelopment. Now these modest but charming 18th-century Neo-Classical buildings are home to a number of different arts and crafts workshops, cosy bars, unusual boutiques, a puppet theatre and interesting art galleries.

One building with a particularly eventful history is Sophienstrasse No. 18. Erected in 1852, the house was remodelled in 1904 on behalf of the Craftsmen's Association, an educational society for blue-collar workers, to serve as their headquarters (Handwerkervereinshaus). The hall in the yard (Sophiensaele) was used as a meeting venue by revolutionary leftists like Rosa Luxemburg and Karl Liebknecht in the 1920s.

↑ The colourful façade of the Handwerkervereinshaus

↑ Soaring tower of the Neo-Romantic Zionskirche

Zionskirche

📍 M2 🏠 Zionskirchplatz
📞 449 21 91 Ⓤ Senefelder-
platz, Rosenthaler Platz
🚊 12, M1 🕐 Hours vary,
call ahead

Located in the square named after it, Zionskirchplatz, this Protestant church was built between 1866 and 1873 – a tranquil oasis in the middle of this lively district. Both the square and the church have always been centres of political opposition. During the Third Reich, resistance groups against the Nazi regime congregated at the church, and when the Communists were in power in East Germany, the alternative "environment library" (an information and documentation centre) was established here. Church and other opposition groups active here played a decisive role in the transformation of East Germany in 1989–90.

Alte and Neue Schönhauser Strasse

📍 N3 🚉 Hackescher Markt
Ⓤ Weinmeisterstrasse
🚊 M1

Alte Schönhauser Strasse is one of the oldest streets in the Spandauer Vorstadt district, running from the centre of Berlin to Pankow and Schönhausen. In the 18th and 19th centuries, this was a popular residential area among wealthy merchants. During World War II, however, its proximity to the neighbouring Jewish district of Scheunenviertel *(p140)*, devastated by the Nazis, decreased its popularity considerably.

For a long time, bars, small factories, workshops and retail shops were the hallmark of this neighbourhood. Small private shops survived longer

↑ Shopping in Neue
Schönhauser Strasse

here than in most parts of
Berlin, and the largely original
houses maintained much of
their pre-1939 atmosphere.
Much has changed, however,
since the fall of the Berlin
Wall. Some of the houses
have been restored, and
many old businesses have
been replaced by fashionable
shops, restaurants and bars,
making it one of the most
expensive retail areas in the
city. Throughout the district,
the old and the new now
stand side by side. One
poignant example is at
Neue Schönhauser Strasse
No. 14. This interesting old
house in the German Neo-
Renaissance style was built
in 1891 to a design by Alfred
Messel. The first-floor rooms
were home to the first public
reading room in Berlin, while
on the ground floor was a
Volkskaffeehaus, a soup
kitchen, with separate
rooms for men and women.
Here the poor of the neighbourhood could get a free
bowl of soup and a cup of
ersatz (imitation) coffee.

EAT

Yam Yam
Popular with locals,
this contemporary
canteen-style restaurant
uses organic Korean
vegetables and hot
spices for owner Sumi
Ha's *cha chang myun*
and *bibimbap*.

📍M3 🏠Alte Schönhauser
Strasse 6 🕐Noon-11pm
Tue-Sat, 5-11pm Sun
🌐yamyam-berlin.de

€€€

Night Kitchen
This cosy spot serves up
personalised Israeli- and
Mediterranean-inspired
small plates. If it's sunny,
grab a seat in the light-
strung garden.

📍L3 🏠Oranienburger
Strasse 32 🕐5pm-
midnight Tue-Sun
🌐nightkitchenberlin.com

€€€

Rutz
A celebrity in Berlin's
gourmet scene, Rutz is a
Michelin-starred venue
offering dishes based on
local recipes served with a
creative twist.

📍K3 🏠Chausseestrasse 8
🕐Hours vary,
check website
🌐rutz-restaurant.de

€€€

Metzer Eck
In its heyday, this
traditional restaurant
was a meeting point for
Prenzlauer Berg's GDR
bohemian luminaries.
It still has oodles of
character and serves
cheap, simple dishes like
meatballs and *Bockwurst*.

📍N2 🏠Metzer Strasse 33
🕐4pm-1am Mon-Fri, 6pm-
1am Sat 🌐metzer-eck.de

€€€

25

Prater

N1 **Kastanienallee 7-9** **44485688** **Eberswalder Strasse** **12, M1**

Prater has been one of Berlin's best-known entertainment institutions for more than a century. The building, along with its quiet courtyard, was constructed in the 1840s and later became the city's oldest and largest beer garden. It now houses a restaurant, serving Berlin specialities, and stages a variety of pop, rock and folk concerts and theatre shows.

Did You Know?

The periphery of the cemetery is reserved for the upper classes; the overgrown centre for the less well off.

 26

Alter Jüdischer Friedhof

M4 **Grosse Hamburger Strasse** **Hackescher Markt** **M1**

The Old Jewish Cemetery was established in 1672 and, until 1827 when it was finally declared full, it provided the resting place for over 12,000 Berliners. After this date, Jewish people were buried in cemeteries in Schönhauser Allee (*p132*) and in Herbert-Baum-Strasse. The Alter Jüdischer Friedhof was destroyed by the Nazis in 1943, and in 1945 the site was turned into a park. Embedded in the original cemetery wall, a handful of Baroque *masebas* (or tombstones) continue to recall the past. A *maseba* stands on the

grave of the philosopher Moses Mendelssohn (*p130*), erected in 1990 by members of the Jewish community.

 27

Synagoge Rykestrasse

O2 **Rykestrasse 53** **88028147** **Senefelderplatz**

This synagogue is one of the few reminders of old Jewish life in Berlin, and one of the few in Germany left almost intact during the Nazi regime. Built in 1904, the red-brick synagogue has a basilica-like nave with three aisles and certain Moorish features. Due to its location inside a huge tenement area, Nazi SA troops did not set it on fire during

> This synagogue is one of the few reminders of old Jewish life in Berlin, and one of the few in Germany left almost intact during the Nazi regime.

the Kristallnacht pogrom on 9 November 1938, when hundreds of other synagogues were razed to the ground. The synagogue welcomes visitors to its public services.

Kulturbrauerei

⃝N1 **⃝Schönhauser Allee 36–39** **⃝Eberswalder Strasse** **🚋12, M1, M10** **⃝10am–6pm Tue–Sun (to 8pm Thu)** **⃝hdg.de**

This vast Neo-Gothic, industrial red-and-yellow-brick building was once Berlin's most famous brewery, Schultheiss, built by architect Franz Schwechten in 1889–92. Now housing the Kulturbrauerei (culture brewery), the huge complex with several courtyards has been revived as a cultural and entertainment centre, with concert venues, restaurants and cafés, and a cinema, as well as artists' ateliers. A popular Christmas market is also held here in December.

Inside the Kulturbrauerei, the Museum Alltagsgeschichte der DDR (Museum of Everyday Life in the GDR) features both permanent and temporary exhibitions on the former East Germany. Don't miss the reconstructed flat, or the "Trabi-Tent", a typically ingenious East German solution to a caravan holiday with no caravan.

Wasserturm

⃝O2 **⃝Knaackstrasse/ Belforter Strasse** **⃝Senefelderplatz**

The unofficial symbol of this district is a 30-m- (100-ft-) high water tower, standing high on the former mill hill in the heart of Prenzlauer Berg. It was here that some of the windmills, once typical in Prenzlauer Berg, produced flour for the city's population. The distinctive brick water tower was built in 1874 by Wilhelm Vollhering and served as a reservoir for the country's first running water system. In the 1930s, the basement served as a makeshift jail, where Nazi SA troops held and tortured Communist opponents. This dark period is marked by a plaque.

↑ The Wasserturm, with its brickwork cladding

↑ Leafy avenue in the Alter Jüdischer Friedhof

SHOP

Goldhahn und Sampson

This charming gourmet food store stocks high-end, high-quality products and a good selection of cookbooks.

⃝O1 **⃝Dunckerstrasse 9** **⃝8am–8pm Mon–Sat** **⃝goldhahnund sampson.de**

Thatchers

A popular women's clothing store, Thatchers sells dresses, skirts and accessories.

⃝N1 **⃝Kastanienallee 21** **⃝11am–7pm Mon–Sat** **⃝thatchers.de**

Saint George's English Bookshop

Book lovers will relish the range of popular literature sold here.

⃝O2 **⃝Wörther Strasse 27** **⃝11am–8pm Mon–Fri (to 7pm Sat)** **⃝saint georgesbookshop.com**

A SHORT WALK
SCHEUNENVIERTEL

Distance 1.5 km (1 mile) **Nearest S-Bahn station** Oranienburger Strasse **Time** 20 minutes

From the 17th century to World War II, Scheunenviertel lay at the heart of Berlin's large Jewish district. During the 19th century, the community flourished, its prosperity reflected in grand buildings such as the Neue Synagoge, which opened in 1866. Left to crumble for nearly 50 years after the double devastations of the Nazis and Allied bombing, the district enjoyed a huge revival after the fall of the Berlin Wall, and a walk in this area will reveal cafés and bars that are home to some of the city's liveliest nightlife.

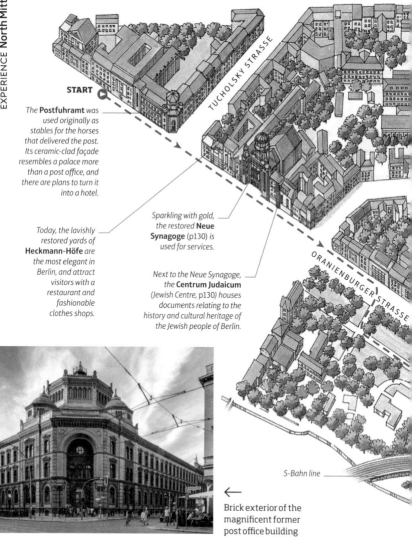

START

The **Postfuhramt** was used originally as stables for the horses that delivered the post. Its ceramic-clad façade resembles a palace more than a post office, and there are plans to turn it into a hotel.

Today, the lavishly restored yards of **Heckmann-Höfe** are the most elegant in Berlin, and attract visitors with a restaurant and fashionable clothes shops.

Sparkling with gold, the restored **Neue Synagoge** (p130) is used for services.

Next to the Neue Synagoge, the **Centrum Judaicum** (Jewish Centre, p130) houses documents relating to the history and cultural heritage of the Jewish people of Berlin.

TUCHOLSKY STRASSE

ORANIENBURGER STRASSE

S-Bahn line

← Brick exterior of the magnificent former post office building

↑ Glazed brick façade of the first courtyard at Hackesche Höfe

NORTH MITTE AND PRENZLAUER BERG

Scheunenviertel

Locator Map
For more detail see p120

Did You Know?

Scheunenviertel translates to "Barn Quarter". It was once home to barns that stored food for livestock.

Grosse Hamburger Strasse *was destroyed by bombs during World War II. Today, it is home to the Missing House memorial (p133), which lists the names of the residents killed.*

FINISH

Sophienkirche (p132) *is a small Protestant church founded by its namesake, Queen Sophia Luisa, in 1712.*

The **Gedenkstätte Grosse Hamburger Strasse** (p133) *memorial to the Jewish people of Berlin stands on the site of the city's first Jewish old-people's home.*

Hackesche Höfe (p130) *is an attractive series of interconnected courtyards, home to many popular entertainment venues.*

GROSSE HAMBURGER STRASSE

The city's oldest Jewish cemetery, **Alter Jüdischer Friedhof** (p138), *is now a tree-filled park after being destroyed by the Gestapo in 1943.*

HACKESCHER MARKT

Once the grounds of a royal palace, the small **Monbijoupark** (p130) *contains a marble bust of the poet Adelbert von Chamisso.*

| 0 metres | 100 |
| 0 yards | 100 |

N ↑

FRIEDRICHSHAIN

This famous district was created in 1920 when several outlying villages were absorbed into the city as part of the Greater Berlin Act. The area was bombed heavily during World War II because of its many factories and, due to the damage, the district's residential buildings were left largely unattended under the GDR regime – which focused on constructing Soviet showstreet Karl-Marx-Allee and erecting its trademark *Plattenbauten* (prefab tower blocks) wherever it could.

After the Berlin Wall fell, the area became a magnet for left-wingers and squatters. Vague traces of the area's dissident culture remain, but most have been driven out by the same gentrifying process that has affected the rest of Berlin's inner-city areas.

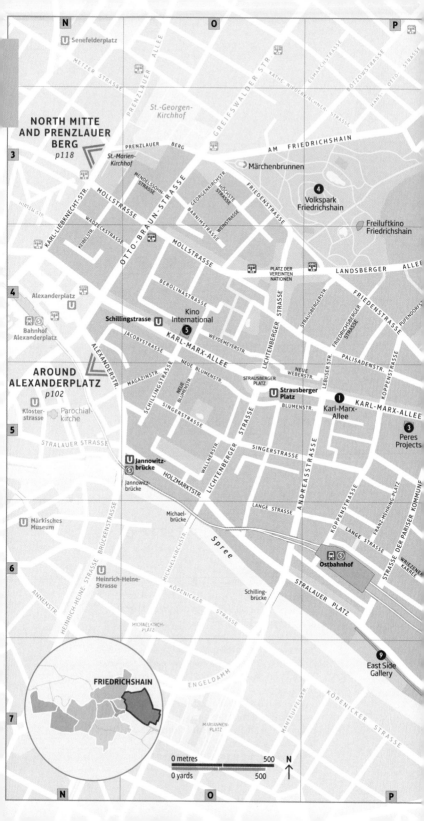

NORTH MITTE AND PRENZLAUER BERG
p118

N Senefelderplatz

St.-Georgen-Kirchhof

St.-Marien-Kirchhof

PRENZLAUER BERG

AM FRIEDRICHSHAIN

Märchenbrunnen

4 Volkspark Friedrichshain

Freiluftkino Friedrichshain

Alexanderplatz

Bahnhof Alexanderplatz

PLATZ DER VEREINTEN NATIONEN

LANDSBERGER ALLEE

AROUND ALEXANDERPLATZ
p102

Kloster-strasse Parochial-kirche

Schillingstrasse Kino International

5

KARL-MARX-ALLEE

WEYDEMEYERSTR.

NEUE WEBERSTR.

Strausberger Platz

STRAUSBERGER PLATZ

1 Karl-Marx-Allee

3 Peres Projects

BLUMENSTR.

SINGERSTRASSE

Jannowitz-brücke

Jannowitz-brücke

HOLZMARKTSTR.

LANGE STRASSE

STRASSE DER PARISER KOMMUNE

Märkisches Museum

Heinrich-Heine-Strasse

Michael-brücke

Spree

Schilling-brücke

Ostbahnhof

STRALAUER PLATZ

FRIEDRICHSHAIN

ENGELDAMM

9 East Side Gallery

KÖPENICKER STRASSE

MARIANNEN-PLATZ

0 metres	500
0 yards	500

N ↑

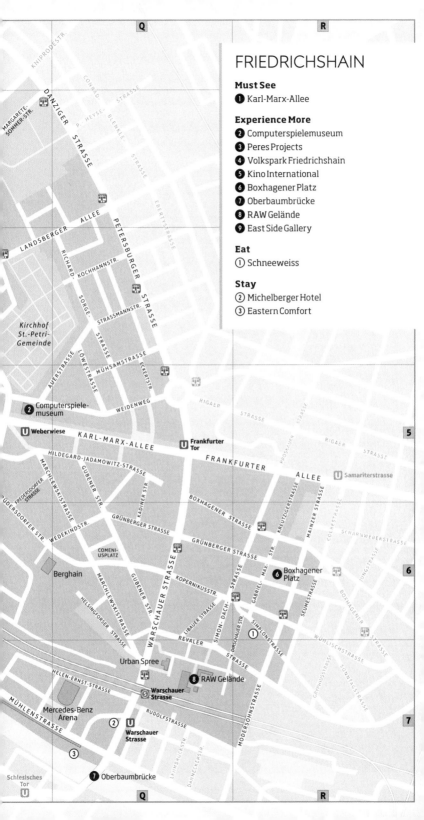

FRIEDRICHSHAIN

Must See
❶ Karl-Marx-Allee

Experience More
❷ Computerspielemuseum
❸ Peres Projects
❹ Volkspark Friedrichshain
❺ Kino International
❻ Boxhagener Platz
❼ Oberbaumbrücke
❽ RAW Gelände
❾ East Side Gallery

Eat
① Schneeweiss

Stay
② Michelberger Hotel
③ Eastern Comfort

❶

KARL-MARX-ALLEE

📍 P5

The area around this 2-km (1-mile) boulevard has a vibrant and relaxed atmosphere. Most residents are in their mid-twenties, drawn here by the alternative cafés and cool bars.

The route leading east to Poland and Moscow was initially called Frankfurter Strasse, and then renamed Stalinallee in 1949. Having suffered severe damage during World War II, the street was chosen as the site for the construction showpiece of the new German Democratic Republic, featuring spacious and luxurious apartments for workers, as well as commercial infrastructure.

← A typical Socialist-era residential block, now in high demand for Berliners

taken from famous Berlin architects Schinkel (p29) and Gontard, as well as from the renowned Meissen porcelain.

GDR Showcase

The avenue was widened to 90 m (300 ft) and, in the course of the next ten years, huge residential tower blocks and a row of shops sprang up along it. The first houses to be built on the street were Modernist in style and quickly denounced as "too Western". They were hidden behind trees while the rest of the street proceeded in a more aptly Socialist style. The next architects followed a style known in the Soviet Union as "pastry chef", which was "nationalistic in form, but socialist in content", and linked the whole work to Berlin's own traditions. Hence there are motifs

The Avenue Today

The buildings on this street, renamed Karl-Marx-Allee in 1961, are now considered historic monuments, and the section between Strausberger Platz and Frankfurter Tor is effectively a huge open-air museum of Socialist Realist architecture. The buildings have been cleaned up and the crumbling details are gradually being restored.

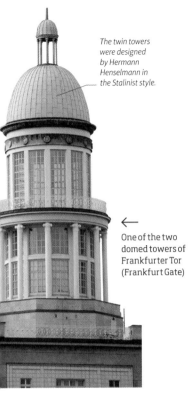

The twin towers were designed by Hermann Henselmann in the Stalinist style.

← One of the two domed towers of Frankfurter Tor (Frankfurt Gate)

WORKER UPRISING

In 1953, Karl-Marx-Allee was the site of a mass worker uprising. Increasing food costs and work quotas led people to begin peaceful protests, which were followed by strikes and marches as their calls fell on deaf ears. The situation escalated, with the uprising spreading across East Germany. The uprising ended on 17 June, when Soviet tanks were called in to help the police suppress a protest in East Berlin. Over 50 workers were killed and many more injured in the revolt.

↑ The tree-lined boulevard stretches from Frankfurter Tor to Strausberger Platz

EXPERIENCE MORE

Computerspiele-museum

📍 P5 🏛 Karl-Marx-Allee 93a
Ⓤ Weberwiese, Strauss-berger Platz 🚌 347, N5
🕙 10am–8pm daily
🌐 computerspiele museum.de

Europe's first museum for video and computer games, the Computer Games Museum has over 300 items, from a life-size Lara Croft to a Wall of Hardware with vintage games and toys. Here, one can find most arcade machines and games consoles ever made, including the Nimrod (1951) and the Brown Box (1959), developed by Ralph H Baer – the inventor of video games for home use. There's also a small penny arcade (no payment required) with vintage slot machine games like Donkey Kong, and more modern game systems like Sony's 3D PlayStation monitor.

3 Peres Projects

📍 P5 🏛 Karl-Marx-Allee 82
Ⓤ Weberwiese, Strauss-berger Platz 🚌 142, N5
🕙 11am–6pm Mon–Fri
🌐 peresprojects.com

Founded by Javier Peres in 2002, this contemporary art space arrived in Berlin in 2005. The well-known art gallery is the latest of a series of venues – a typically box-shaped room with concrete columns, large, street-facing windows and pristine white-painted walls. Known for championing artists early in their careers as well as the occasional established name, it shows consistently innovative works from inter-national contemporary figures ranging from North American artists like James Franco and Brent Wadden to locals such as the German painter David Ostrowski.

4 Volkspark Friedrichshain

📍 P3 🏛 Am Friedrichshain/
Friedenstrasse 🚌 142, 200
🚊 M5, M6, M8, M10

The extensive park complex of Friedrichshain, with its picturesque nooks and crannies, was one of Berlin's first public parks. It was laid out in the 1840s on the basis of a design by landscape architect Peter Joseph Lenné, with the idea of creating an alternative

↑ Bust of Frederick the Great in Volkspark Friedrichshain

Tiergarten for the eastern districts of the city. The greatest attraction here is the Fountain of Fairy Tales (or Märchenbrunnen) by Ludwig Hoffmann, built in 1902–13. It is a spectacular feature in a Neo-Baroque style, its fountain pools decorated with small statues of turtles and other animals. The fountain is surrounded by characters from the fairy tales by the Brothers Grimm. There's a sports and games area and a challenging outdoor climbing wall. Trails cross over Mont Klamott, an artificial hill constructed from the rubble of buildings destroyed in World War II.

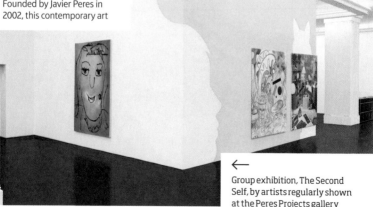

← Group exhibition, The Second Self, by artists regularly shown at the Peres Projects gallery

Goods for sale *(inset)* at Boxhagener Platz's weekend market

Kino International

📍O4 🚉 Karl-Marx-Allee 33
Ⓢ&Ⓤ Alexanderplatz
Ⓤ Schillingstrasse 🚌 N5
🌐 kino-international.com

One of the most eye-catching buildings on the Karl-Marx-Allee, this large, blocky and historic cinema was a landmark in the GDR and remains so today – not least for its cameo role in the classic movie *Goodbye Lenin* and, since 1995, its UNESCO-heritage status. Used for hosting premieres until the fall of the Wall, it still operates as a cinema, with state-of-the-art facilities and a good rotation of commercial and arthouse movies. It's worth taking a moment to inspect the sandstone reliefs on the outside as well as the distinctly retro-looking foyer.

EAT

Schneeweiss

One of Friedrichshain's few upmarket restaurants, "Snow White" combines a minimalist aesthetic with an Alpine menu that straddles Italian, Austrian and south German dishes: think Wiener schnitzel and Bavarian pasta.

📍R6 🚉 Simplonstrasse 16 🕐 5-10pm Mon-Sat, 10am-3pm & 5-10pm Sun
🌐 schneeweiss-berlin.de

€€€

6

Boxhagener Platz

📍R6 Ⓢ&Ⓤ Frankfurter Allee Ⓤ Frankfurter Tor
🚌 240, N40 🚊 M5, M10, M13, 21

The most famous square in Friedrichshain, Boxhagener Platz (locally known as "Boxi") serves as both a historical centrepoint for the area and a social hub. Named after the former nearby manor farm and hamlet of Boxhagen, these days it's surrounded by shops, bars, galleries and restaurants that draw a real mix of Berliners. At weekends Boxi is especially popular due to its excellent markets. The Saturday food market has been held here since 1903 and offers an array of fruit and vegetables, but also food stalls selling everything from falafel to grilled fish. And at the Sunday flea market you can find a variety of items such as jewellery and vinyl and second-hand clothes.

The streets leading off from the square – Grünberger Strasse, Krossener Strasse, Gärtnerstrasse and Gabriel-Max-Strasse – are also worth exploring for their cafés, boutiques, restaurants and bars, while nearby Simon-Dach-Strasse and RAW Gelände *(p150)* are well known for their upbeat weekend nightlife.

> **The extensive park complex of Friedrichshain, with its picturesque nooks and crannies, was one of Berlin's first public parks.**

STAY

Michelberger Hotel

This alternative hotel is one of Friedrichshain's funkiest, with quirky rooms, a great lounge and restaurant, plus live music in the courtyard.

 Q7 Warschauer Strasse 39/40
michelbergerhotel.com

€€€

Eastern Comfort

This floating hostel on a solar-powered boat on the Spree is a perennial backpacker favourite.

 Q7
Mühlenstrasse 73
eastern-comfort.com

€€€

 7

Oberbaumbrücke

Q7 & Warschauer Strasse Schlesisches Tor 300, 347 M10

This pretty bridge crossing the Spree river was built in 1896 to a design by Otto Stahn. It is made from reinforced concrete, but the arches are faced with red brick. The central arch is marked by a pair of crenellated Neo-Gothic towers. The most decorative element of the bridge, a Neo-Gothic arcade, supports a line of the U-Bahn.

Prior to reunification, the bridge linked districts from opposing sides of the Wall, and only pedestrians with the correct papers were able to cross. It is now open to traffic.

 8

RAW Gelände

Q7 Revaler Strasse 99 & Warschauer Strasse 347 M5, M10, M13

Formerly a 19th-century repair yard owned by the national railway (its official name was "Reichsbahn-Ausbesserungs-Werk", hence RAW), this sprawling complex of graffiti-spattered warehouses and buildings today represents one of the most prominent alternative cultural spaces in the city. It's fun to stroll around any time of day, especially if you're a street-art fan, though it really comes alive in the evenings at weekends. The 70,000-sq-m (750,000-sq-ft) site incorporates a slew of clubs and bars, a couple of places to eat, an indoor skate hall and a climbing wall that was once a World War II bunker. Haubentaucher is a trendy event and concert

venue with an outdoor pool and beer garden for the warmer months.

One of the most exciting enterprises here is **Urban Spree**, a masterpiece in post-apocalyptic urban styling. The 1,700-sq-m (18,000-sq-ft) space is devoted to "urban cultures", most notably street and graphic art. Its monthly changing art shows mostly involve high-profile local and international street artists who often paint the entire compound, including all 15 m (50 ft) of its 8-m- (25-ft-) high flagship "Artist Wall".

Urban Spree
 Noon-midnight Tue-Sun (to 3am Fri & Sat)
urbanspree.com

←

Street food stalls and a tattoo parlour at Urban Spree in the RAW Gelände complex

← The graffiti-covered East Side Gallery, bringing back memories of the Wall era

⑨ East Side Gallery

 P7 🏛 Mühlenstrasse
Ⓢ & Ⓤ Warschauer Strasse
Ⓢ Ostbahnhof 🚌 24, 140,
300 🚊 M10 🌐 eastside
gallery-berlin.com

Running alongside the River Spree, the East Side Gallery is the longest surviving stretch of the Berlin Wall – as well as the most colourful, thanks to the numerous paintings that have adorned its surface since 1990. More than 100 artists have contributed to the gallery, and millions of visitors to the city come here every year to enjoy their work.

Although it's not the city's official Berlin Wall memorial, this 1.3-km (0.8-mile) stretch is the longest section of the Wall that still exists today. Located in the former East Berlin district of Friedrichshain,

the Wall was protected by border guards and watch-towers until the collapse of the GDR in 1989. Soon after, dozens of artists began using it as a political canvas, decorating it with murals, slogans and paintings. The improvised gallery was appointed an official one in 1990 and given protected memorial status the following year. The gallery was repainted for its 20th anniversary in 2009, with some original artists refusing to repaint or retouch their artworks for reasons of authenticity. In 2016, a multimedia museum opened at the south end of the East Side Gallery, giving an overview of the Berlin Wall era through screens, interactive displays, original newsreel footage and filmed interviews with Berliners who lived through it.

BERGHAIN

Often voted the best techno club in the world, this former power station features a cavernous main room, a smaller Panorama Bar upstairs and an experimental music area on the ground floor. Its minimal, industrial design aesthetic is as uncompromising as the notorious door policy – but if you can get in, expect some of the best DJs playing all through the weekend. Weekday concerts tend to be ticket-only and are much easier to get into; check website for further details (*berghain.de*).

TIERGARTEN

Once a royal hunting estate, the Tiergarten became a park in the 18th century. In the 19th century, a series of buildings – mostly department stores and banks – was erected at Potsdamer Platz. Many of these were destroyed during World War II, and the division of Berlin into East and West changed the character of the area even further. The Tiergarten ended up on the west side of the Wall, and later regained its glory with the creation of the Kulturforum and the Hansaviertel. The area around Potsdamer Platz, however, fell in East Berlin and became a wasteland.

Following reunification, this area witnessed exciting development. Together with the government offices near the Reichstag, this ensures that the Tiergarten area is at the centre of Berlin's political and financial district.

TIERGARTEN

Must Sees

1. The Reichstag
2. Gemäldegalerie
3. Potsdamer Platz

Experience More

4. Philharmonie und Kammermusiksaal
5. St-Matthäus-Kirche
6. Kunstgewerbe Museum
7. Kupferstichkabinett
8. Staatsbibliothek
9. Musikinstrumenten-Museum
10. Neue Nationalgalerie
11. Urban Nation
12. Potsdamer Strasse
13. Schwules Museum
14. Bauhaus-Archiv
15. Villa von der Heydt
16. Bendlerblock
17. Diplomatenviertel
18. Tiergarten
19. Grosser Stern
20. Haus der Kulturen der Welt
21. Sowjetisches Ehrenmal
22. Schloss Bellevue
23. Memorial to Homosexuals Persecuted Under Nazism
24. Regierungsviertel
25. Siegessäule
26. Hansaviertel

Eat

① Café am Neuen See
② Lindenbräu
③ Vox
④ Ristorante essenza
⑤ Teehaus im Englischen Garten
⑥ Oh Panama
⑦ Joseph Roth Diele
⑧ FACIL

Drink

⑨ Kumpelnest 3000
⑩ Victoria Bar
⑪ Tiger Bar

Stay

⑫ Das Stue

Shop

⑬ Andreas Murkudis

AROUND KURFÜRSTENDAMM
p196

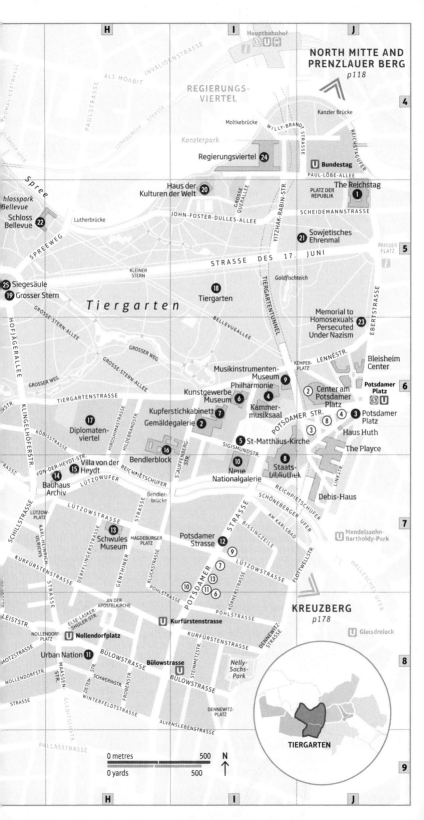

Hauptbahnhof

NORTH MITTE AND PRENZLAUER BERG *p118*

Kanzler Brücke

REGIERUNGS-VIERTEL

ALT-MOABIT

PAULSTRASSE

INVALIDENSTRASSE

THOMAS USTRASSE

Moltkebrücke

Kanzlerpark

WILLY-BRANDT-STRASSE

REICHSTAGUFER

U Bundestag

Regierungsviertel 24

PAUL-LÖBE-ALLEE

GROSSE QUERALLEE

YITZHAK-RABIN-STR.

PLATZ DER REPUBLIK

The Reichstag 1

Spree

hlosspark Bellevue

Haus der Kulturen der Welt 20

Lutherbrücke

JOHN-FOSTER-DULLES-ALLEE

SCHEIDEMANNSTRASSE

Schloss Bellevue 22

SPREEWEG

Sowjetisches Ehrenmal 21

PARISER PLATZ

STRASSE DES 17. JUNI

KLEINER STERN

Goldfischteich

25 Siegessäule

19 Grosser Stern

GROSSE-STERN-ALLEE

T i e r g a r t e n

Tiergarten 18

TIERGARTENTUNNEL

Memorial to Homosexuals Persecuted Under Nazism 23

EBERTSTRASSE

HOFJÄGERALLEE

GROSSE-STERN-ALLEE

BELLEVUEALLEE

LENNÉSTR.

Bleisheim Center

GROSSER WEG

GROSSER WEG

KEMPER-PLATZ

Potsdamer Platz

GROSSER WEG

GROSSE-STERN-ALLEE

TIERGARTENSTRASSE

Musikinstrumenten-Museum 9

Philharmonie

Center am Potsdamer Platz 2

Potsdamer Platz 6

KLINGELHÖFERSTR.

KÖBISSTRASSE

17 Diplomaten-viertel

HIRSCHMSTRASSE

HILDEBRANDTR.

Kunstgewerbe Museum 6

Kupferstichkabinett 7

Kämmer-musiksaal 4

POTSDAMER STR.

3 Potsdamer Platz

8

4

Haus Huth

Gemäldegalerie 2

STAUFFENBERG-STR.

St-Matthäus-Kirche 5

SIGISMUNDSTR.

The Playce

VON-DER-HEYDT-STR.

Villa von der Heydt 15

REICHPIETSCHUFER

Bendlerblock 16

Neue Nationalgalerie 10

Staats-bibliothek 8

14 Bauhaus Archiv

LÜTZOWUFER

LÜTZOWPLATZ

LÜTZOWSTRASSE

Bendler-brücke

SCHÖNEBERGER UFER

REICHPIETSCHUFER

Debis-Haus

SCHILLSTRASSE

KARL-HEINRICH-ULRICHS-STR.

DERFFLINGERSTRASSE

STRASSE

MAGDEBURGER PLATZ

Schwules Museum 13

Potsdamer Strasse 12

STRASSE

BISSINGZEILE

AN KARLSBAD

FLOTTWELLSTR.

U Mendelssohn-Bartholdy-Park

HALLESCHES UFER

KURFÜRSTENSTRASSE

GENTHINER

KLUCKSTRASSE

POHLSTRASSE

9

LÜTZOWSTRASSE

KÖRNERSTRASSE

7

13

10 11 6

POHLSTRASSE

KREUZBERG *p178*

U Gleisdreieck

LEISTSTR.

AN DER APOSTELKIRCHE

ELSE-LASKER-SCHÜLER-STR.

U Kurfürstenstrasse

KURFÜRSTENSTRASSE

DENNEWITZ-STRASSE

NOLLENDORFPLATZ

U Nollendorfplatz

Urban Nation 11

BÜLOWSTRASSE

U Bülowstrasse

Bülowstrasse

STEINMETZSTR.

Nelly-Sachs-Park

MOTZSTRASSE

MAASSEN-STR.

DIETEN-STR.

SCHWERINSTR.

ERDBENSTR.

NOLLENDORFSTR.

STRASSE

WINTERFELDTSTRASSE

BÜLOWSTRASSE

DENNEWITZ-PLATZ

ALVENSLEBENSTRASSE

PALLASSTRASSE

GLEDITSCHSTR.

0 metres   500

0 yards   500

N ↑

TIERGARTEN

The historic Reichstag topped with a modern glass dome ↑

①

THE REICHSTAG

⚲ J5 **△** Platz der Republik **Ⓢ** Brandenburger Tor
Ⓤ Bundestag **🚌** 100, 245, M85 **🕓** 8am–midnight daily;
bookings for a time slot to visit or for a restaurant
reservation are required at least a few days in advance
🌐 bundestag.de

One of Berlin's most recognizable landmarks, the
Reichstag, seat of Germany's parliament, has survived
fascism, fire, bombardment and being wrapped in
fireproof polypropylene fabric by artists to become a
symbol of a modern, politically transparent Germany.

The Reichstag was built between 1884 and 1894 to a Neo-
Renaissance design by German architect Paul Wallot. In 1933, a fire
destroyed the main hall, and World War II delayed rebuilding for
years. In the 1960s, the structure underwent a partial restoration
that included the removal of most of the ornamentation on the
façade. After German reunification in 1990, the Reichstag once
again became the home of the German parliament. The
magnificent rooftop glass dome, with its photogenic curves,
mirrored columns and stellar views across the city, was added in
1999 by British architect Norman Foster. A permanent exhibition
at the dome recalls key events in German parliamentary history.

EAT

Dachgarten-Restaurant
The only government
building restaurant in
the world with public
access offers gourmet
German cuisine and fine
views of eastern Berlin.

△ Platz der Republik 1
🌐 feinkost-kaefer.de/
berlin

€€€

The magnificent rooftop glass dome, with its photogenic curves, mirrored columns and stellar views across the city, was added in 1999.

↑ The Reichstag dome, offering stunning views inside and out

Timeline

5 December 1894

△ Designed by Paul Wallot, the Reichstag is dedicated, the final stone being laid by Kaiser Wilhelm II.

27 February 1933

▽ Fire destroys the Reichstag. Many believe this was ordered by the Nazis to obtain emergency powers.

7 July 1995

Artists wrap the Reichstag in plastic.

19 April 1999

▽ The building receives a spectacular new glass dome, which was designed by Norman Foster.

② ⌖ Ⓜ ▢ 🛍

GEMÄLDEGALERIE

📍I6 🏛Matthäikirchplatz 4-6 Ⓢ&ⓊPotsdamer Platz ⓊMendelssohn-Bartholdy-Park 🚌200, M29, M41, M48, M85 🕐10am-6pm Tue-Sun (to 8pm Thu) 🌐smb.museum

The Picture Gallery is the central attraction of the Kulturforum complex. Circling a striking inner courtyard, the gallery contains many of the world's finest 13th- to 18th-century European paintings.

The paintings in the Picture Gallery collection have been carefully chosen by specialists who, from the beginning of the 19th century, systematically acquired pictures to ensure that all the major European schools of painting were represented. After the division of the city in 1945, the collection was split over several sites in East and West Berlin. Following reunification, with the building of a new home as part of the Kulturforum development, this unique set of paintings was united again.

The building itself was designed by Heinz Hilmer and Christoph Sattler, and its exhibition space offers a superb environment in which to view the paintings. The pictures are gently lit by the diffused daylight that streams in from above, while the walls are covered in light-absorbing fabric. The vast hall that occupies the centre of the building allows the visitor to take a break from sightseeing at any time. The hall, with a futuristic sculpture by Walter de Maria set in a water-filled pool, provides an ideal place for moments of quiet contemplation and rest.

GALLERY GUIDE

The main gallery contains about 1,000 masterpieces grouped according to their country of origin and period. The educational gallery on the lower floor houses about 400 13th- to 18th-century European paintings and a digital gallery.

→

The sloped approach to the Kulturforum, obscuring the building within

Highlights

c 1480

△ *Virgin and Child Enthroned with Saints*, by Italian Renaissance artist Carlo Crivelli.

c 1489

Saint John on Patmos, an oil on oak painting by Dutch artist Hieronymus Bosch.

1559

△ Pieter Bruegel managed to illustrate more than 100 proverbs in his painting *Dutch Proverbs*.

c 1636

Landscape with Juno and Argus, Nicolas Poussin.

1641

▽ *Double portrait of the Mennonite preacher Cornelis Claesz Anslo and his wife Aeltje Gerritsdr Schouten*, Rembrandt.

Did You Know?

A walk taking in the gallery's most famous masterpieces would be 2 km (1 mile) long.

High ceilings and natural light help show off the gallery's masterpieces ↑

↑ *Portrait of a young man* (c 1490–1500) by Davide Ghirlandaio

Italian Painting

The collection of Italian paintings contains exemplary works by 14th- and 15th-century masters, including later works by Raphael, such as the *Madonna di Terranuova*, painted after Raphael's arrival in Florence around 1505.

The Venetian school is also well represented: *Portrait of a Young Man* by Giorgione is a vibrant and colourful study; there is also Titian's *Venus and the Organ Player* and Tintoretto's *Virgin and the Child Adored by Saints Mark and Luke*. It is interesting to compare Caravaggio's *Cupid Victorious*, whose provocative and distinctly human sexuality contrasts with the spiritual orthodoxy of *Heavenly and Earthly Love*, by Giovanni Baglione. Similar in style, the two paintings convey opposing ideologies.

Works by Old Masters such as Giovanni Battista Tiepolo, Francesco Guardi and Antonio Canaletto represent the art of 18th-century Venice.

> **All the most famous Dutch painters are represented but the works of Jan Vermeer and Rembrandt attract the greatest amount of interest.**

Dutch and Flemish Painting

Within the large collection of excellent Flemish paintings, you can marvel at the Baroque vitality and texture evident in the canvases of friends and sometime collaborators Peter Paul Rubens, Jacob Jordaens, Jan Brueghel the Elder and Frans Snyders. The exceptional portraits of Anthony van Dyck are indicative of the artist at the height of his powers.

The gallery of 17th-century Dutch paintings probably holds the richest collection in the museum. Included among these are portraits by Frans Hals that perfectly illustrate his enormous artistic talents.

All the most famous Dutch painters are represented, but the works of Jan Vermeer and Rembrandt attract the greatest amount of interest. Rembrandt's works include the paintings *Samson and Delilah*, *Susanna and the Two Elders* and *Joseph and the Wife of Potiphar*. It is also worth taking time to view *The Man with the Golden Helmet*, a sad yet noble painting originally attributed to Rembrandt, which carbon-dating has shown to be the work of members of his studio. It is a magnificent tribute to his skill as a teacher.

 INSIDER TIP
Gallery Tours

The museum runs some useful tours, including an "Art in the Evening" tour with changing thematic focuses, and a one-hour "Best of the Gallery" tour, which provides a good overview for those on a tight schedule.

French, English and Spanish Painting

The collection of French art includes highlights such as *The Madonna with Child* (c 1410), one of the oldest preserved works of art painted on a canvas. Nicolas Poussin, the mainspring of the French Classical tradition, and Claude Lorrain, famous for his idealized landscapes, showcase 17th-century French painting. The 18th century is represented by Jean-Antoine Watteau, Jean-Baptiste Siméon Chardin and François Boucher.

The smaller Spanish collection contains a portrait by Diego Velázquez, while the English collection includes good portraits by rivals Sir Joshua Reynolds and Thomas Gainsborough.

↑ *Jupiter as a child nourished by the goat Amalthea* (1639) by Nicolas Poussin

↑ Hans Multscher's 15th-century *Wurzach Altar*

German Painting

The German collection comprises works from the 13th to 18th centuries. It includes a fine body of religious art – notably the side panels of the 15th-century *Wurzacher Altar*, ascribed to Hans Multscher.

A real rarity is the *Nativity* by Martin Schongauer. Often thought of primarily as an engraver, he was one of the most significant painters of the late 15th century but few of his paintings have survived. Another artist known for both his engravings and paintings, Albrecht Dürer was a major figure in Renaissance art in northern Europe. His works here include *Madonna with the Siskin* and two portraits of Nürnberg patriarchs.

The 17th and 18th centuries are represented by the works of notable artists such as Adam Elsheimer and Johann Heinrich Tischbein.

EAT

Café am Neuen See
For a picturesque, lakeside break between museums, take a stroll to this Tiergarten beer garden.

📍G6
Lichtensteinallee 2
🌐cafeamneuensee.de

€€€

Lindenbräu
This popular watering hole serves Bavarian specialities and home-brewed fruit-flavoured wheat beer.

📍J6
Bellevuestrasse 3-5
🌐bier-genuss.berlin

€€€

Vox
This elegant hotel restaurant serves a modern fusion of Asian and international dishes.

📍J6
Marlene-Dietrich-Platz 2
🌐vox-restaurant.de

€€€

Ristorante essenza
Enjoy top-notch, creative Italian fare at this pleasant restaurant. The menu is matched with an extensive list of wines and champagnes.

📍J6
Potsdamer Platz 1
🌐ristorante-essenza.de

€€€

3

POTSDAMER PLATZ

📍 J6 ⓈⓊ Potsdamer Platz 🚌 200, M41, M48, M85, N2
🌐 potsdamerplatz.de

There is no better place to experience the vibrant energy of Berlin than Potsdamer Platz, which has evolved into a thriving city within the city since the fall of the Wall

Originally a green park in 1831, this square evolved into a major traffic hub thanks to the construction of a railway station, where the city's first ever train made its maiden journey. During the Roaring Twenties, it was Europe's busiest plaza and a bustling entertainment centre, frequented by famous artists and authors. The square was almost destroyed during World War II and was left as a derelict wasteland for several decades. Redevelopment began in 1992, and Potsdamer Platz became Europe's largest construction site, where a total of $25 billion has been invested. Now the city's old hub is once again a dynamic centre, with an array of entertainment, shopping and dining opportunities in splendid modern buildings designed by architects such as Renzo Piano, Helmut Jahn and Arata Isozaki.

→
④
Leipziger Platz
100 m (110 yd)

📷 PICTURE PERFECT
Light Festival

Potsdamer Platz plays a leading role in Berlin's annual Festival of Lights in October. The illuminated installations and light displays are different every year, and are always unforgettable.

→

Looking down on the Center am Potsdamer Platz piazza from the roof

Center am Potsdamer Platz

⑨J6 **⌂** Potsdamer Strasse 4 **⏰**24 hours daily **ⓦ**sonycenter.de

The Center am Potsdamer Platz is one of Berlin's most exciting architectural complexes, a glitzy steel-and-glass construction covering a breathtaking 4,013 sq m (43,195 sq ft). Designed by architect Helmut Jahn, the Center opened in 2000 and was formerly known as the Sony Center. Today, the piazza at the heart of the Center has become one of Berlin's most popular attractions. Set under a soaring tent-like roof, it is dominated by a pool with constantly changing fountains. The light and airy piazza is surrounded by offices and an apartment complex, as well as a number of restaurants.

One of the main attractions in the Center am Potsdamer Platz is the **Museum für Film und Fernsehen** (Museum of Film and Television), which gives visitors a backstage glimpse of Hollywood and

↑ The Center am Potsdamer Platz under its soaring roof, lit up in the evening

> The Center am Potsdamer Platz is one of Berlin's most exciting architectural complexes, a glitzy steel-and-glass construction covering a breathtaking 4,013 sq m (43,195 sq ft).

the historic UFA (Universum Film AG) film studios. The museum chronicles the development of cinema from the first silent movie hits to the latest science fiction productions. However, the main focus is on German films from the glorious UFA days in the 1920s, when Germany's leading film company produced one smash hit after another at the Babelsberg studios (p265). Films such as *The Cabinet of Dr Caligari*, directed by Robert Wiene, and *Metropolis*, by Fritz Lang, are presented with costumes, set sketches, original scripts, models and photos. Exhibits also explore the use of film during the Nazi era, when filmmaking became part of the propaganda machine. In addition, the museum documents the life and work of the actor Kurt Gerron, who died in Auschwitz. The museum also features

a range of other exhibitions with changing themes and special film programmes.

Just outside the Center am Potsdamer Platz you'll find the **LEGOLAND® Discovery Centre**. It provides a wonderland of indoor adventure for young visitors, including rides and a 4D cinema, as well as hands-on activities like model-building workshops. There's also a LEGO® factory tour.

Museum für Film und Fernsehen
Ⓐⓑⓒⓓ **⌂**Potsdamer Strasse 4 **⏰**10am-6pm Tue, Wed & Fri-Sun (to 8pm Thu) **ⓦ**deutsche-kinemathek.de

LEGOLAND® Discovery Centre
Ⓐⓑⓒ **⌂**Potsdamer Strasse 4 **⏰**10am-7pm daily (last entry 5pm) **ⓦ**legolanddiscovery centre.de/berlin

② Theatre Complex

J6 **Marlene-Dietrich-Platz**

Sited in a square dedicated to the actress Marlene Dietrich, the city's largest musical stage is housed in the **Theater am Potsdamer Platz**.

Spielbank Berlin, the largest casino in Germany, can be found here, too. It has 40 gaming tables, 500 modern slot machines and a restaurant.

The theatre complex is also the main forum for the annual film festival, the Berlinale. Book ahead if you wish to attend.

Theater am Potsdamer Platz

Marlene-Dietrich-Platz 1 **8am-8pm daily** **tapp.berlin**

Spielbank Berlin

Marlene-Dietrich-Platz 1 **11am-3am daily** **spielbank-berlin.de**

---

③ The Playce

J6/7 **Alte Potsdamer Strasse 7** **10am-9pm Mon-Sat; Manifesto Market: 11am-10pm daily (to midnight Fri-Sat)** **potsdamer-platz.de**

This entertainment and shopping complex is spread over three floors, and includes a variety of stores and boutiques. The expansive food court, Manifesto Market, spans two floors and is home to a large collection of restaurants and bars.

---

④ Leipziger Platz

J6

This small square located just east of Potsdamer Platz is becoming an exciting hub of its own.

The **Mall of Berlin** now occupies the site of the former Wertheim department store, once the largest in Europe. It contains shops and restaurants of every variety as well as a hotel, a running club and the XXL slide that winds from the second floor all the way to the ground-floor atrium.

At the southern end of Leipziger Platz is the **Deutschland Museum**, a 4D multimedia museum that takes you through 2,000 years of German history. A few doors down is the **German Spy Museum**, a multimedia museum exploring the history of secret services around the world, with an emphasis on

The buildings of the Daimler Quartier, sharply angled to admit light

Did You Know?

Potsdamer Platz was the centre of the city's black market during the post-war years.

espionage in Cold War-era Berlin. The museum exhibits collections of original and replica espionage equipment, and offers various interactive experiences such a laser maze and Facebook data puzzle.

Mall of Berlin
Leipziger Platz 12 **10am-9pm Mon-Sat, 1-7pm Sun** **mallofberlin.de**

Deutschland Museum
Leipziger Platz 7 **10am-8pm daily** **deutschlandmuseum.de**

German Spy Museum
Leipziger Platz 9 **10am-8pm daily** **deutschesspionage-museum.de**

↑ Potsdamer Platz contains an eclectic mix of modern architectural designs

⑤ Daimler Quartier

 J6

This vast complex comprises 19 modern buildings, all designed in different styles according to an overall plan by architects Renzo Piano and Christoph Kohlbecker. The buildings form a long column of magnificent architecture leading from Potsdamer Platz all the way down to the Landwehr Canal. The green traffic-light tower marking the beginning of the Daimler Quartier is a replica of the first automatic traffic light in Europe, which was erected on this very spot in 1924.

One of the highlights of this avenue is the Kollhoff Tower skyscraper, which is topped by a 96-m- (315-ft-) high observation platform called **Panoramapunkt** (Panorama Point). It offers a breathtaking view and can be reached via Europe's fastest elevator.

The Daimler Quartier also contains the only historic building on Potsdamer Platz to escape destruction in World War II: the grey limestone building of Haus Huth, built for the wine dealer Christian Huth in 1912. The best view of the building is from its south side, where a tiny park offers a place to rest.

Today, the offices of the famous car manufacturers Daimler are located here, along with a restaurant, a small café and an upmarket wine shop. Haus Huth is also home to **Daimler Contemporary**, a small exhibition featuring key works and new additions to the corporation's collection of 20th-century art.

Panoramapunkt

♿ ☺ ⬛ Potsdamer Platz 1
🕐 Hours vary, check website
🌐 panoramapunkt.de

Daimler Contemporary

♿ ☺ ⬛ Alte Potsdamer Strasse 5 🕐 11am–6pm daily
🌐 art.daimler.com

MARLENE DIETRICH (1901–1992)

Born in Schöneberg, Marlene Dietrich was a film star of the 1920s. She landed a contract with Paramount in Hollywood following the success of the film *Der Blaue Engel* (*The Blue Angel*). With her smoky voice and andro-gynous style, she quickly became a cinema and fashion icon. She lived polygamously in an open marriage and had relationships with many actors, including Greta Garbo and Frank Sinatra. When World War II began, she spoke out against the Nazis and renounced her German citizenship, becoming an American citizen; she later joined the American armed forces as an entertainer. From the 1950s, she worked almost exclusively as a cabaret artist, performing in theatres around the world.

EXPERIENCE MORE

Philharmonie und Kammermusiksaal

🚇 I6 🏛 Herbert-von-Karajan-Strasse 1 📞 25 48 88 00 Ⓢ & Ⓤ Potsdamer Platz Ⓤ Mendelssohn-Bartholdy-Park 🚌 200, 300, M41, M48, M85

Home to one of the most renowned orchestras in Europe, the Philharmonic and Chamber Music Hall is among the finest postwar architectural achievements in Europe. The Philharmonic, completed in 1963 to a design by Hans Scharoun, pioneered a new concept in concert hall interiors. The orchestra's podium occupies the central section of the pentagonal hall, around which are galleries for the public, designed to blend into the perspective of the five corners.

The Berlin Philharmonic was founded in 1882 and the orchestra has since attained renown not only for its concerts, but also through its prolific symphony recordings.

The smaller Chamber Music Hall was added in the 1980s.

Designed to complement Scharoun's existing architecture, it features a central multi-sided space covered by a fanciful tent-like roof.

St-Matthäus-Kirche

🚇 I6 🏛 Matthäikirchplatz Ⓢ & Ⓤ Potsdamer Platz Ⓤ Mendelssohn-Bartholdy-Park 🚌 148, 200, M41, M48, M85 🕐 11am–6pm Tue–Sun 🌐 stiftung-stmatthaeus.de

St Matthew's Church once stood in the centre of a small square surrounded by buildings. After bomb damage in World War II, the structure was restored, making it the focal point of the Kulturforum. The church was originally built between 1844 and 1846 to a design by Friedrich August Stüler and Hermann Wentzel, in a style based on Italian Romanesque temples.

Each of the three naves is covered by a separate two-tier roof, while the eastern end of the church is closed by a semi-circular apse. The exterior is covered in a two-tone brick

façade arranged in yellow and red lines. Today, this pretty church with its slender tower offers an intriguing contrast to the many ultramodern and sometimes extravagant buildings of the Kulturforum.

Kunstgewerbe-museum

🚇 I6 🏛 Matthäikirchplatz 8 Ⓢ & Ⓤ Potsdamer Platz Ⓤ Mendelssohn-Bartholdy-Park 🚌 200, M29, M41, M48, M85 🕐 10am–6pm Tue–Fri, 11am–6pm Sat & Sun 🌐 smb.museum

The Kunstgewerbe Museum embraces many genres of craft and decorative art, from the early Middle Ages to the modern day. Goldwork is especially well represented, and among the most valuable exhibits is a collection of medieval gold pieces from the church treasuries of Enger, near Herford, and the Guelph treasury from Brunswick. The museum also takes great pride in its collection of late Gothic and Renaissance silver from the town of Lüneburg's civic

← The striking home of the Berlin Philharmonic

Das Stue

Located inside a former embassy, Das Stue ("living room" in Danish), has a plush Nordic-style interior that houses a Michelin-starred restaurant, Susanne Kaufmann Spa and a cool cocktail bar.

📍G6 🏠Drakestrasse 1 🌐das-stue.com

€€€

treasury. There are fine examples of Italian majolica, and 18th- and 19th-century German, French and Italian glass, porcelain and furniture. Exhibits also include Jugendstil and Art Deco glassware and furniture, and Bauhaus and contemporary design.

Kupferstichkabinett

📍I6 🏠Matthäikirchplatz 8 🚇&Ⓤ Potsdamer Platz Ⓤ Mendelssohn-Bartholdy-Park 🚌200, M29, M41, M48, M85 ⏰10am-6pm daily 🌐smb.museum

The print collections of galleries in the former East and West Berlin were united in 1994 in the Print Library, located in the Kulturforum (p176). These displays originated with a collection started by the Great Elector (p215) in 1652, which has been open to the public since 1831. Despite wartime losses, it has an imposing breadth and has around 2,000 engravers' plates, over 520,000 prints and around 110,000 drawings and watercolours. Sadly, only a small fraction of these delicate treasures can be even briefly exposed to daylight; therefore

the museum does not have a permanent exhibition, only galleries with temporary displays of selected works.

The collection includes works of artists from the Middle Ages to contemporary times. Well represented is the work of Botticelli (including illustrations for Dante's *Divine Comedy*), Dürer, Rembrandt and the Dutch Masters, Watteau, Goya, Daumier and painters of the *Brücke* art movement.

8

Staatsbibliothek

📍I7 🏠Potsdamer Strasse 33 🚇&Ⓤ Potsdamer Platz 🚌200, M29, M48, M85 ⏰9am-9pm Mon-Fri (to 7pm Sat) 🌐staats bibliothek-berlin.de

An unusually shaped building with a gilded dome, the State Library is home to one of the largest collections of books and manuscripts in Europe and is fondly referred to by Berliners as the "Stabi". After World War II, East and West Berlin each inherited part of the prewar state library collection and the Staatsbibliothek was built to house the part belonging to West Berlin. The building itself was designed by Hans Scharoun and Edgar Wisniewski, and constructed between 1967 and 1978.

It is a building where the disciplines of function and efficiency take precedence over that of form. The store rooms hold about five million volumes; the hall of the vast reading room is open-plan, with an irregular arrangement of partitions and floor levels; general noise and the sound of footsteps is muffled by fitted carpets, making the interior a very quiet and cosy place. The library itself houses more than four million books and a fine collection of manuscripts. It is linked to the Staatsbibliothek on Unter den Linden (p68).

↑ Street organ in the Musikinstrumenten-Museum collection

9

Musikinstrumenten-Museum

📍I6 🏠Tiergartenstrasse 1 🚇&Ⓤ Potsdamer Platz 🚌200, 300, M41, M48, M85 ⏰Hours vary, see website for details 🚫Mon 🌐sim.spk-berlin.de

Hidden behind the Philharmonie, the fascinating Museum of Musical Instruments houses over 750 exhibits in a collection dating from 1888. Intriguing displays enable you to trace each instrument's development, from the 16th century to the present day. You can marvel at the harpsichord of Jean Marius, once owned by Frederick the Great, and the violins made by Amati and Stradivarius.

Most spectacular of all is the silent-film-era cinema organ, a working Wurlitzer dating from 1929. With a range of sounds that extends even to locomotive impressions, the demonstrations of its powers every Saturday at noon attract enthusiastic crowds. The sounds of other exhibited instruments can be heard via recordings.

DRINK

Potsdamer Strasse has come on in leaps and bounds over the last decade, with plenty of great drinking spots among the cool boutiques and galleries.

Kumpelnest 3000

📍 I7 🏠 Lützowstrasse 23 🕐 7pm-6am Mon-Thu, 7pm-8am Fri & Sat 🌐 kumpelnest3000.com

---

Victoria Bar

📍 I7 🏠 Potsdamer Str 102 🕐 6:30pm-3am Sun-Thu, 6:30pm-4am Fri & Sat 🌐 victoriabar.de

---

Tiger Bar

📍 I7 🏠 Oh Panama, Potsdamer Strasse 91 🕐 6pm-midnight Tue-Sat 🌐 oh-panama.com

---

Neue Nationalgalerie

📍 I7 🏠 Potsdamer Strasse 50 Ⓢ & Ⓤ Potsdamer Platz Ⓤ Mendelssohn-Bartholdy-Park 🚌 200, M29, M41, M48, M85 🕐 Hours vary, check website 🌐 smb.museum

The magnificent collection of modern art housed in the New National Gallery has a troubled history. The core of the collection consisted of 262 paintings that belonged to banker J H W Wagener. In the late 1860s, when Wagener died, he bequeathed them to Crown Prince Wilhelm, who housed them in the National-galerie on Museumsinsel.

However, in 1937, a Nazi programme of cultural cleansing meant that over 400 of the works in the collection, which had grown to include paintings by Monet, Manet and Renoir, were confiscated.

After World War II, the Berlin municipal authority decided to rebuild the collection and authorized the construction of a suitable building in West Berlin to house it. The commission was given to the elder states-man of modern architecture, the 75-year-old Mies van der Rohe. The result is a striking, minimalist building with a flat steel roof over a glass hall, which appears to float in mid-air supported only by six slender interior struts.

The collection comprises largely 20th-century art, but begins with artists of the late 19th century, such as Edvard Munch, Ferdinand Hodler and Oskar Kokoschka. German movements, such as *Die Brücke (p30)*, are well represented, with pieces by Karl Schmidt-Rottluff and Ernst Ludwig Kirchner (notably his evocative oil painting *Potsdamer Platz*).

As well as the Bauhaus movement, represented by Paul Klee and Wassily Kandinsky, the gallery shows works by exponents of a stark realism, such as Otto Dix and George Grosz. Celebrated artists of other European countries are also included – Pablo Picasso, Fernand Léger, de Chirico, Dalí, René Magritte and Max Ernst. Post-World War II art is represented by Barnett Newman, Frank Stella and many others. The sculpture garden houses important works, both figurative and abstract.

Following reunification, new works by artists from the former East Germany were added. Some of the art is sometimes shown at the Hamburger Bahnhof *(p124)*, as both museums draw on the same collection.

Urban Nation

📍 H8 🏠 Bülowstrasse 7 Ⓤ Nollendorfplatz 🚌 106, 187, M19 🕐 10am-6pm Tue-Wed, noon-8pm Thu-Sun 🌐 urban-nation.com

The Urban Nation Museum for Contemporary Art opened in 2017 in Schöneberg, though its roots as an organization stretch back to 2013. Whereas the collective behind it, under the curation of Yasha Young, had previously used the city's surfaces as canvases for outdoor street art and installations, now there is an indoor space to show them off, too. As well as exhibiting the work of international and local artists, the nonprofit venue hosts workshops and events – and it's still possible to find much of their work on

→ Exhibits at the Schwules Museum, mapping the history of the LGBTQ+ community

the streets around the gallery; look out for the large mural on the corner of Bülowstrasse and Frobenstrasse.

⑫ Potsdamer Strasse

🗺 I7 🚇 & 🚇 Potsdamer Platz
🚇 Kurfürstenstrasse,
Bülowstrasse, Kleistpark
🚌 104, 106, 187, 204, M19,
M29, M41, M45, M48

A few years ago, Schöneberg's main drag, Potsdamer Strasse, was known for its sex shops and run-down casinos. These days, only slight traces of this insalubrious past remain, as gentrification has ushered in a new generation of shops, galleries, cafés and bars. Sitting alongside established spots like the Victoria Bar (No. 102) and the charming Joseph Roth-Diele at No. 75 are shiny newcomers: art galleries such as Circle Culture (No. 75) and Esther Schipper (No. 81e), stylish restaurants such as Oh Panama (No. 91) and luxury designer shops like Andreas Murkudis (p170).

← Contemporary art shown by the nonprofit art collective Urban Nation

⑬ Schwules Museum

🗺 H7 🏠 Lützowstrasse 73
🚇 Nollendorfplatz,
Kurfürstenstrasse
🌐 schwulesmuseum.de

This is the world's first museum dedicated to LGBTQ+ history. Containing more than 50,000 objects, it has four exhibition spaces hosting temporary exhibits, which recount the history and culture of LGBTQ+ communities in Berlin and beyond. Exhibits have included the queer history of video games and LGBTQ+ movements in Germany following Stonewall. The museum also offers film screenings, guided tours and talks on subjects such as celebrity culture and coming out.

⑭   Bauhaus-Archiv

🗺 H7 🏠 Klingelhöfer-
strasse 14 📞 25 40 02 78
🚇 Nollendorfplatz 🚌 100,
106, 187, M29 🚫 For
restoration

The Bauhaus school of art, started by Walter Gropius in 1919, was one of the most influential

art institutions of the 20th century. The belief of the Bauhaus group was that art and technology should combine in harmonious unity.

Originally based in Weimar, and from 1925 in Dessau, this school provided inspiration for numerous artists and architects. Staff and students included Mies van der Rohe, Paul Klee, Wassily Kandinsky, Theo van Doesburg and László Moholy-Nagy. The school moved to Berlin in 1932, but was closed down by the Nazis in 1933.

After the war, the Bauhaus-Archiv was relocated to Darmstadt. In 1964, Walter Gropius designed a building to house the collection, but it was never realized. The archive was moved to Berlin in 1971, where the design was adapted to the new site. The gleaming white building with its distinctive glass-panelled gables was completed in 1979, and while the interior is closed for renovation, the exterior is magnificent. Some of the archive (together with its Bauhaus shop) can be seen in its temporary home in the Hardenberg Haus, on the corner of Knesebeckstrasse and Hardenbergstrasse, not far from Berlin Zoo (p203).

EXPERIENCE Tiergarten

15

Villa von der Heydt

Q H7 **⌂** Von-der-Heydt-Strasse 18 **☎** 266 41 28 88 **U** Nollendorfplatz 🚌 100, 200, M29

One of the last remaining villas in the Tiergarten neighbourhood, Villa von der Heydt was built between 1860 and 1862 as a private residence for Baron August von der Heydt. This fine villa, designed by Hermann Ende and G A Linke and built in a late Neo-Classical style, is one of the few surviving reminders that the southern side of the Tiergarten area was one of the most expensive and beautiful residential areas of Berlin.

The neatly manicured gardens and railings around the villa are adorned with busts of Christian Daniel Rauch and Alexander von Humboldt. The statues, by Reinhold Begas, originally lined the Triumphal Avenue in the Tiergarten before being moved here. After restoration in 1980, the villa became the headquarters of one of the most influential cultural bodies, the Foundation of Prussian Cultural Heritage.

SHOP

Andreas Murkudis
One of the first establishments to kick off the ongoing gentrification of this formerly gritty street, this huge, white, bright space stocks a selection of luxury goods curated by the eponymous owner.

Q I7 **⌂** Potsdamer Strasse 81 **⊙** 10am–9pm Mon–Sat **w** andreasmurkudis.com

16

Bendlerblock (Gedenkstätte Deutscher Widerstand)

Q H6 **⌂** Stauffenbergstrasse 13–14 **☎** 26 99 50 00 **U** Potsdamer Platz, Kurfürstenstrasse 🚌 M29, M48 **⊙** 9am–6pm Mon–Fri (to 8pm Thu), 10am–6pm Sat & Sun

The collection of buildings known as the Bendlerblock was originally built during the Third Reich as an extension to the German State Naval Offices. During World War II, these buildings were the headquarters of the Wehrmacht (German Army). It was here that a group of officers planned their famous and ultimately unsuccessful assassination attempt on Hitler on 20 July 1944. Four of the conspirators were shot in the Bendlerblock courtyard, and a monument commemorating this event, designed by Richard Scheibe in 1953, stands where the executions were carried out. On the upper floor of the building is an exhibition documenting the history of the German anti-Nazi movements.

17

Diplomatenviertel

Q H6 **U** Nollendorfplatz, Potsdamer Platz 🚌 100, 106, 187, 200

Although a number of consulates existed in the Tiergarten area as early as 1918, the establishment of a Diplomatic Quarter along the southern edge of the Tiergarten, between Stauffenbergstrasse and Lichtensteinallee, did not take place until

Tiergarten in autumn *(inset)* and summer

the period of Hitler's Third Reich, when large embassies representing the Axis Powers, Italy and Japan, were built here.

Despite the fact that these monumental buildings were designed by a number of different architects, the Fascist interpretation of Neo-Classicism and the influence of Albert Speer as head architect meant that the group was homogenous, if bleak. Few buildings survived World War II bombing.

Today, the diplomatic area is bounded by Tiergarten-strasse. The Austrian embassy, designed by Hans Hollein, stands at the junction of Stauffenbergstrasse, next door to the embassies of India and the Republic of South Africa. At Tiergartenstrasse Nos. 21–3, the pre-World War II Italian embassy still stands, while next door is a copy of the first Japanese embassy. Between Klingelhöfer-strasse and Rauchstrasse stands an imposing complex of five embassies. Completed in 1999, these represent Norway, Sweden, Denmark, Finland and Iceland. The complex has an art gallery and café open to the public.

Tiergarten

◊ I5 ◎ Tiergarten, Bellevue
▭ 100, 106, 187, 200, N26

This is the largest park in Berlin. Situated at the geographical centre of the city, it occupies a surface area of more than 200 ha (495 acres). Once a forest used as the Elector's hunting reserve, it was transformed into a landscaped park by Peter Joseph Lenné in the 1830s. A Triumphal Avenue was built in the eastern section of the park at the end of the 19th century, lined with statues of the country's rulers and statesmen.

World War II inflicted huge damage on the Tiergarten, including the destruction of the Triumphal Avenue, many of whose surviving monuments can now be seen in the Zitadelle Spandau (*p239*). Replanting, however, has now restored the Tiergarten, which is a fav-ourite meeting place for Berliners. Its avenues are lined with statues of figures such as Johann Wolfgang von Goethe and Richard Wagner.

By the lake known as Neuer See and the Landwehrkanal are memorials to the murdered leaders of the Spartacus movement, Karl Liebknecht and Rosa Luxemburg. Also worth finding is a collection of gas lamps, displayed near the Tiergarten S-Bahn station.

PETER JOSEPH LENNÉ

Born to a court gardener from Bonn, Peter Joseph Lenné (1789-1866) was destined to follow in his father's footsteps and become one of Prussia's most renowned landscape architects. As Director-General of Royal Prussian Gardens, his impact on shaping Berlin and Potsdam's green spaces was profound. From the regal vistas at Sanssouci to the storybook magic of Pfaueninsel, many of Lenné's parks are now UNESCO World Heritage Sites.

EAT

Teehaus im Englischen Garten

Slightly hidden in a small corner of the Tiergarten, this cosy café-restaurant is nestled in a cottage with a thatched roof and surrounded by a small formal garden.

📍G5 🚇Altonaer Str. 2 Nov-Mar 🌐 das-teehaus.jimdo.com

€€

Oh Panama

Swanky spot, with an artsy interior, offering global fusion food.

📍I8 🚇Potsdamer Strasse 91 🌐oh-panama.com

€€€

Joseph Roth Diele

Named after an Austrian Jewish writer, this atmospheric venue serves German cuisine.

📍I7 🚇Potsdamer Strasse 75 🌐joseph-roth-diele.de

€€€

FACIL

This two-Michelin-starred restaurant offers a seasonal menu.

📍J6 🚇Potsdamer Strasse 3 🌐facil.de

€€€

 19

Grosser Stern

📍G5 🚆Bellevue 🚇Hansa-platz 🚌100, 106, 187, N26

The Great Star roundabout at the centre of the Tiergarten is so-named for the five large roads that radiate from it. At its centre is the Siegessäule

↑ The squat structure and parabolic roof of the Haus der Kulturen der Welt

(Victory Column; p174). Surrounding it are monuments brought over from the nearby Reichstag building (p156) in the late 1930s. During the same period, the Strasse des 17 Juni was widened to twice its original size, the square surrounding the roundabout was enlarged and much of the existing statuary removed.

In the northern section of the square stands a vast bronze monument to the first German Chancellor, Otto von Bismarck (1815–98). Around it stand allegorical figures, the work of late 19th-century sculptor Reinhold Begas. Other statues represent various national heroes, including Field Marshal Helmuth von Moltke (1800–91), chief of the Prussian general staff between the years 1858 and 1888, who won the Franco-German war.

 20

Haus der Kulturen der Welt

📍I5 🚇John-Foster-Dulles-Allee 10 🚆&🚇Haupt-bahnhof, Bundestag 🚌100 🕙10am-7pm daily 🌐hkw.de

The House of World Culture, designed by the American architect Hugh Stubbins, was intended as the American entry in the international architecture competition "Interbau 1957", from which the Hansaviertel apartment

blocks also originated. It soon became a symbol of freedom and modernity in West Berlin during the Cold War, particularly when compared to the GDR-era architecture of Karl-Marx-Allee (p146) in East Berlin.

Unfortunately its roof failed to withstand the test of time and the building partially collapsed in 1980. After reconstruction it was reopened in 1989, with a change of purpose: to bring world cultures to a wider German audience via events, exhibitions and performances. It is known for its jazz festivals in particular.

Standing nearby is the black tower of the Carillon, built in 1987 to commemorate the 750th anniversary of Berlin. Suspended in the tower is the largest carillon in Europe, comprising 67 bells. Daily, at noon and 6pm, the bells give a computer-controlled concert.

 21

Sowjetisches Ehrenmal

📍J5 🚇Strasse des 17 Juni 🚆&🚇Brandenburger Tor 🚌100, 245

The huge Monument to Soviet Soldiers near the Brandenburg Gate was unveiled on 7 November 1945, on the anniversary of the start of the October Revolution in Russia. Flanked by the first two tanks into the city, the monument commemorates over 300,000 Soviet soldiers who perished in the Battle of Berlin at the end of World War II. The vast column was made from marble taken from the headquarters of the Chancellor of the Third Reich when it was being dismantled.

The monument is also a cemetery for around 2,500 Soviet casualties. Following the partition of Berlin, the site ended up in the British sector, but formed a kind of non-territorial enclave to which Soviet soldiers posted to East Berlin had access.

Schloss Bellevue

G5 **Spreeweg 1**
S Bellevue **100, 187**

The captivating Bellevue Palace with its dazzlingly white Neo-Classical façade is now the official residence of the German Federal President, and is a very pretty sight from the northern edge of the Tiergarten park. Built in 1786 to a design by Michael Philipp Boumann for the Prussian Prince August Ferdinand, the palace served as a royal residence until 1861. In 1935, it was refurbished to house a Museum of German Ethnology. Refurbished again in 1938, it became a hotel for guests of the Nazi government.

Following bomb damage during World War II, the palace was carefully restored to its former glory, with the oval ballroom rebuilt to a design by Carl Gotthard Langhans. The palace is set within an attractive park laid out to the original late 18th-century design, though unfortunately the picturesque garden pavilions that once stood here did not survive World War II.

Memorial to Homo-sexuals Persecuted Under Nazism

J6 **Ebertstrasse, Tiergarten**

Between 1933 and 1945, tens of thousands of gay men were persecuted, arrested and killed by the Nazis under *Paragraph 175*, a section of Germany's criminal code that made sexual relations between men illegal; around 15,000 of them were sent to concentration camps. This memorial, established in 2008, is dedicated to their memory, and also acts as a symbol against intolerance and exclusion of the LGBTQ+ community. Designed by Michael Elmgreen and Ingar Dragset, it comprises a single grey concrete cube that is reminiscent of the concrete slabs or "stelae" from the Holocaust Denkmal *(p77)*. A window opens into its interior, where a film is projected; the film alternates biennially, one showing two men kissing and one showing two women kissing.

The display screen *(inset)* at the
Memorial to Homosexuals
Persecuted Under Nazism ↑

㉔ Regierungsviertel

📍I4 ⑤Brandenburger Tor
Ⓤ Bundestag 🚌100, 248

This bold concept for a
government district fit
for a 21st-century capital
was the winning design in
a competition held in 1992.
Construction of the complex
was completed in 2003.
Axel Schultes and Charlotte
Frank's grand design pro-
posed a rectangular site
cutting across the meander
of the Spree just north of
the Reichstag (p156).

While many of the buildings
have been designed by other
architects to fit within the
overall concept, Schultes and
Frank designed the Bundes-
kanzleramt, opposite the
Reichstag – the official
residence of the German
Chancellor. The whole project
is complemented by the
neighbouring Hauptbahnhof
railway station, an impressive
glass-and-steel construction
with several levels above
and below ground. The
U-Bahn line U5 has been
extended and now connects
Hauptbahnhof with the
Brandenburg Gate (p78), Unter
den Linden, Museum Island
and Alexanderplatz (p106).

㉕ Siegessäule

📍G5 🏛Grosser Stern
📞391 29 61 ⑤Bellevue
Ⓤ Hansaplatz 🚌100, 106,
187 🕐Apr-Oct: 9:30am-
6:30pm daily; Nov-Mar:
10am-5pm daily

The Victory Column is
based on a design by Johann
Heinrich Strack and was
built to commemorate
Prussia's triumph in the
Prusso-Danish war of 1864.

After further Prussian
victories, "Goldelse", a gilded
figure by Friedrich Drake
representing Victory, was
added to the top. The
monument stood in front of
the Reichstag building until
the Nazi government moved
it here in 1938. The base is
decorated with bas-reliefs
commemorating battles.
Higher up the column, a
mosaic frieze depicts the
1871 founding of the German
Empire. An observation
terrace at the top offers
magnificent vistas over Berlin.

㉖ Hansaviertel

📍G4 ⑤Bellevue
Ⓤ Hansaplatz
🚌100, 106, 187

This area to the west of
Schloss Bellevue (p173) is
home to some of the most
interesting modern archi-
tecture in Berlin, built for an
international exhibition in
1957. Taking on a World War II

bomb site, prominent architects from around the world designed 45 projects, of which 36 were realized, to create a varied residential development set in an environment of lush greenery. The list of distinguished architects involved in the project included Walter Gropius (Händelallee Nos. 3–9), Alvar Aalto (Klopstock-strasse Nos. 30–32) and Oscar Niemeyer (Altonaer Strasse Nos. 4–14). The development also includes a school, a commercial services building and two churches.

In 1960, a new headquarters for the **Akademie der Künste** (Academy of Arts) was built at Hanseatenweg No. 10. Designed by Werner Düttmann, the academy has a concert hall, an exhibition area, archives and a library. In front of the main entrance is a magnificent piece,

90

The percentage of Hansaviertel's original buildings that were destroyed during World War II.

Reclining Figure, by eminent British sculptor Henry Moore.

The area is also home to the **Buchstabenmuseum** (Letter Museum). This quirky collection is made up of over 1,000 examples of abandoned 3D letters, logos and signs, many of which have been rescued from across Berlin itself. It's an eclectic mix, with glowing neon letters hanging alongside old shop signs and long-forgotten logos. As well as being visually stunning, the collection helps to document

↑ The Regierungsviertel's Marie-Elisabeth-Lüders-Haus office building (2003), named for one of Germany's first female politicians

otherwise forgotten aspects of the city's past, with historical and typographical infor-mation provided on many of the items. Highlights include Berlin's oldest neon sign and a letter "e" used in Quentin Tarantino's *Inglourious Basterds*.

Akademie der Künste
◈ ❷ G5 ⌂ Hanseatenweg 10 ⏱ 11am-8pm Tue-Sun
ⓦ adk.de

Buchstabenmuseum
◈ ❷ G4 Stadtbahnbogen 424 ⏱ 1pm-5pm Thu-Sun
ⓦ buchstabenmuseum.de

A SHORT WALK
AROUND THE KULTURFORUM

Distance 1 km (0.5 miles) **Nearest station** Potsdamer Platz **Time** 15 minutes

The idea of creating a new cultural centre in West Berlin was put forward in 1956. The first building to go up was the Berlin Philharmonic concert hall, built to an innovative design by Hans Scharoun in 1961. Most of the plans for the various other components of the Kulturforum were realized between 1961 and 1987, and came from such famous architects as Ludwig Mies van der Rohe. The area is now a major cultural centre with fascinating museums and stunning architecture to enjoy as you explore.

The **Kunstgewerbemuseum** *(Museum of Arts and Crafts, p166) contains a unique collection of items including fashion and furniture, dating from the Middle Ages to the present day (p166).*

The **Kupferstichkabinett** *(Gallery of Prints and Drawings, p167)*

The **Kunstbibliothek** *(Art Library) has a rich collection of books, graphic art and drawings, many of which are displayed in its exhibition halls.*

Important works by Old Masters such as Jan van Eyck and Jan Vermeer are exhibited in the **Gemäldegalerie** *(p158).*

REICHPIETSCHUFER

LANDWEHRKANAL

← Gallery of fashion at the Kunstgewerbemuseum

Did You Know?

Hans Scharoun was a key architect during the reconstruction of Berlin after World War II.

Its outside covered in a layer of golden aluminium, the **Berlin Philharmonie** (p166) concert hall is known all over the world for its superb acoustics.

TIERGARTEN

Around the Kulturforum

Locator Map
For more detail see p154

The **Musikinstrumenten-Museum** *(Museum of Musical Instruments,w p167) contains a unique collection of instruments dating from the 16th to the 20th centuries.*

St-Matthäus-Kirche (p166) *is a picturesque 19th-century church that stands out among the modern buildings of the Kulturforum.*

SCHAROUNSTRÄSSE

Hans Scharoun designed the public lending and research **Staatsbibliothek** *(State Library, p167) in 1978.*

MATTHÄI KIRCH PLATZ

POTSDAMER STRASSE

SIGISMUNDSTRASSE

FINISH

| 0 metres | 100 | N |
| 0 yards | 100 | ↑ |

START

Sculptures by Henry Moore and Alexander Calder stand outside the streamlined building of the **Neue Nationalgalerie** *(p168), designed by Ludwig Mies van der Rohe.*

→ The bright exterior of St-Matthäus-Kirche

KREUZBERG

The area covered in this chapter is only a part of the district of the same name. The evolution of Kreuzberg began in the late 19th century, when it was a working-class neighbourhood. After World War II, unrepaired buildings were abandoned by those who could afford to move, leaving behind a population of artists, immigrants and low-income households.

Kreuzberg has become an area of contrasts, with luxury apartments inhabited by affluent young professionals located next to dilapidated buildings. It's also home to a variety of cultures and cuisines. Some parts of Kreuzberg are Turkish and the district's attractions are its wealth of restaurants and Turkish bazaars, as well as an interesting selection of nightclubs, cinemas, theatres and galleries.

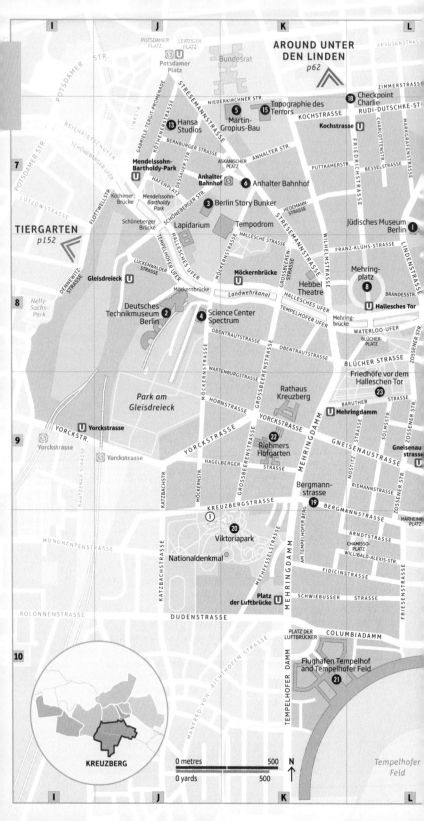

AROUND UNTER
DEN LINDEN
p62

KRAUSENSTRASSE

POTSDAMER
PLATZ

LEIPZIGER
PLATZ

ZIMMERSTRASSE

Potsdamer
Platz

Bundesrat

18 Checkpoint
Charlie

NIEDERKIRCHNER STR.

5 **15** Topographie des
Terrors

RUDI-DUTSCHKE-ST

POTSDAMER STR.

LINKSTR.

GABRIELE-TERGIT-PROMENADE

REICHPIETSCHUFER

SCHÖNEBERGER UFER

KÖTHENERSTRASSE

STRESEMANNSTRASSE

BERNBURGER STRASSE

Martin-
Gropius-Bau

KOCHSTRASSE

Kochstrasse U

CHARLOTTENSTR.

FRIEDRICHSTRASSE

MARKGRAFENSTRASSE

BESSELSTRASSE

13 Hansa
Studios

ANHALTER STR.

PUTTKAMERSTR.

7

Mendelssohn-
Bartholdy-Park
U

HAFENPLATZ

DESSAUER STR.

ASKANISCHER
PLATZ

SCHÖNEBERGER STR.

**Anhalter
Bahnhof** Ⓢ

6 Anhalter Bahnhof

HEDEMANN-
STRASSE

WILHELMSTRASSE

FRANZ-KLÜHS-STRASSE

**Jüdisches Museum
Berlin** ❶

LINDENSTRASSE

POTSDAMER STR.

LÜTZOWSTRASSE

Köthener
Brücke

FLOTTWELLSTR.

Mendelssohn-
Bartholdy
Park

3 Berlin Story Bunker

STRESEMANNSTRASSE

TIERGARTEN
p152

DENNEWITZ STRASSE

LUCKENWALDER
STRASSE

Schöneberger
Brücke

Lapidarium

TEMPELHOFER UFER

HALLESCHES UFER

Tempodrom

HALLESCHE STRASSE

MÖCKERNSTRASSE

Möckernbrücke
U

HALLESCHE STRASSE

GROSSBEERENSTRASSE

Hebbel
Theatre

**Mehring-
platz**

8

BRANDESSTR.

ZOSSENER STR.

8

Nelly-
Sachs-
Park

Gleisdreieck U

Möckernbrücke

Landwehrkanal

HALLESCHES UFER

TEMPELHOFER UFER

Mehring-
brücke

U **Hallesches Tor**

WATERLOO-UFER

BLÜCHER-
PLATZ

**Deutsches
Technikmuseum
Berlin** **2**

4 Science Center
Spectrum

OBENTRAUTSTRASSE

OBENTRAUTSTRASSE

BLÜCHER STRASSE

BLÜCHER STRASSE

ZOSSENER STR.

Park am
Gleisdreieck

MÖCKERNSTRASSE

WARTENBURGSTRASSE

GROSSBEERENSTRASSE

Rathaus
Kreuzberg

Friedhöfe vor dem
Halleschen Tor

23

STRASSE

U **Yorckstrasse**

Ⓢ Yorckstrasse

YORCKSTR.

HORNSTRASSE

YORCKSTRASSE

YORCKSTRASSE

U **Mehringdamm**

BARUTHER

STRASSE

SOLMSSTR.

ZOSSENER STR.

9

BAUTZENER STRASSE

KATZBACHSTR.

MÖCKERNSTR.

HAGELBERGER

GROSSBEERENSTRASSE

STRASSE

22
Riehmers
Hofgarten

MEHRINGDAMM

GNEISENAUSTRASSE

NOSTIZSTR.

RIEMANNSTRASSE

ZOSSENER STR.

**Gneisenau
strasse**
U

Bergmann-
strasse

19

BERGMANNSTRASSE

MARHEINE-
PLATZ

MONUMENTENSTRASSE

KREUZBERGSTRASSE

Ⓘ

20

Viktoriapark

Nationaldenkmal

METHFESSELSTRASSE

AM TEMPELHOFER BERG

MEHRINGDAMM

ARNDTSTRASSE

CHAMISSO-
PLATZ

WILLIBALD-ALEXIS-STR.

FIDICINSTRASSE

FRIESENSTRASSE

KOLONNENSTRASSE

**Platz
der Luftbrücke**

DUDENSTRASSE

SCHWIEBUSSER

STRASSE

10

TEMPELHOFER DAMM

MANFRED-VON-RICHTHOFEN STRASSE

PLATZ DER
LUFTBRÜCKER

COLUMBIADAMM

Flughafen Tempelhof
and Tempelhofer Feld

21

Tempelhofer
Feld

KREUZBERG

0 metres   500

0 yards   500

N↑

I   J   K   L

Waldeckpark

Engel-
becken

Berlinische
Galerie

König Gallery
(St Agnes)

KREUZBERG

Moritzplatz

Prinzessinnen-
garten

FHXB
Museum

SO36

Kottbusser
Tor

Prinzenstrasse

Sommerbad
Kreuzberg

Waterloobrücke

Landwehrkanal

Böckler-
park

Baerwaldbrücke

Urbanhafen

Admiralbrücke

Kottbusser
Brücke

Schönleinstrasse

KREUZBERG

Must Sees

1. Jüdisches Museum Berlin
2. Deutsches Technik-
   museum Berlin

Experience More

3. Berlin Story Bunker
4. Science Center Spectrum
5. Martin-Gropius-Bau
6. Anhalter Bahnhof
7. Sommerbad Kreuzberg
8. Mehringplatz
9. Admiralbrücke
10. SO36
11. Kottbusser Tor
12. FHXB Museum
13. Hansa Studios
14. Berlinische Galerie
15. Topographie des Terrors
16. König Gallery (St Agnes)

17. Moritzplatz
18. Checkpoint Charlie
19. Bergmannstrasse
20. Viktoriapark
21. Flughafen Tempelhof
    and Tempelhofer Feld
22. Riehmers Hofgarten
23. Friedhöfe vor dem
    Halleschen Tor

Eat

1. Tomasa
2. Defne
3. Cocolo

Drink

4. Luzia

Shop

5. Voo Store

1 🖎 🖾 🖵 🛍

JÜDISCHES MUSEUM BERLIN

📍L7 🏛Lindenstrasse 9-14 🚇Halleshes Tor, Kochstrasse
🚌M29, M41, 248 🕐10am-7pm daily 🚫Some Jewish hols 🌐jmberlin.de

The Jewish Museum is a mix of exhibition spaces, archives and gardens that bring the memories and stories of Jewish culture alive.

Designed by Daniel Libeskind, a Polish-Jewish architect based in the United States, the Jüdisches Museum complex is an exciting and imaginative example of late 20th-century architecture. The complex contains a library and gardens, but the highlight is the Libeskind Building itself, whose shape, style and interior arrangement are part of a philosophical programme to illustrate the history and culture of Germany's Jewish community, and the repercussions of the Holocaust. The long, narrow galleries with slanting floors and sharp zigzagging turns are designed to evoke the feeling of loss and dislocation. These are interspersed by "voids" that represent the vacuum left behind by the destruction of Jewish life and culture.

Iron plate faces *(inset)* crying up at visitors where they lie discarded on the floor in Menashe Kadishman's *Shalekhet* installation

↑ The Libeskind Building,
sometimes likened to a
deconstructed Star of David

↑ The Garden of Exile, symbolizing
the forced exile of Germany's
Jewish population under Nazi rule

MUSEUM GUIDE

Entrance to the main museum
(the Libeskind Building) is via
an underground tunnel. The
exhibition is divided into 14
sections, taking visitors through
German Jewish history and
culture from early history up
to the present day.

2 🛠️ ✂️ 🍴 💻 🛍️

DEUTSCHES TECHNIKMUSEUM BERLIN

📍 J8 🏠 Trebbiner Strasse 9 🚇 Gleisdreieck 🚌 M29, M41 🕐 9am–5:30pm Tue–Fri, 10am–6pm Sat & Sun 🌐 technikmuseum.berlin

The Museum of Technology takes visitors on a multimedia journey through recent human history by exploring its technological achievements.

The museum was established by grouping together more than 100 smaller, specialized collections under one roof. The current collection is arranged on the site of a former trade hall, the size of which allows many of the museum's exhibits – such as locomotives, aircraft, boats and water towers – to be displayed full-size and in their original condition. Highlights of the collection include vintage cars and motorcycles, and dozens of locomotives and railway carriages from different eras. There are also exhibitions dedicated to flying, printing, weaving, engineering and computer technology. Live demonstrations of machinery are held regularly, with schedule information available at the information desk in the entrance hall. Adjacent to the museum is a beautiful park containing two windmills and the museum's rail transport exhibit in the former Anhalter Bahnhof station.

↑ Modern exterior of the Deutsches Technikmuseum Berlin on the banks of the Landwehr Canal

EAT

Tomasa

This red-brick villa has a well-stocked playroom, a great kids' menu and a courtyard and garden. It's a good spot for breakfast or brunch before the museum, which is a pleasant 1.5-km (1-mile) walk away through Park am Gleisdreieck.

📍 J10 🏠 Kreuzbergstrasse 62 🕐 9am–midnight Sun–Wed (to 1am Thu) 🌐 tomasa.de

€€€

Did You Know?

The plane on the museum's roof is a Douglas C-47B Skytrain "Raisin Bomber" dating from 1948–9.

↑ Model ships on display in the shipping and navigation galleries

↑ Swiss Air Force Bü 131
biplane in the superb
Aerospace exhibition

EXPERIENCE MORE

Berlin Story Bunker

📍 J7 🏠 Schöneberger Strasse 23A
Ⓢ Anhalter Bahnhof
Ⓤ Mendelssohn-Bartholdy-Park 🚌 M29, M41
🕙 10am–7pm daily
🌐 berlinstory.de

The bunker that houses this idiosyncratic museum was used during the war by those working in and living around the nearby Anhalter Bahnhof train station, which is now a memorial ruin. Today it contains the Berlin Story Museum, which illuminates some of the most significant aspects of Berlin's 800-year history through multimedia stations that combine photographs, films and art installations.

A separate exhibition was added in 2017 entitled "Hitler – how could it happen." It follows the timeline of Adolf Hitler's rise and fall via photographs, films, documents and recreations of parts of the infamous Führerbunker *(p76)*.

DRINK

Luzia

One of the district's most popular pre-club bars. A welcoming and quirky mix of exposed brick walls, street art murals and floor-to-ceiling windows that are ideal for people-watching.

📍 O7 🏠 Oranienstrasse 34 📞 30 81 79 99 58
🕙 Noon–5am daily

↑ Colour-mixing, just one of the absorbing interactive activities on offer at the Science Center Spectrum

Science Center Spectrum

📍 J8 🏠 Möckernstrasse 26
Ⓢ Anhalter Bahnhof
Ⓤ Möckernbrücke, Gleisdreieck 🚌 M29, M41, 248
🕙 Hours vary, check website
🌐 sdtb.de/spectrum

This annexe to the Deutsches Technikmuseum *(p184)* focuses on interactive exhibits. With its own distinct building next to the main museum, it occupies some 1,400 sq m (15,000 sq ft) of space across four floors, and features around 150 interactive exhibits arranged by themes such as Sound, Light & Sight and Power. There's a big room full of cars and motorbikes, a rainbow suspended in the air without the use of water, and masses of hands-on experiments, including swings and bridges to operate, the option to create colour tones by mixing light surfaces originating from real sunlight, and a Foucault's Pendulum that shows how the earth rotates. There's also a fun hall of mirrors for some stretchy selfies.

Martin-Gropius-Bau

📍 K7 🏠 Niederkirchner Strasse 7 (corner of Stresemannstrasse) 📞 25 48 60 Ⓢ & Ⓤ Potsdamer Platz 🚌 200, M29, M41
🕙 10am–7pm Wed–Mon

The innovative Martin-Gropius-Bau building was originally built to fulfil the requirements of an arts and crafts museum. It was designed by Martin Gropius with the participation of Heino Schmieden and constructed in 1881. The building's style is reminiscent of an Italian Renaissance palace, with a magnificent glazed interior courtyard, an impressive atrium and unusual, richly decorated elevations. Located between the windows are the crests of German cities, and within the friezes are reliefs illustrating different arts and crafts. In the plaques between the windows of the top storey are beautiful mosaics containing allegorical figures representing the cultures of different eras and countries.

From 1922, Martin-Gropius-Bau accommodated the Museum of Ethnology, but after World War II the building was abandoned and left in ruins. Although plans for an inner-city motorway threatened it until the 1970s, a reconstruction programme eventually commenced in 1981, led by architects Winnetou Kampmann and Ute Weström.

This was followed in 1999 by a further refurbishment, and since then the building has housed a changing series of exhibitions on art, photography and architecture.

Anhalter Bahnhof

◎K7 ⚐Askanischer Platz 6-7 ⓢAnhalter Bahnhof ⓤPotsdamer Platz, Mendelssohn-Bartholdy-Park ⛍M29, M41

Only a tiny fragment now remains of the Anhalter Bahnhof station, which was named after the Saxon royal family. It was once Berlin's largest, and Europe's second-largest, railway station.

The hugely ambitious structure was designed by Franz Schwechten and constructed in 1880. The station was intended to be the biggest and most elegant in Europe in order to impress official visitors to the capital of the German Empire. Some of the most famous people to alight at Anhalter Bahnhof were the Italian King Umberto, who was welcomed by Kaiser Wilhelm II himself, and the Russian Tsar Nicholas.

The station was taken out of public use in 1943 after its roof was destroyed by Allied bombing. Only the front portico remains, crowned by still-damaged sculptures and the hole that housed a large electric clock, as well as fragments of its once glorious façade. On the vast grounds behind rises the soaring, tent-like roof of the entertainment venue, Tempodrom.

Did You Know?

Kreuzberg is also known as X-Berg (based on "kreuz", which means "cross" in German).

KREUZBERG'S LGBTQ+ COMMUNITY

While Schöneberg is the most famous LGBTQ+ area in Berlin, Kreuzberg is the other main district of queer life in the city. Since the 1960s, this district has been known for its libertarian and tolerant way of life, with students, activists, artists and immigrants all living in the area. Today, the epicentre of queer nightlife here is the area around Kottbusser Tor U-Bahn station, which is home to LGBTQ+ friendly cafés and bars.

Fragment of the Anhalter Bahnhof, once the gateway to southern Germany ↓

SHOP

Voo Store

Situated inside a former locksmiths, this swanky industrial-design shop sells a highly curated mix of clothing, home decor and fashion accessories. Great coffee shop, too.

⬛ O8 🏠 Oranienstrasse 24 🕐 11am-7pm Mon-Sat 🌐 vooberlin.com

Sommerbad Kreuzberg

⬛ M8 🏠 Prinzenstrasse 113-9 📞 30 22 19 00 11 Ⓤ Prinzenstrasse 🚌 140, 248 🕐 7am-8pm daily

Known more commonly as Prinzenbad due to its proximity to the Prinzenstrasse U-Bahn station, this cult Kreuzberg swimming pool was made famous by its appearance in Sven Regener's 2001 book *Herr Lehmann* – and it subsequently featured in the hit film, too. While not the most refined of the city's pools, its two 50-m (164-ft) pools are hugely popular not only for their outdoor location, but also because they're big on character. Expect to find a rich and varied mix of people, including hipsters, Middle Eastern families, elderly Berliners and water-sliding youngsters, gathered here on any warm day.

Mehringplatz

⬛ L8 Ⓤ Hallesches Tor 🚌 248, M41

Mehringplatz was planned in the 1730s when the boundaries of the city were extended. Its original name was Rondell, meaning "circus", an appropriate name, as Wilhelmstrasse, Friedrichstrasse and Lindenstrasse all converged here.

Rondell was originally the work of Philipp Gerlach; then, in the 1840s, Peter Joseph Lenné designed the decoration of the square. At the centre is the Column of Peace, commemorating the Wars of Liberation in 1815. The column is crowned by the figure of Victory by Christian Daniel Rauch. Two sculptures were added in the 1870s: *Peace* by Albert Wolff and *Clio* (the Muse of History) by Ferdinand Hartzer. In the 19th and early 20th centuries, the area was populated with politicians, diplomats and aristocrats, and in 1947 the square was named after the writer Franz Mehring. The current buildings date from the 1970s.

Admiralbrücke

⬛ N9 🏠 Fraenkelufer/ Planufer Ⓤ Kottbusser Tor, Schönleinstrasse 🚌 140, M41

Built in 1882, the oldest steel-made bridge in Berlin is like a cultural heritage site and a popular hangout spot for locals and tourists. Connecting the banks of the Landwehrkanal, the bridge attracts a mostly young crowd who come here on sunny summer days to stroll along the canal's banks, chat, drink store-bought

People relaxing on the Admiralbrücke in the evening ↑

↑ People outside alternative music venue SO36, known for its techno and indie sounds

Did You Know?

The name SO36 is a reference to the district's Berlin Wall-era postal code.

beer and listen to street musicians, who play well into the night.

SO36

📍O8 🏠Oranienstrasse 190 Ⓤ Kottbusser Tor 🚌M29, 140 🕐9pm-5am Tue-Sat 🌐so36.de

One of Berlin's best-known alternative music venues, SO36 grew famous during the 1970s and 1980s, when it was run by artist Martin Kippenberger and hosted punk and post-punk acts such as Einstürzende Neubauten, Iggy Pop and Nick Cave. Today it regularly hosts big-name bands, mostly of a rock and indie persuasion, as well as up-and-coming local bands in its basic, large main room. Look out also for regular specials such as roller discos, Turkish LGBTQ+ pop event Gayhane and even the occasional flea market.

⑪ Kottbusser Tor

📍N8 🏠Kottbusser Strasse Ⓤ Kottbusser Tor 🚌140, M29, N8

Kottbusser Tor is the lively centre of the eastern part of Berlin's district of Kreuzberg. Nicknamed "Little Istanbul", Kottbusser Tor has long been the Turkish heartland of inner city Berlin. Originally a city gate leading to the city of Cottbus, today it's ostensibly a roundabout surrounded by 1970s- and 1980s-era residential housing bedecked with tell-tale satellite dishes (so that residents can tune into Turkish and Middle Eastern TV channels). It's a vibrant area both day and night, with a constant flow of foot and car traffic and a procession of food markets, street vendors and coffee shops. Although its reputation for low-level crime can't be disregarded, these days it's mostly frequented by a mix of local families and hipsters who congregate at weekends in search of the many inconspicuous bars and clubs – Monarch, Palermo, Möbel Olfe – as well as the mix of cheap falafel spots and trendy US-style burger joints like The Bird.

⑫ FHXB Museum

📍O8 🏠Adalbertstrasse 95A Ⓤ Kottbusser Tor 🚌140, M29 🕐Noon-8pm Tue-Thu, 10am-8pm Fri-Sun 🌐fhxb-museum.de

Housed in an old furniture factory away from the hustle and bustle of nearby Kottbusser Tor, the FHXB Museum, named after Berlin's Friedrichshain-Kreuzberg borough, charts the tumultuous and, at times, radical past of this vibrant neighbourhood. Permanent exhibitions at this community museum explore how 40 years of urban regeneration policies have defined the area, and the protest movements against its gentrification. An interactive exhibit enables visitors to listen to locals' stories, and they can walk over a large map of Kreuzberg, discovering various places in the district from the perspective of residents and refugee new Berliners. A lively roster of talks and workshops cover themes such as immigration and the housing crisis, which are top of mind to residents.

⑬ Hansa Studios

📍J7 🏠Köthener Strasse 38 🕐For tours only; book via the website 🌐musictours-berlin.de

Hansa Studios is one of Berlin's most famous music recording studios. Built in 1912, it has recorded albums by such internationally renowned names as David Bowie, Depeche Mode, U2 and R.E.M., as well as German luminaries such as Nina Hagen and Udo Jürgens. Only one studio is active these days, but it's possible to tour the building and also see the rooms where many of these prominent artists once recorded.

↑ A juxtaposition of white space and colour *(inset)* at the Berlinische Galerie

The museum's collection of sketches, prints and posters encompasses the Berlin Dadaists George Grosz, Hannah Höch and Werner Heldt, as well as works by Ernst Ludwig Kirchner and Hanns Schimansky.

Among the architectural items held by the Galerie are drawings and models for buildings that were never built, offering fascinating glimpses into how the city might have looked. A fine example is the shell-like Expressionist Sternkirche (Star Church), designed by Otto Bartning in 1922.

⑭

Berlinische Galerie

⑨L7 ⌂Alte Jakobstrasse 124-8 ⓊKochstrasse ⓫248, M29 ⊙10am-6pm Wed-Mon ⓦberlinische galerie.de

The city's museum for modern art, design and architecture is one of the finest regional museums in the country. Changing themed exhibitions draw upon its huge collection of German, East European and Russian paintings, photographs, graphics and architectural artifacts.

One of the highlights is the 5,000-strong painting collection, which covers all the major art movements from the late 19th century until today. It includes works by Max Liebermann *(p245)*, Otto Dix, Georg Baselitz, Alexander Rodchenko, Iwan Puni and Via Lewandowsky.

⑮

Topographie des Terrors

⑨K7 ⌂Stresemannstrasse 110 (entrance on Nieder-kirchner Strasse 8) Ⓢ&ⓊPotsdamer Platz, Kochstrasse ⓈAnhalter Bahnhof ⓫M29, M41 ⊙10am-8pm daily ⓦtopographie.de

During the Third Reich, three of the most terrifying Nazi political departments had their headquarters in a block here, making this area the government district of National Socialist Germany. Prinz-Albrecht palace at Wilhelmstrasse No. 102 became the headquarters of the Third Reich's security ser-vice (SD). Prinz-Albrecht-Strasse

THE BERLIN BLOCKADE (1948-9)

On 24 June 1948, due to rising tensions between East Germany and West Berlin, Soviet authorities blockaded all the roads leading to West Berlin. In order to ensure food and fuel for the residents, US General Lucius Clay ordered that provisions be flown into the city. British and American planes made a total of 212,612 flights, transporting almost 2 million tonnes (2.3 million tons) of goods, among which were parts of a power station. In April 1949, at the height of the airlifts, planes were landing every 63 seconds. The blockade ended in May 1949. Although the airlifts were successful, there were casualties: 70 airmen and 8 ground crew lost their lives.

No. 8 was occupied by the head of the Gestapo, Heinrich Müller, while the Hotel Prinz Albrecht at No. 9 became the headquarters of Himmler's SS.

After World War II, the ruins of the heavily bombed buildings were pulled down. In 1987, however, an exhibition was installed on this site by committed citizens of Berlin. This well-researched and exhaustive exploration of Nazi crimes and terror in all its forms, including propaganda, deportation, forced labour and genocide, builds a chilling picture of the decisions that must have been taken on this very site. A preserved section of the Berlin Wall runs alongside the building, on Niederkirchner Strasse.

16

König Gallery (St Agnes)

Q M8 **A** Alexandrinenstrasse 118-121 **U** Prinzenstrasse, Moritzplatz **🚌** 140, 248, N41 **🕐** 11am-7pm Tue-Sat, noon-7pm Sun **W** koeniggalerie.com

The striking, almost windowless Brutalist church of St Agnes was built in the 1960s. It houses the Johann König Gallery, which opened here in 2015 following a renovation by Arno Brandlhuber.

The gallery features two distinctive spaces – one on the main floor and the other on an upper floor supported by a concrete slab – plus a sculpture garden that also forms part of the exhibitions. In addition to both solo and group shows, the gallery hosts regular readings, performances and presentations. There's a pleasant café inside too, and some of the surrounding buildings are used by artists during their residencies.

17

Moritzplatz

Q N7 **U** Moritzplatz **🚌** 140, M29

For several decades – before and after the fall of the Wall – the area around Moritzplatz was a somewhat bleak vision of 1970s residential blocks and the occasional kebab shop. Since then, it has been transformed almost beyond recognition by a flurry of developments. It has been joined by the creative centre Aufbau Haus, which houses the Aufbau publishing group, a well-stocked bookshop, arts and design shops, a crafts supplier called Modular, a CLB-Berlin project space for contemporary art and urbanism, and the Kai Dikhas contemporary Sinti and Roma art gallery.

18

Checkpoint Charlie

Q L7 **A** Friedrichstrasse 43-45 **U** Kochstrasse **🚌** M29

Between 1961 and 1990, Checkpoint Charlie was the only crossing point for foreigners between East and West Berlin. During that time, it acted as a symbol of both freedom and separation for the many East Germans trying to escape from the GDR regime. It was also witness to dramatic events during the Cold War, including a tense two-day standoff between Russian and American tanks in 1961.

Little remains of the checkpoint: no gates, barriers or barbed wire. Instead, there is a replica checkpoint booth and the famous huge sign on the old Western side that reads "You are leaving the American Sector".

At the museum nearby, **Haus am Checkpoint Charlie**, look out for exhibits connected with the escape attempts of East Germans to the West. The ingenuity and bravery of these escapees are astonishing, using devices such as secret compartments built into cars and specially constructed suitcases.

Haus am Checkpoint Charlie

🅐🅑🅒 **Q** 9am-10pm daily **W** mauermuseum.de

→
Replica of
Checkpoint Charlie

↑ Outdoor dining in summer on busy Bergmannstrasse

EAT

Defne

Long-running, canalside restaurant whose Turkish and Mediterranean menu includes delicious classics like *imam bayildi*, lamb skewers and seafood pasta.

QN9 **A**Planufer 92C **O**Hours vary, check website **W**defne-restaurant.de

€€€

Cocolo

The second branch of Berlin's best ramen spot. Cocolo's menu is small but consistently top-notch: think ramen with sweet pork belly or miso and vegetables, plus extras like Japanese dumplings.

Q08 **A**Paul-Lincke-Ufer 39 **O**Noon-11pm Mon-Sat **W**kuchi.de/restaurant/cocolo-x-berg

€€€

⑲ Bergmannstrasse

QK9 **U**Südstern, Geneisenaustrasse **248, N7, N6, N42**

Kreuzberg is unofficially divided between its gritty and hip east side and its more gentrified western counterpart. Here, entire blocks of 19th-century houses have been restored and the area's main artery, Bergmannstrasse, has been revitalized. Pedestrianized and furnished with antique streetlamps to enhance the atmosphere, it bristles with independent shops, galleries, cafés and restaurants. Also refreshed is the popular Marheineke Markthalle: a covered market filled with not only fruit and vegetables but also cafés, delis and even exhibitions. Just off the street is the charming Chamissoplatz, which draws crowds to its Saturday morning organic farmers' market. To the west, the street leads to one of the main parks in the area, Viktoriapark, ideal for a green breather after the bustle of the streets.

⑳ 🖻 Viktoriapark

QK10 **U**Platz der Luftbrücke **104, 140, M19**

This rambling park, with several artificial waterfalls, short trails and a small hill, |was designed by Hermann Mächtig and built between 1884 and 1894. The Neo-Gothic Memorial to the Wars of Liberation at the summit of the hill is the work of Karl Friedrich Schinkel *(p29)*, which commemorates the Prussian victory against Napoleon's army in the Wars of Liberation. The cast-iron tower is well ornamented. In the niches of the lower section are 12 allegorical figures by Christian Daniel Rauch, Friedrich Tieck and Ludwig Wichmann. Each figure symbolizes a battle and is linked to a historic figure – either a military leader or a member of the royal family.

→ Viktoriapark's Neo-Gothic memorial

The park contains the popular Golgotha pub and beer garden, perfect for refreshment after a stroll.

Flughafen Tempelhof and Tempelhofer Feld

 K10 ⬛ Platz der Luftbrücke ☎ 200 03 74 41 Ⓤ Platz der Luftbrücke 🚌 104, 248

The disued Tempelhof Airport was once Germany's biggest. Built in 1923, it was enlarged during the Third Reich. You can take a guided tour of the building (1:30pm on Wed, Fri, Sat and Sun), which is typical of Third Reich architecture, even though the eagles that decorate it predate the Nazis. In 1951, a monument was added in front of the airport. Designed by Eduard Ludwig, it commemorates the airlifts of the Berlin Blockade (p190). The three spikes on the top symbolize the air corridors used by Allied planes. The airport was permanently closed to air traffic in 2008. It has now been transformed into a park that is popular with cyclists, roller-bladers and skaters who come here to enjoy the unobstructed airport runways. Open-air concerts, like the three-day Tempelhof Sounds festival, also take place here.

㉒

Riehmers Hofgarten

 K9 ⬛ Yorckstrasse 83-86, Grossbeerenstrasse 56-57 & Hagelberger Strasse 9-12 Ⓤ Mehringdamm 🚌 140, 248, M19

Riehmers Hofgarten is the name given to the 20 or so exquisite houses arranged around a picturesque garden within the area bordered by the streets Yorckstrasse, Hagelberger Strasse and Grossbeerenstrasse. These houses were built between 1881 and 1899 to the detailed designs of Wilhelm Riehmer and Otto Mrosk, respected architects who not only

The elaborate Yorckstrasse gateway to the 19th-century Riehmers Hofgarten

 GREAT VIEW
Top of the World

Berlin's highest natural peak can be found at the top of Kreuzberg's Viktoriapark, alongside a tumbling waterfall, a war memorial by Karl Friedrich Schinkel and stellar views towards the city centre.

designed the houses' intricate, Renaissance-style and Neo-Baroque façades but also gave equal splendour to the elevations overlooking the courtyard garden. The streets of Riehmers Hofgarten have been carefully restored and Yorckstrasse also has quite a few cafés. Next to Riehmers Hofgarten is the church of St Bonifaz, designed by Max Hasak. Adjacent to the church is a similar complex of houses built in an impressive Neo-Gothic style.

㉓

Friedhöfe vor dem Halleschen Tor

 L9 ⬛ Mehringdamm, Blücher-, Baruther & Zossener Strasse ☎ 691 61 38 Ⓤ Hallesches Tor 🚌 140, 248, M41 ⏰ Hours vary, call ahead

Beyond the city walls, next to the Halleches Gate, are four cemeteries established in 1735. The beautiful gravestones commemorate some of the great Berlin artists including the composer Felix Mendelssohn-Bartholdy, architects Georg Wenzeslaus von Knobelsdorff, David Gilly and Carl Ferdinand Langhans, and the writer, artist and composer E T A Hoffmann.

A SHORT WALK
MEHRINGPLATZ AND FRIEDRICHSTRASSE

Distance 1.5 km (1 mile) **Nearest station** Potsdamer Platz **Time** 20 minutes

The areas north of Mehringplatz are the oldest sections of Kreuzberg. Now full of modern developments such as the Friedrichstadt Passagen – a huge complex of shops, apartments, offices, galleries and restaurants – only a few buildings recall the earlier splendour of this district, which was laid out in 1734. However, a walk through this area is a must for those who want to know more about World War II- and GDR-era Berlin, as it's home to some key sights such as the Jüdisches Museum Berlin and Checkpoint Charlie.

A small hut marks the place of **Checkpoint Charlie** *(p191), the notorious border crossing between East and West Berlin.*

Martin-Gropius-Bau *(p186) is an interesting, multicoloured Neo-Renaissance building that houses the city's main temporary art exhibition space.*

START ▶

KOCHSTRASSE

WILHELMSTRASSE

FRIEDRICHSTRASSE

PUTTKAMERSTRASSE

HEDEMANNSTRASSE

A shocking exhibition known as **Topographie des Terrors** *(Topography of Terror, p190) details Nazi crimes.*

← Stretch of the Wall incorporated in the Topographie des Terrors

Locator Map
For more detail see p180

↑ The jagged edges of the Jüdisches Museum Berlin

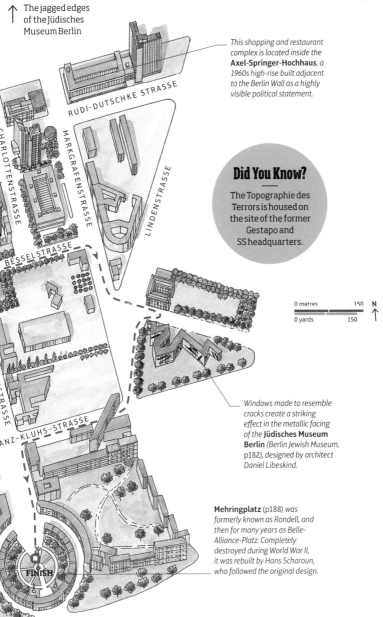

This shopping and restaurant complex is located inside the **Axel-Springer-Hochhaus**, *a 1960s high-rise built adjacent to the Berlin Wall as a highly visible political statement.*

Did You Know?

The Topographie des Terrors is housed on the site of the former Gestapo and SS headquarters.

0 metres 150 N
0 yards 150

Windows made to resemble cracks create a striking effect in the metallic facing of the **Jüdisches Museum Berlin** *(Berlin Jewish Museum, p182), designed by architect Daniel Libeskind.*

Mehringplatz (p188) was formerly known as Rondell, and then for many years as Belle-Alliance-Platz. Completely destroyed during World War II, it was rebuilt by Hans Scharoun, who followed the original design.

KaDeWe seen from Wittenbergplatz U-bahn station

AROUND KURFÜRSTENDAMM

The area around Kurfürstendamm boulevard (the Ku'damm) was developed in the 19th century. Luxurious buildings were constructed along the avenue, while the areas of Breitscheidplatz and Wittenbergplatz became replete with hotels and department stores.

After World War II, with the old centre (Mitte) situated in East Berlin, this area became the centre of West Berlin. Traces of wartime destruction were removed very quickly and it was transformed into the heart of West Berlin, and dozens of new company headquarters and trade centres were built. The situation changed after the reunification of Berlin and, although many tourists concentrate on the Mitte district, the heart of the city continues to beat around Kurfürstendamm.

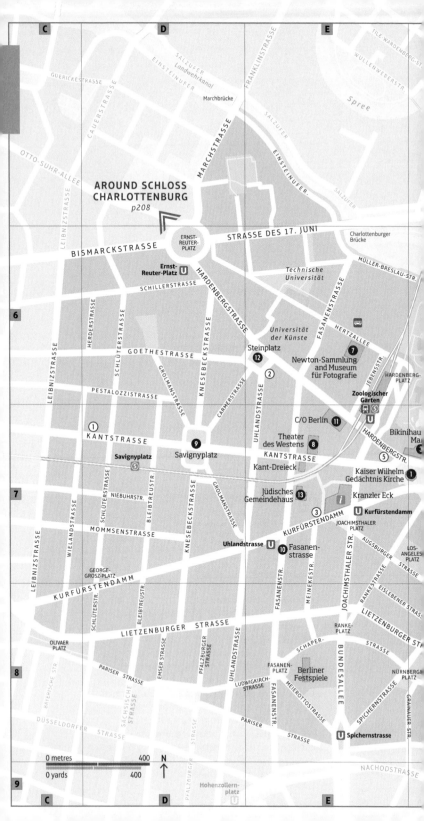

AROUND KURFÜRSTENDAMM

Must See

1 Kaiser Wilhelm
Gedächtnis Kirche

Experience More

2 KaDeWe
3 Bikinihaus Mall
4 Europa-Center
5 Zoo Berlin
6 Tauentzienstrasse
7 Newton-Sammlung and
Museum für Fotografie
8 Theater des Westens
9 Savignyplatz

10 Fasanenstrasse
11 C/O Berlin
12 Steinplatz
13 Jüdisches Gemeindehaus

Eat & Drink

① Lon Men's Noodle House
② Bar am Steinplatz

Stay

③ Hotel Zoo
④ 25hours Hotel Bikini
⑤ Waldorf Astoria

KAISER WILHELM GEDÄCHTNIS KIRCHE

F7 ⌂ Breitscheidplatz ⓢ & Ⓤ Zoologischer Garten Ⓤ Kurfürstendamm
🚌 100, 109, 110, 200, 204, 245, M19, M29, M46, X10, X34 ⏰ 9am–7pm daily
🌐 gedaechtniskirche-berlin.de

The damaged tower of Kaiser Wilhelm Memorial Church is a symbol of peace and the city's determination to rebuild after World War II.

This church-monument is one of Berlin's most famous landmarks, surrounded by a lively crowd of Berliners, including street traders and buskers. The vast Neo-Romanesque church was designed by Franz Schwechten and consecrated in 1895. It was almost completely destroyed by Allied bombs in 1943, and after World War II the ruins were removed, leaving only the massive front tower at the base of which the Gedenkhalle (Memorial Hall) is situated. This hall documents the history of the church and contains some of its original ceiling mosaics, marble reliefs and liturgical objects. In 1961, Egon Eiermann designed an octagonal church in blue glass and a new freestanding bell tower.

↑ The vast figure of *Christ on the Cross* is the work of Karl Hemmeter

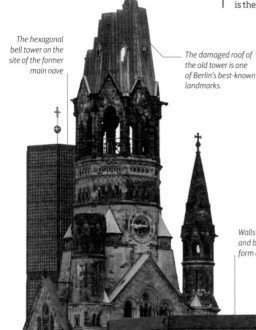

The hexagonal bell tower on the site of the former main nave

The damaged roof of the old tower is one of Berlin's best-known landmarks.

Walls of concrete and blue glass form a dense grid

COVENTRY AND BERLIN

In the main entrance of the old church you'll find a surprisingly modest crucifix. It was fashioned from nails found in the ashes of Coventry Cathedral, England, which was destroyed during German bombing raids in 1940.

← The old spire, completed in 1895, and the new church and bell tower, completed in 1961

Splendid mosaics decorate the arches, walls and ceilings of the old church

↑ Food with a view at legendary department store KaDeWe

EXPERIENCE MORE

❷ KaDeWe

📍 F7 🏠 Tauentzienstrasse 21–4 Ⓤ Wittenbergplatz 🚌 M19, M29, M46 🕐 10am–8pm Mon–Thu, 10am–9pm Fri, 9:30am–8pm Sat 🌐 kadewe.de

Kaufhaus des Westens, or KaDeWe, is the largest department store in Europe. It was built in 1907 to a design by Emil Schaudt, but it has been extended several times. From the very beginning it was Berlin's most exclusive department store, with a slogan that ran "In our shop a customer is a king, and the king is a customer". After World War II, KaDeWe became the symbol of the economic success of West Berlin.

You can buy everything here; however, the main attraction must be the Food Hall, a gourmet's paradise, with fresh fruits and vegetables, live fish and seafood, 100 varieties of tea, more than 2,400 wines and a host of other gastronomic delights. KaDeWe also has a restaurant, the Wintergarten.

❸ Bikinihaus Mall

📍 F7 🏠 Budapester Strasse 38–50 Ⓢ & Ⓤ Zoologischer Garten Ⓤ Kurfürstendamm 🚌 100, 110, 200, 204, 245, 249, M45 🕐 10am–8pm Mon–Sat 🌐 bikiniberlin.de

The three-floor Bikinihaus Mall, named for the 1950s building that houses it, has an inspired feature: its ground floor houses 70 wooden "pop-ups", crate-like mini-shops that independent stores can rent for up to a year. This keeps things fresh and exciting while the surrounding brand outlets – Carhaart, Scotch & Soda, Gant – offer a solid range of mid-range fashion and home design.

❹ Europa-Center

📍 F7 🏠 Breitscheidplatz Ⓢ & Ⓤ Zoologischer Garten 🚌 100, 109, 200

The Europa-Center stands on the site of the legendary Romanisches Café, a famous meeting place for Dada artists in the 1920s. The current building dates from 1965, and since that time it has been one of the largest complexes of its type in the whole of Germany. Designed by Helmut Hentrich and Hubert Petschnigg, it comprises a group of low-rise buildings housing a trade centre, numerous restaurants and pubs, the deluxe Hotel Palace Berlin and the political cabaret *Die Stachelschweine*.

Around the centre are some intriguing fountains, including the "Flow of Time Clock", designed by Bernard Gitton. Seconds,

---

 GREAT VIEWS
Monkey Bar

As well as amazing cocktails, the Monkey Bar at the 25hours Hotel Bikini has a wrap-around terrace with excellent views over the adjacent zoo and Kaiser Wilhelm Gedächtnis Kirche.

minutes and hours are measured in vials and spheres of green liquid.

Zoo Berlin

F7 **Hardenbergplatz 8/ Budapester Strasse 34** & **Zoologischer Garten** **100, 109, 110, 200, 204, 245, 249, M45, M46, M49, X10, X34** **Hours vary, check website** **zoo-berlin.de**

Zoo Berlin is one of Berlin's most popular attractions and over 1,000 species are to be found here. Part of the Tiergarten (p171), it dates from 1844, which makes it the oldest zoo in Germany. You can enter from Hardenbergplatz through the Lion's Gate, and from Budapester Strasse through the decorative Elephant Gate.

The zoo offers a number of attractions, including the monkey house, with its family of gorillas, and a darkened pavilion for nocturnal animals. The hippopotamus pool has a glazed wall so they can be seen underwater. Since 2017, the zoo has also been home to a pair of giant pandas. The aquarium, one of the largest in Europe, contains sharks, piranhas and unusual animals from coral reefs. There is also a huge terrarium with an overgrown jungle that is home to a group of crocodiles.

6

Tauentzienstrasse

F7 **Wittenbergplatz** **M19, M29, M46**

This is one of the most important streets for trade and commerce in this part of Berlin. Some shops here are not as expensive or as elegant as on Kurfürstendamm – but they attract more visitors. One of the highlights of the street is the façade of the department store Peek & Cloppenburg. Designed by Gottfried Böhm, the walls of the building are covered with transparent, undulating "aprons".

Also unmissable, literally, is the amazing sculpture, *Berlin*. Representing the divided Berlin of the Wall era, it was installed in 1987 to mark the 750th anniversary of the city.

7

Newton-Sammlung and Museum für Fotografie

E6 **Jebensstrasse 2** & **Zoologischer Garten** **10am–6pm Tue, Wed & Fri–Sun (to 8pm Thu)** **smb.museum**

Society and art photographer Helmut Newton (1931–2004) bequeathed his life's work to the city of Berlin. Newton, who was born and received his first training as a photographer in Berlin, became one of the 20th century's most well-known photographers with his stark black-and-white images of nudes and portraits of the rich and famous.

This museum serves as the city's museum of photography, and is constantly expanding its collections. It displays photographs dating back to the 19th century, and its exhibits on Newton contain selections of his work, as well as a collection of his cameras.

STAY

Hotel Zoo
Right on the Ku'damm, this former mansion became an upscale hotel in 1911. It houses a grand living room and a lovely rooftop terrace.

E7 **Kurfürsten-damm 25** **hotelzoo.de**

€€€

25hours Hotel Bikini
This trend-setting hotel has rooms that overlook the adjacent zoo, plus a buzzing top-floor bar and restaurant.

F7 **Budapester Strasse 40** **25hours-hotels.com**

€€€

Waldorf Astoria
A slick five-star hotel with luxurious rooms and glamorous spa, as well as an American-themed cocktail bar and fine dining.

E7 **Hardenberg-strasse 28** **waldorf astoriaberlin.de**

€€€

←

The interior of the Museum of Photography (Museum für Fotografie) in Berlin

Theater des Westens

E7 **Kantstrasse 9-12**
0180 544 44
& **Zoologischer Garten**
100, 109, 110, 200, M49, X10, X34

The Theatre of the West, one of the most attractive of all Berlin's theatres, was built in 1896 to a design by Bernhard Sehring. The composition of its façade links Neo-Classical elements with Palladian and Art Nouveau details. The interior of the theatre has been designed in a splendid Neo-Baroque style, while the back and the section that houses the stage have been rebuilt within a Neo-Gothic structure, incorporating the decorative elements of a chess set.

From its very beginning the theatre focused on lighter forms of musical entertainment. Operettas and vaudeville have been staged here, and in more recent times musicals such as *Les Misérables*. Some of the world's greatest stars have appeared on the stage here, including Josephine Baker, who performed her famous banana dance in 1926. Near the theatre is the renowned Delphi cinema and popular jazz club Quasimodo.

Savignyplatz

D7 **Savignyplatz**
M49, X34

Savignyplatz is enclosed on the south side by the arcade of a railway viaduct, under which Sally (Liza Minnelli) and Brian (Michael York) scream in the film *Cabaret* by Bob Fosse. During the day the square does not look interesting – there are no remarkable buildings, only carefully tended greenery and flowerbeds. However, the area around the square truly comes alive at night, when the dozens of cafés and restaurants fill up. During summer, the entire edge of Savignyplatz and neighbouring streets turn into one big garden filled with tables and umbrellas. People come from outlying districts to visit popular restaurants and cafés such as Dicke Wirtin. The arcades in the viaduct contain many cafés and bars, and one section has been taken up by the Bücherbogen bookshop.

> **During summer, the entire edge of Savigny Platz and neighbouring streets turn into one big garden filled with tables and umbrellas.**

Fasanenstrasse

E7 **Uhlandstrasse**
109, 110, M49, X10, X34

The discreet charm of Fasanenstrasse, particularly between Lietzenburger Strasse and Kurfürstendamm, has attracted the most exclusive designer shops in the world. *Fin-de-siècle* villas set in tranquil gardens and elegant shop windows of jewellers, art galleries and fashion shops will all entice you to take an afternoon stroll along this street.

It is worth seeing the villas at No. 23–5, which are called the Wintergarten-Ensemble – No. 23 dates from 1889. Tucked away in a garden, the villa is home to the Literaturhaus, which organizes interesting exhibitions and readings (closed for renovations until 2027). It also houses a café that extends into a conservatory. No. 25, built in 1892 by Hans Grisebach, accommodates an auction house and art gallery.

C/O Berlin

E7 **Hardenbergstrasse 22-4** **Zoologischer Garten** **100, 200, 245, M49, X10, X34** **11am-8pm daily** **co-berlin.org**

This photography exhibition centre showcases work by renowned photographers as well as young talent, and holds artist talks, lectures and guided tours. It is housed in Amerika Haus, the former American culture and information centre,

↑ The magnificent façade of the Theater des Westens, matched by an equally opulent interior

built during the international building exhibition in 1956–7 to a light and airy design by Bruno Grimmek.

12 Steinplatz

 E6 🚇 Steinplatz Ⓢ & Ⓤ Ernst-Reuter-Platz, Zoologischer Garten 🚌 245, M45, N2

Because of the two nearby universities (Berlin University of the Arts and the Technical University of Berlin), this square was a popular meeting place for artists, intellectuals and students in the years of West Berlin. A green oasis surrounded by beautiful architecture, the square is still a lovely meeting spot, and makes a great place to take a break while exploring the galleries and stores along Hardenbergstrasse, and in the streets between here and Savignyplatz.

The square also contains a monument dedicated to the victims of Stalinism and National Socialism. It is made of stones from Fasanen-strasse Synagogue, which was destroyed during World War II.

13 Jüdisches Gemeindehaus

🔲 E7 🚇 Fasanenstrasse 79/80 📞 88 02 80 Ⓢ & Ⓤ Zoologischer Garten Ⓤ Uhlandstrasse or Kurfürstendamm 🚌 245, M49, X10, X34

The Jewish Community House is the headquarters of the local Jewish community, constructed on the site of a synagogue that was burned down by the Nazis and their supporters during Kristall-nacht on 9 November 1938. The new building, designed by Dieter Knoblauch and Heinz Heise, was constructed in 1959. The only reminders of the splendour of the former synagogue are the portal at the entrance to the building and some decorative frag-ments on the façade.

Inside, there are offices and a prayer room covered by three glazed domes. At the rear there is a courtyard with a place of remembrance. There is also an emotive statue at the front of the building, depicting a broken scroll of the Torah (the holy book of Jewish law).

↑ Crowds outside the C/O Berlin photography exhibit centre

EAT

Lon Men's Noodle House

Family-run Taiwanese that's small in size but big on taste. Try the dumplings or ask for the homemade noodles.

🔲 D7 🚇 Kantstrasse 33 📞 030 31 51 96 78 🕐 Noon–10:30pm daily

€€€

DRINK

Bar am Steinplatz

This famous and stylish hotel bar was a meeting place for artists in West Berlin in the 1960s. Since its rebirth in 2014 it is again attracting up-market bar-hoppers.

🔲 E6 🚇 Steinplatz 4 🌐 barsteinplatz.com

A SHORT WALK
BREITSCHEIDPLATZ AND KU'DAMM

Distance 1.5 km (1 mile) **Nearest U-Bahn station** Kurfürstendamm **Time** 20 minutes

The area surrounding the eastern end of the Ku'damm – especially Tauentzienstrasse and Breitscheidplatz – is the centre of the former West Berlin. Years ago, this ultra-modern district attracted visitors from all over the world. In terms of shopping and leisure, it's becoming overshadowed by Potsdamer Platz and the arcades of Friedrichstrasse, but the Ku'damm still retains its unique character and is the perfect place for a city stroll. Nowhere else in Berlin is there a place so full of life as Breitscheidplatz, a department store with such style as KaDeWe, or streets as refined as Fasanenstrasse.

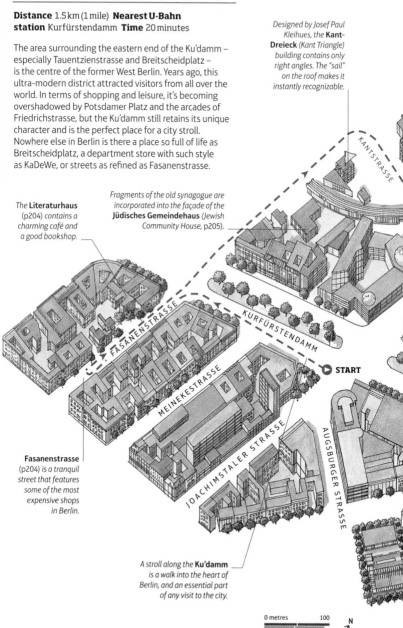

*Designed by Josef Paul Kleihues, the **Kant-Dreieck** (Kant Triangle) building contains only right angles. The "sail" on the roof makes it instantly recognizable.*

*The **Literaturhaus** (p204) contains a charming café and a good bookshop.*

*Fragments of the old synagogue are incorporated into the façade of the **Jüdisches Gemeindehaus** (Jewish Community House, p205).*

Fasanenstrasse (p204) *is a tranquil street that features some of the most expensive shops in Berlin.*

*A stroll along the **Ku'damm** is a walk into the heart of Berlin, and an essential part of any visit to the city.*

0 metres 100
0 yards 100

N

The structure of the **Berlin Stock Exchange** at Ludwig-Erhard-Haus is based on parabolic arches.

The façade of the **Theater des Westens** (p204) is fittingly decorated with dancing women.

Bahnhof Zoo

AROUND KURFÜRSTENDAMM

Breitscheidplatz and Ku'damm

Locator Map
For more detail see p198

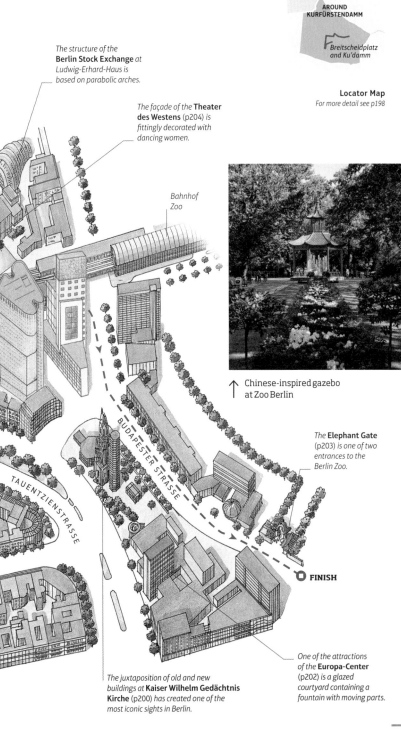

↑ Chinese-inspired gazebo at Zoo Berlin

The **Elephant Gate** (p203) is one of two entrances to the Berlin Zoo.

BUDAPESTER STRASSE

TAUENTZIENSTRASSE

○ **FINISH**

The juxtaposition of old and new buildings at **Kaiser Wilhelm Gedächtnis Kirche** (p200) has created one of the most iconic sights in Berlin.

One of the attractions of the **Europa-Center** (p202) is a glazed courtyard containing a fountain with moving parts.

AROUND SCHLOSS CHARLOTTENBURG

The area surrounding Schloss Charlottenburg is one of the most enchanting regions of the city, full of greenery and attractive buildings dating from the end of the 19th century. Originally a small settlement called Lützow, it was only when Elector Friedrich III (later King Friedrich I) built his wife's summer retreat here at the end of the 17th century that this town attained significance. Initially called Schloss Lietzenburg, the palace was renamed Schloss Charlottenburg after the death of Queen Sophie Charlotte.

By the 18th century, Charlottenburg had become a town, and was for many years an independent administration, inhabited by wealthy people living in elegant villas. It became officially part of Berlin in 1920 and, despite World War II and the ensuing division of the city, the central section of this area has kept its historical character.

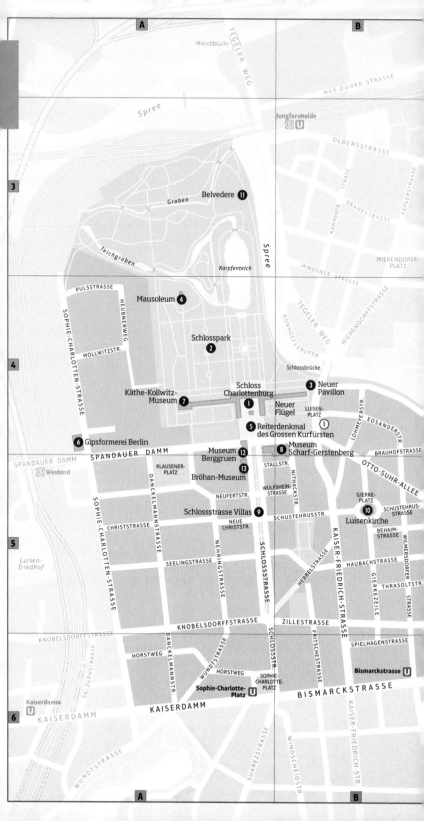

AROUND SCHLOSS CHARLOTTENBURG

Must See

❶ Schloss Charlottenburg

Experience More

❷ Schlosspark
❸ Neuer Pavillon
❹ Mausoleum
❺ Reiterdenkmal des Grossen Kurfürsten
❻ Gipsformerei Berlin
❼ Käthe-Kollwitz-Museum
❽ Museum Scharf-Gerstenberg
❾ Schlossstrasse Villas
❿ Luisenkirche
⓫ Belvedere
⓬ Museum Berggruen
⓭ Bröhan-Museum

Eat

① Brauhaus Lemke am Schloss

AROUND KURFÜRSTENDAMM
p196

AROUND SCHLOSS CHARLOTTENBURG

0 metres   400
0 yards   400

N

❶ ⧖ ⧗

SCHLOSS CHARLOTTENBURG

📍A4 🏛Spandauer Damm 20-24 🚈Jungfernheide, Westend Ⓤ Richard-Wagner-Platz, Sophie-Charlotte-Platz 🚌109, 309, M45 🕐Apr–Oct: 10am–5:30pm Tue–Sun; Nov–Mar: 10am–4:30pm Tue–Sun 🌐spsg.de

This opulent Baroque place was once the home of the Hohenzollern dynasty, rulers of the region for over 500 years. It is made up of two magnificent buildings: the Altes Schloss (Old Palace) and Neuer Flügel (New Wing).

Built in 1695, the palace in Charlottenburg was intended as a summer home for Sophie Charlotte, Friedrich I's wife. Between 1701 and 1713, Johann Friedrich Eosander enlarged the palace, crowning it with a cupola and adding the orangery wing. This section of the palace is now known as the Altes Schloss. The Neuer Flügel extension was undertaken by Frederick the Great (Friedrich II), and designed by Georg Wenzeslaus von Knobelsdorff in the mid-18th century. Restored to its former elegance after World War II, the palace's collection of lavish interiors is unequalled in Berlin.

Highlights of the Altes Schloss include the Portrait Gallery and the fine Japanese and Chinese ceramics in the Porcelain Cabinet, while the Neuer Flügel showcases Friedrich II's exquisite apartments. Each building has its own entrance, with separate tickets required.

↑ Some of the delicate ceramics on display in the Porcelain Cabinet

The palace's cupola, topped by a statue of the goddess of fortune ↑

↑ The Goldene Galerie, a Rococo garden ballroom, dating from 1746

💬 INSIDER TIP
Get Festive

The Orangerie was once used as a setting for court festivities in the summer months. Today, it continues to entertain as a unique events venue, hosting everything from Baroque classical concerts to Christmas dinners.

↑ The stunning exterior
of the Altes Schloss

↑ Cherubs striking playful poses in royal Schlosspark

EXPERIENCE MORE

 2

Schlosspark

🚩 A4 🔼 Luisenplatz
Ⓢ Westend Ⓤ Richard-Wagner-Platz, Sophie-Charlotte-Platz
🚌 109, 309, M45

The extensive palace park that surrounds Schloss Charlottenburg (p212), crisscrossed with tidy gravel paths, is a favourite place for Berliners to stroll at the weekend. The park is largely the result of reconstruction work carried out after World War II, when 18th-century prints were used to help recreate the varied layout of the original grounds.

Immediately behind Schloss Charlottenburg is a French-style Baroque garden, made to a strict geometrical design with a vibrant patchwork of flower beds, carefully trimmed shrubs and ornate fountains. Further away from the palace, beyond the curved carp lake, is a less formal English-style landscaped park, originally laid out in the 1820s under the direction of the renowned royal gardener, Peter Joseph Lenné (p171). The lakes and waterways of the park are the habitat of various waterfowl,

including herons. A bike path runs along the Spree from the palace park to the Tiergarten (p171) and beyond.

 3

Neuer Pavillon (Schinkel-Pavillon)

🚩 B4 🔼 Luisenplatz (Schlosspark Charlottenburg) 📞 30 32 09 11
Ⓢ Westend Ⓤ Richard-Wagner-Platz, Sophie-Charlotte-Platz 🚌 109, 309, M45 🕐 Apr-Oct: 10am-5:30pm Tue-Sun; Nov-Mar: noon-4pm Tue-Sun

This charming Neo-Classical pavilion, with its clean lines and first-floor balcony, was built for Friedrich Wilhelm III and his second wife, Princess Auguste von Liegnitz. During a visit to Naples, the king was so impressed by the Villa Reale del Chiamonte that he commissioned Karl Friedrich Schinkel (p29) to build him something similar. The pavilion was finished for the king's birthday on 3 August 1825. Schinkel designed a two-storey structure with a central staircase and ranged the rooms around it in perfect

symmetry. Pillared galleries on the first floor added variety to the eastern and western elevations. A cast-iron balcony runs around the entire structure. Like many other Schloss Charlottenburg buildings, the pavilion burned down completely in World War II and was rebuilt in 1960.

EAT

Brauhaus Lemke am Schloss

Set right beside Schloss Charlottenburg, this classic brewhouse makes a convenient spot for post-tour sustenance. The interior is as reassuringly traditional as the menu, which features home-brewed beer and filling, meat-heavy German food.

🚩 B4 🔼 Luisenplatz
🕐 Noon-midnight daily
🌐 lemke.berlin

€€€

The display inside the pavilion reveals the original splendour of the aristocratic interiors, enhanced with pictures and sculptures of the period. The prize picture is a renowned panorama of Berlin dated 1834, painted by Eduard Gärtner from the roof of the Friedrichswerdersche Kirche. You can also admire paintings by Schinkel, not only a great architect but also a fine painter of fabulous architectural fantasies.

Mausoleum

 A4 **Luisenplatz (Schlosspark Charlottenburg)** 32 09 14 46 **Westend** **Richard-Wagner-Platz, Sophie-Charlotte-Platz** 109, 309, M45 **Apr-Oct: 10am-5:30pm Tue-Sun** **Nov-Mar**

Queen Luise, the beloved first wife of Friedrich Wilhelm III, was laid to rest in this modest, dignified building, set among the trees in Schlosspark. The mausoleum was designed by Karl Friedrich Schinkel, in the style of a Doric portico-fronted temple.

In the original design, the queen's sarcophagus was housed in the crypt while the tombstone (a cenotaph sculpted by Christian Daniel Rauch) stood in the centre of the mausoleum. After the death of Friedrich Wilhelm in 1840, the mausoleum was refurbished, an apse added and the queen's tomb moved to one side, leaving room for her husband's tomb, also designed by Rauch. The second wife of the king, Princess Auguste von Liegnitz, was also buried in the crypt of the mausoleum.

Between 1890 and 1894, the tombs of Kaiser Wilhelm I and his wife, Auguste von Sachsen-Weimar, were added to the crypt. Both monuments are the work of Erdmann Encke.

5

Reiterdenkmal des Grossen Kurfürsten

A4 **Luisenplatz** **Westend** **Richard-Wagner-Platz, Sophie-Charlotte-Platz** 109, 309, M45

The Monument to the Great Elector (Friedrich Wilhelm) was paid for by his son, Elector Friedrich III (later King Friedrich I) and is a masterpiece of Baroque sculpture. Designed by Andreas Schlüter to be cast in one piece, the statue was completed in 1703, and erected near the former Berlin palace, by Lange Brücke (now called Rathausbrücke). The statue was moved to safety in World War II, but ironically, on the return journey, the barge transporting the monument sank in the port of Tegel.

In 1949, the statue was retrieved intact from the water and erected here on a copy of the base. The original base finally ended up in the Bode-Museum topped with a replica of the statue.

The statue portrays the Great Elector on horseback with figures of prisoners of war around the base. The base itself is decorated with patriotic reliefs of allegorical scenes. One scene depicts the

kingdom surrounded by figures representing Peace, History and the Spree river; another shows it protected by embodiments of Bravery, Faith and Strength (represented by the figure of Hercules).

6

Gipsformerei Berlin

 A4 **Sophie-Charlotten-Strasse 17-18** 32 67 69 11 **Westend** **Sophie-Charlotte-Platz** 309, M45 **9am-4pm Mon-Fri (to 6pm Wed); may vary during exhibitions**

Founded by Friedrich Wilhelm III in 1819, the Berlin Replica Workshop produces original-sized replicas from items in Berlin museums and other collections, and also repairs damaged sculptures. Visitors are welcome to this modest brick building west of Schloss Charlottenburg and can purchase items on the spot or choose from catalogues to have them made to order and shipped home. Sculptures are generally copied in white plaster or painted true to the original. Most moulds originate from the Middle Ages, the Renaissance and the 19th century.

THE GREAT ELECTOR (1620-88)

The Elector Friedrich Wilhelm was one of the most famous rulers of the Hohenzollern dynasty. He inherited the position of ruler of Brandenburg-Prussia in 1640, and one of his first duties was to rebuild the region after the devastation of the Thirty Years' War (1618-48). In 1660, he wrested the Duchy of Prussia territory from Poland. During the course of his reign, Berlin became a powerful city, and rich families from all over Europe - fleeing persecution in their own land - chose to settle here.

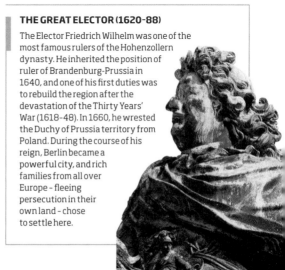

7

Käthe-Kollwitz-Museum

⚑A4 ⌂ Spandauer Damm 10 **Ⓢ** Westend **Ⓤ** Richard-Wagner-Platz, Sophie-Charlotte-Platz 🚌 109, 309, M45 🕐 Hours vary, check website 🌐 kaethe-kollwitz.berlin

This museum showcases the work of Käthe Kollwitz (1867–1945). Born in Königsberg, the artist settled in Berlin, where she married a doctor who worked in Prenzlauer Berg, a working-class district (p118). Her drawings and sculptures portrayed the social problems of the poor, as well as human tragedy and suffering. She frequently took up the theme of motherhood and war after losing a son and grandson in World Wars I and II.

8

Museum Scharf-Gerstenberg

⚑B4 ⌂ Schlossstrasse 70 **Ⓤ** Richard-Wagner-Platz, Sophie-Charlotte-Platz **Ⓢ** Westend 🚌 309, M45 🕐 10am-6pm Tue-Fri, 11am-6pm Sat & Sun 🌐 smb.museum

The two 1850s pavilions on either side of Schlossstrasse were intended as officers'

← Spiral staircase below the cupola of the Museum Scharf-Gerstenberg

barracks for the King's Guard du Corps. Adjoining the eastern one is the Marstall, or stable block, and in this can be found the Museum Scharf-Gerstenberg. The museum presents paintings, sculptures, works on paper and even films by Surrealist and associated artists such as Dalí, Magritte, Max Ernst, Paul Klee and Jean Dubuffet, and also older works by Goya, Piranesi and Redon. More than 250 objects are presented over three floors, explaining the history of surreal art, with pieces from almost all the leading Surrealists.

9

Schlossstrasse Villas

⚑A5 ⌂ Schlossstrasse 65-7 **Ⓤ** Sophie-Charlotte-Platz 🚌 309

Most of the historic villas and buildings that once graced Schlossstrasse no longer exist. However, careful restoration of a few villas enables the visitor to get a feel for what the atmosphere must have been like at the end of the 19th century. It is worth taking a stroll down Schlossstrasse to look at the renovated villas, especially no. 67, which was built in 1873 in a Neo-Classical style to a design by Georg Töbelmann. If you continue the walk down nearby Schustehrusstrasse, you'll see an interesting school building at No. 39–43. Just up the road at No. 55 is the fine Villa Oppenheim, home of the Charlottenburg-Wilmersdorf Museum, open to the public except on Mondays.

Did You Know?

Charlottenburg was named after Sophie Charlotte of Hanover after she died in 1705.

10

Luisenkirche

⚑B5 ⌂ Gierkeplatz 4 📞 341 90 61 **Ⓤ** Richard-Wagner-Platz, Sophie-Charlotte-Platz 🚌 109, M45 🕐 9am-1pm Mon, Tue, Thu & Fri, 2-6pm Wed

This small church dates back to 1716, but its original Baroque styling was removed in rebuilding undertaken by Karl Friedrich Schinkel (p29) in the 1820s, when the church was renamed in memory of Queen Luise (1776–1810).

The shape of the church is based on a traditional Greek cross, with a tower at the front. The interior fixtures and fittings are not the originals, and the elegant stained-glass windows were made in 1956.

11

Belvedere

⚑A3 ⌂ Spandauer Damm 20-24 (Schlosspark Charlottenburg) 📞 32 09 10 **Ⓢ** Westend **Ⓤ** Richard-Wagner-Platz, Sophie-Charlotte-Platz 🚌 109, 309, M45 🕐 Apr-Oct: 10am-5:30pm Tue-Sun ⊘ Nov-Mar

The Belvedere is a summer house in the Schlosspark which served as a tea pavilion for Friedrich Wilhelm II and, in times of war, as a watchtower. It dates from 1788 and was designed by Carl Gotthard Langhans. The architect mixed Baroque and Neo-Classical elements, giving the building an oval central structure with

→ A formal green avenue leading up to the Belvedere

four straight-sided annexes. The building is crowned by a low dome topped with a sculpture of three cherubs supporting a basket of flowers.

Though the Belvedere was ruined during World War II, the summer house was reconstructed between 1956 and 1960 and adapted to serve as an exhibition space. The exhibition is a large collection of exquisite porcelain from the Berlin Königliche Porzellan-Manufaktur (Royal Porcelain Workshop), which has pieces from the Rococo period up to late Biedermeier, including some outstanding individual items.

The Belvedere is a summer house in the Schlosspark which served as a tea pavilion for Friedrich Wilhelm II and, in times of war, as a watchtower.

to the city of his birth. The museum opened in what was once the west pavilion of the barracks using space freed up by moving the Antiken-sammlung to Museumsinsel. The exhibition halls were modified according to the designs of Hilmer and Sattler, who also designed the layout of the Gemäldegalerie *(p158)*. The Museum Berggruen is particularly well known for its large collection of quality paintings, drawings and gouaches by Pablo Picasso. The collection begins with a drawing from his student days in 1897 and ends with works he painted in 1972, one year before his death.

In addition to these, the museum displays more than 60 works by Swiss artist Paul Klee and more than 20 works by Henri Matisse. The museum also houses paintings by other major artists, such as Georges Braque and Paul Cézanne. The collection is supplemented by some excellent sculptures, particularly those of Henri Laurens and Alberto Giacometti.

Museum Berggruen

 A4 Schlossstrasse 1 ⑤ Westend Ⓤ Richard-Wagner-Platz, Sophie-Charlotte-Platz ▦109, 309, M45 ⌚ For renovation until 2025 ⓦ smb.museum

Heinz Berggruen assembled this tasteful collection of art, dating from the late 19th and first half of the 20th century. Born and educated in Berlin, he emigrated to the US in 1936, spent most of his later life in Paris, but later entrusted his collection

13

Bröhan-Museum

A5 Schlossstrasse 1a ⑤ Westend Ⓤ Richard-Wagner-Platz, Sophie-Charlotte-Platz ▦109, 309, M45 ⌚ 10am–6pm Tue–Sun ⓦ broehan-museum.de

This small but interesting museum, set in a late Neo-Classical building, houses a collection of decorative arts amassed by Karl H Bröhan, who from 1966 collected works of art from the Art Nouveau (Jugendstil or Secessionist) and Art Deco periods. The paintings of the artists particularly connected with the Berlin Secessionist movement, such as Karl Hagemeister and Hans Baluschek, are especially well represented. Alongside the paintings there are fine examples of arts and crafts in other media: furniture, ceramics, silverwork and textiles. There is glasswork by Émile Gallé and porcelain from some of the finest European manufacturers.

A SHORT WALK
AROUND THE SCHLOSS

Distance 2 km (1.5 miles) **Nearest U-Bahn station** Richard-Wagner-Platz **Time** 30 minutes

The park surrounding the former royal summer residence in Charlottenburg is one of the most picturesque places in Berlin, making for a beautiful walk in every season. Visitors are drawn here by the luxury Baroque complex and outlying structures, which were meticulously rebuilt after World War II. The marvellous interiors were once home to Prussian nobles, and now the wings of the palace and its pavilions house interesting exhibitions.

| 0 metres | 150 |
| 0 yards | 150 |

N

↑ French-style garden in the Schlosspark

The central section of **Schloss Charlottenburg** *(p212) is called Nering-Eosanderbau, in honour of the architects who designed the building.*

Did You Know?

Charlottenburg was an independent city until 1920.

Kleine Orangerie

The monument to the **Great Elector** *(p215) at the entrance of Schloss Charlottenburg was funded by his son King Friedrich I and designed by Andreas Schlüter.*

START

Neuer Flügel, *the palace's newest wing, was once home to the royal art collection. Today, the building houses changing art and history exhibits.*

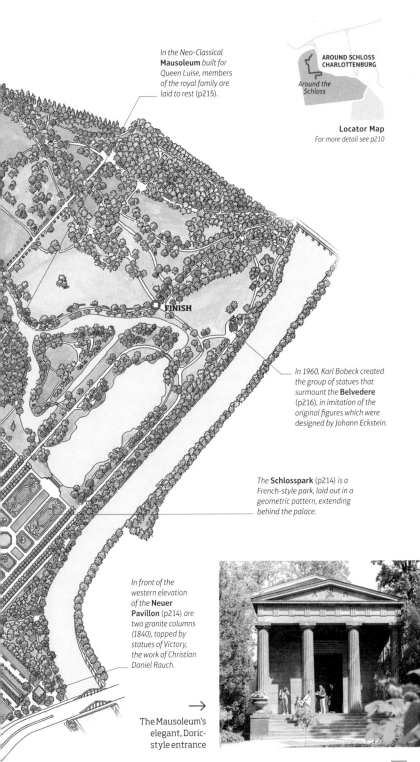

In the Neo-Classical **Mausoleum** built for Queen Luise, members of the royal family are laid to rest (p215).

AROUND SCHLOSS CHARLOTTENBURG

Around the Schloss

Locator Map
For more detail see p210

FINISH

In 1960, Karl Bobeck created the group of statues that surmount the **Belvedere** (p216), in imitation of the original figures which were designed by Johann Eckstein.

The **Schlosspark** (p214) *is a French-style park, laid out in a geometric pattern, extending behind the palace.*

In front of the western elevation of the **Neuer Pavillon** (p214) *are two granite columns (1840), topped by statues of Victory, the work of Christian Daniel Rauch.*

→ The Mausoleum's elegant, Doric-style entrance

BEYOND THE CENTRE

In 1920, seven towns were incorporated into Berlin, along with 59 communes and 27 country estates – each of which had been evolving independently for many years. Over the following decades the faces of many of these boroughs changed, but some places have kept their small-town or rural character. Thanks to this diversity, a stay in Berlin can simultaneously equate to visiting several cities. A short journey by S-Bahn enables you to travel from the cosmopolitan city centre of the 21st century to the vast forests of the Grunewald or the beach at Wannsee lake. You can explore everything from Dahlem's tranquil streets lined with villas, to Spandau's Renaissance citadel, cobbled lanes and the vast Gothic church of St-Nikolai-Kirche – all just half an hour away from the centre of Berlin and well worth a visit.

BEYOND THE CENTRE

Höhen Neuendorf

B96

L172

A111

Hennigsdorf

Frohnau

Hermsdor

Heiligensee

SCHLOSS TEGEL 22

VILLA BORSIG 20   Tegel

Tegeler See

A111

Hakenfelde

Berlin Tegel Airport ✈

L172

Haselhorst

SPANDAU 26

Spree

A111

OLYMPIA-STADION   GEORG-KOLBE-MUSEUM

Wilhelm-stadt

HAUS DES RUNDFUNK

27

25   16

LE CORBUSIER HAUS 21

FUNKTURM 24

23   Halens

MESSEGELÄNDE

A100

Grunewald   Schmargendorf

GRUNEWALDTURM

31   A115

See Dahlem map, p247

Berliner Forst Grunewald

Havel

DAHLEM 36

B1

STRANDBAD WANNSEE   Zehlendorf

28

B2

See Potsdam map, p251

HAUS DER WANNSEE-KONFERENZ 32

VILLENKOLONIE ALSEN 35   Wannsee   Nikolassee

B1   MUSEUMSDORF DÜPPEL

34

GRABSTÄTTE VON 33
HEINRICH VON KLEIST

B1

Kleinmachnow   Schönow

POTSDAM 37

Teltow

L77

Babelsberg

A115

L794

Stahnsdorf

Templiner See

L40

B2   Drewitz   L40   B101

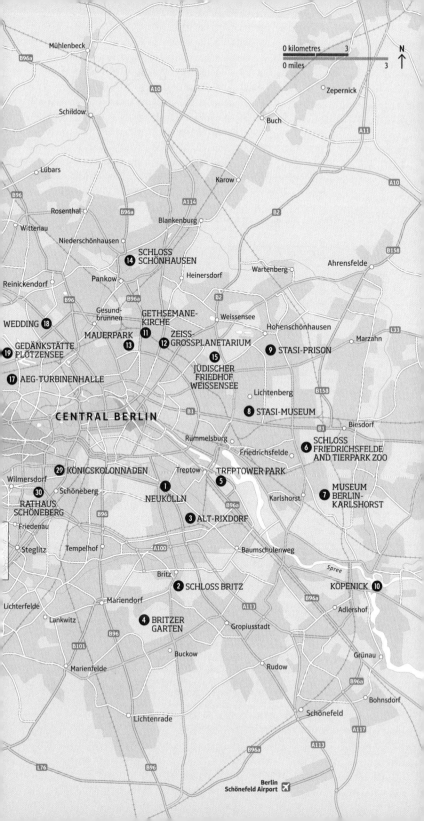

GETTING TO KNOW
BEYOND THE CENTRE

Although most visitors to Berlin will spend their time roaming the inner city, the *Ortsteile* (localities) in the surrounding boroughs offer plenty more sights and surprises. The GDR-era museums and architecture of the East, the mellow districts in the northwest and the sparkling lakes of the southwest are all just an S-Bahn or bicycle ride away.

PAGE 226

EAST OF THE CENTRE

East of Friedrichshain lie the less gentrified districts of Lichtenberg, Hohenschönhausen, Marzahn and Treptow-Köpenick. Largely demonised in the nineties, the areas' prefabricated residential blocks today draw a mix of former East Berliners, immigrants and students priced out of the city centre. You'll find a clutch of GDR-era sights well worth exploring, including the Gedenkstätte Hohenschönhausen and the Stasi-Museum Berlin, plus more natural attractions such as the charming but low-key Tierpark.

Best for
GDR history and architecture, strolls, local culture

Home to
Neukölln, Tierpark, Stasi-Museum, Köpenick, Mauerpark

Experience
The cobbled streets of medieval Alt-Rixdorf

PAGE 236

NORTHWEST OF THE CENTRE

The many forests, parks, lakes and rivers of the northwest act as a natural magnet for city-dwellers looking for a weekend getaway. The area is also dotted with local attractions and impressive structures that exemplify key moments in Berlin's fascinating history: from the medieval Spandau and its Renaissance citadel to the enormous Third Reich-era Olympiastadion and the modernist (and monolithic) Le Corbusier Haus.

Best for
Architecture, strolls, culture

Home to
Zitadelle Spandau, Olympiastadion

Experience
The area's natural splendour or the architecture and history at the Nazi-era Olympiastadion on a tour

PAGE 240

SOUTHWEST OF THE CENTRE

This area contains some of the city's finest natural beauty and is the place to head in the summer months. The sandy lido at the villa-lined lake Wannsee is a major warm-weather destination, and there is a plethora of beautiful outdoor attractions in the towns of Dahlem and Potsdam. For German culture and history, you can find a top-notch collection of German Expressionism at the Brücke Museum and a medieval atmosphere at Museumsdorf Düppel.

Best for
Nature, walks, beaches

Home to
Strandbad Wannsee, Rathaus Schöneberg

Experience
A stroll along the crisscrossing pathways of Grunewald forest to the striking hilltop Grunewaldturm

❶
NEUKÖLLN

🚇 Hermannplatz 🚌 171, 194, M29, M41, N7, N9, N94

This thriving neighbourhood has become home to a large population of people from around the world, as young students, creatives and professionals flock here for the cheap rents and cool atmosphere.

Characterized by a vibrant mixture of international expats, Neukölln is one of the city's fastest-growing – and fastest-gentrifying – districts. Some tourists would ignore the neighbourhood after seeing traffic-heavy drags like Sonnenallee and the bleak main square, Hermannplatz – but those willing to explore further will soon see why it's so popular with the locals. Areas such as those around Schillerstrasse and Weserstrasse – not to mention Kreuzkölln – are lined with bistros, galleries and boutiques. While there aren't many major sights in the area there are still a few places worth visiting, such as the pretty Körnerpark, the Kindl Centre for Contemporary Art, Schloss Britz *(p228)*, Britzer Garten and Neukölln's historic centre, Alt-Rixdorf.

The central Berlin skyline from Klunkerkranich rooftop bar ↓

KREUZKÖLLN

Reuterstrasse and Hobrechtstrasse are the streets directly south of the Landwehrkanal between Kotbusser Damm and Pannierstrasse. They have been nicknamed Kreuzkölln since they overlap both the Kreuzberg and Neukölln districts. These streets are characterized by a particularly dense concentration of boutiques, bars, galleries, cafés and restaurants. The Maybachufer embankment of the canal also hosts a vibrant Turkish market on Tuesdays and Fridays, and a flea market on Sundays.

 Neukölln's verdant Körnerpark, an attractive spot for many Berliners on sunny days

← Britzer Garten, one of the city's best green spots

Did You Know?

Neukölln is the name of both the district and the borough in which it is located.

EAST OF THE CENTRE

❷

Schloss Britz

🏠 Alt-Britz 73 🚇 Parchimer Allee 🚌 181, M44, M46
🕐 11am-6pm Tue-Sun
🌐 schlossbritz.de

Originally a small manor house built in 1706 for Sigismund von Erlach, Schloss Britz was extended to its current size in the 1880s to a design by Carl Busse. It is a one-storey palace with a modest Neo-Classical aspect adorned with Baroque statues and a tower. As well as housing a museum, the building is often used as a venue for concerts and exhibitions. The palace displays furnishings from the *Gründerzeit* – the years after the founding of the German Empire in 1871. The 19th-century interiors are excellent, but it is also worth strolling through the lovely park, where there is a bust of one of the palace's former owners, Rüdiger von Ilgen, which once stood in the Tiergarten.

Next to the palace there stands a housing estate called Hufeisensiedlung (Horseshoe Colony), built in the late 1920s to a design by Bruno Taut and Bruno Schneidereit. The architects' aim was to create spacious and affordable housing for Berliners.

---

❸

Alt-Rixdorf

Ⓢ & 🚇 Berlin-Neukölln
Ⓢ Sonnenallee
🚇 Karl-Marx-Strasse
🚌 171, M41, N7

Nestled gently between the bustling and unattractive thoroughfares of Karl-Marx-Strasse and Sonnenallee, charming Alt-Rixdorf (Old Rixdorf) is a wonderful hidden spot to explore. This is the historical heart of the Neukölln neighbourhood, with pretty Richardplatz at the centre, founded in the mid-18th century by Protestant refugees from Bohemia. The cobbled streets lined with historical buildings still retain their old-world charm. Along Kirchgasse are the mid-19th-century remnants of the Bohemian village, whose history is told at the nearby **Museum im Böhmischen Dorf** (Museum in a Bohemian Village) via exhibits on the traditions, beliefs, art, crafts and lives of its inhabitants, then and now. Other attractions include picturesque Bethlehemskirche, which sometimes hosts small concerts; the old village forge, dating back to 1624 and still working today; and a similarly historical coach house.

Museum im Böhmischen Dorf

🏠 Kirchgasse 5 🕐 2-5pm Thu, noon-2pm 1st & 3rd Sun of the month 🌐 museum imboehmischendorf.de

---

❹

Britzer Garten

🏠 Sangerhauser Weg 1
🚇 Alt-Mariendorf 🚌 179, 181, M44 🕐 Hours vary, check website 🌐 gruen-berlin.de/britzer-garten

This 4-ha (10-acre) park is something of a city secret. Located in the south of Neukölln (p226), it's vast enough to contain a multitude of sights, from scenic lakes and springs, themed gardens and playgrounds to a domestic animal enclosure with sheep, goats and donkeys, and several café-restaurants. Its size and rolling terrain make it feel more natural than its landscaped heritage suggests, with patches of grassland, streams and shrubs mixed in with rose and herb gardens, and a tremendous, crowd-pulling display of tulips (over 500,000) in spring. Other attractions include a "witch garden", a small train that carries visitors around and the largest sundial in Europe.

↑ Pretty Schloss Britz, occasionally a venue for exhibitions and concerts

↑ Steps leading to the Red Army monument, rising above Treptower Park

2,500,000

The number of Red Army soldiers involved in the Battle of Berlin.

Of the three restaurants, the one inside the Britzer Mühle (mill) is the most interesting, though the Britzer Seeterrassen has the nicest views from its outdoor tables.

5

Treptower Park

🚇 Alt-Treptow
Ⓢ Treptower Park
🚌 166, 265

The vast park in Treptow was laid out in the 1860s on the initiative and design of Johann Gustav Meyer. In January 1919 it was where revolutionaries Karl Liebknecht, Wilhelm Pieck and Rosa Luxemburg assembled a 150,000-strong group of striking workers during the Spartacist uprising.

The park, however, is best known for the colossal Soviet War Memorial. Built between 1946 and 1949, it stands on the grave of 5,000 Soviet soldiers killed in the Battle of Berlin in 1945. The gateway is marked by a vast granite sculpture of a grieving Russian Motherland surrounded by statues of Red Army soldiers. This leads to the mausoleum, topped by an 11-m- (35-ft-) high figure of a soldier rescuing a child and resting his mighty sword on a smashed swastika.

In the furthest section of the park is the astronomical observatory, **Archenhold Sternwarte**, built for a decorative arts exhibition held here in 1896. Given a permanent site here in 1909, the observatory was used by Albert Einstein for a lecture on the Theory of Relativity in 1915. It is also home to the longest refracting telescope in the world (21 m, or 70 ft) and a small planetarium. You can take a tour at 3pm on weekends and at 8pm on Thursdays.

Archenhold Sternwarte
Alt-Treptow 1
🕐 2–4:30pm Wed–Sun
🌐 planetarium.berlin

EAT

Zenner

Situated in Treptower Park on the Spree river, this leafy space is one of the largest and oldest beer gardens in Berlin. As well as plenty of beer, it also serves up light lunches and often has live music. It's good for families, who enjoy the playground and the ice cream parlour nearby.

🚇 Alt Treptow 15
🕐 Noon–8pm Mon–Thu, 11am–9pm Fri–Sun
🌐 zenner.berlin

€€€

The grand Schloss Friedrichsfelde, and a cherub figurine outside the palace *(inset)*

Schloss Friedrichsfelde

Am Tierpark 125
Tierpark 194, 296, 396 27, 37, M17
Summer: 10am-6pm daily; rest of year: 10am-4:30pm daily schloss-friedrichsfelde.de

The Baroque Friedrichsfelde Palace was built for Dutchman Benjamin von Raule around 1695, to a design by Johann Arnold Nering. A redesign in 1786 gave the residence its present-day appearance, typical of the style during the transition from Baroque to Neo-Classical. It now houses a museum of interiors, chiefly furnished with 18th- and 19th-century pieces.

The palace's park was remodelled to become the East Berlin **Tierpark Zoo**

in 1957. The animal inhabitants include all of the usual favourites, and there are masses of family-friendly experiences.

Tierpark Zoo

Nov-Feb: 9am-4:30pm daily; Mar, Sep & Oct: 9am-6pm daily; Apr-Sep: 9am-6:30pm daily tierpark-berlin.de

Museum Berlin-Karlshorst

Zwieseler Strasse 4/ Rheinsteinstrasse
Karlshorst 296
27, 37, M17 10am-6pm Tue-Sun museum-karlshorst.de

This building was erected in the 1930s for the engineering corps of the Wehrmacht (the armed services of the Third Reich). It was here on the night of 8 May

1945 that Hitler's successor, Grossadmiral Karl Dönitz, Field Marshal Wilhelm Keitel, Admiral Hans-Georg von Friedeburg and General Hans-Jürgen Stumpff signed the unconditional surrender of Germany's armed forces. You can visit the officers' mess

EAT

Inselcafé

The main restaurant on the Insel der Jugend (Island of Youth) has a menu that stretches to goulash, coconut curry and pasta dishes, as well as coffee, cake and waffles throughout the day. In summer there are deckchairs set out right by the river.

Insel der Jugend
Apr-Oct: noon-6pm daily; Nov-Mar: noon-6pm Sun
inselberlin.de

hall in which the signing took place and see an exhibition documenting the history of World War II.

Stasi-Museum

🏠 Ruschestrasse 103 (Haus 1) Ⓤ Magdalenen-strasse ⏰ 10am–6pm Mon–Fri, 11am–6pm Sat & Sun 🌐 stasimusem.de

Under the GDR, this huge complex of buildings housed the Ministry of the Interior and the infamous Stasi (GDR secret service) head-quarters. The Stasi was, without doubt, one of the most effective and repressive intelligence and secret police agencies ever to have existed.

One of the buildings houses a museum that describes the organizational structure, history and ideology of the Stasi. It includes photographs and documents depicting the Stasi's activities. The breakup of the Stasi is covered, as well as an overview of subsequent events leading up to the reunification of Germany.

A model of the head-quarters is on display, as well as equipment used for bugging and spying on citizens. You can see the office of the infamous Stasi chief Erich Mielke, commander of the Ministry for State Security

Spy camera designed to be concealed under clothing, on show at the Stasi-Museum

and a Big Brother-like figure. Mielke's legacy of suffering still lives on in the memory of millions of German citizens. The interior is just as it was when the Stasi used the complex. Tours are held in English on Saturday, Sunday and Monday at 3pm.

Stasi-Prison (Gedenkstätte Berlin-Hohenschönhausen)

🏠 Genslerstrasse 13a Ⓢ & Ⓤ Lichtenberg, then 🚌 256 to Liebenwalder-strasse/Genslerstrasse 🚋 16 to Genslerstrasse, M5 to Freienwalder, M6 ⏰ 9am–6pm daily 🌐 stiftung-hsh.de

This museum is housed in the former custody building of the Stasi – the dreaded security service of the GDR. The custody building was part of a huge complex built in 1938. In May 1945, the

occupying Russian authorities created a special transit camp here, in which they interned war criminals sub-sequently transported to Siberia. Shortly thereafter they started to bring anyone under political suspicion to the camp. During this time more than 20,000 people passed through here.

From 1946, this group of buildings was refashioned into the custody area for the KGB, and in 1951 it was given over for the use of the Stasi.

Visitors can see prisoners' cells and interrogation rooms. Housed in the cellars was the "submarine" – cells for the most "dangerous" suspects.

Tours are offered daily in both German and English. Many of the German-language guides are former inmates.

> **The Stasi was, without doubt, one of the most effective and repressive intelligence and secret police agencies ever to have existed.**

The grim Stasi-Prison, a memorial to the victims of the East German regime

Köpenick

 Spindlersfeld, then 167 or Köpenick, then 164
60, 61, 62, 67, 68

Köpenick is much older than Berlin. In the 9th century CE, this island contained a fortified settlement called Kopanica, inhabited by Slavs. From the late 12th century, Köpenick belonged to the Margrave of Brandenburg. In about 1240 a castle was built, around which a town began to evolve, though over the years it lost out in importance to Berlin. Crafters settled here, and after 1685, a large colony of Huguenots followed suit.

In the 19th century, Köpenick recreated itself as an industrial town. Despite wartime devastation, it has retained its historic character. By the old market square and in nearby streets, such as Alt Köpenick and Grünstrasse, modest houses have survived which recall the 18th century, next to buildings from the end of the 19th century.

At Alt Köpenick No. 21 is a vast brick town hall designed in the style of the Brandenburg Neo-Renaissance by Hans Schütte and Hugo Kinzer. It was here on 16 October 1906 that a famous swindle took place. Wilhelm Voigt dressed himself in a Prussian officer's uniform and proceeded to "arrest" the mayor and then fraudulently empty every-thing from the city treasury. This incident inspired a comedy, *The Captain from Köpenick* by Carl Zuckmayer, which is still popular today.

Köpenick's greatest attraction is a magnificent palace, **Schloss Köpenick**, on the island in the southern part of town. It was built in the late 17th century for the heir to the throne, Friedrich (later King Friedrich I), to a design by the Dutch architect Rutger van Langefeld. The three-storey Baroque building that resulted was extended to a design by Johann Arnold Nering, but until 1693 only part of the extension was completed: the chapel, entrance gate and a small gallery wing. In 2004, the Kunstgewerbemuseum *(p166)* opened a series of Renaissance and Baroque rooms in the Köpenick palace.

Schloss Köpenick

Schlossinsel 1
11am–5pm Tue–Sun
smb.museum

HIDDEN GEM
Müggelsee

Köpenick is home to Müggelsee, Berlin's largest lake. It's a great city escape for both locals and tourists, with hills, forests and plenty of bathing areas.

Köpenick's robustly grand town hall, completed in 1904

Stunning imagery at the Zeiss-Gross-planetarium ↑

 11

Gethsemanekirche

🅰 Stargader Strasse 77
Ⓢ & Ⓤ Schönhauser Allee
🅦 ekpn.de

The Neo-Gothic red-brick building of Gethsemane Church is perhaps the most famous church in northeast Berlin, playing as it did a crucial role in East Germany's peaceful revolution. This Protestant church, solidly built in oxblood-red brick in 1890, dominates the neighbourhood. It was one of several built on the order of Emperor Wilhelm II, who wanted to increase religious worship among the mostly Social Democratic working classes living in Prenzlauer Berg and other areas. The building was designed by August Orth, one of the period's most important architects of churches and railway stations.

The Protestant community of Gethsemanekirche is proud to have pioneered civil rights movements, and hosted anti-Nazi rallies from 1933 to 1945. The congregation also questioned the Socialist regime after World War II, while the church itself served as an assembly hall for peaceful opponents in October 1989. On 2 October that year, the praying crowd was brutally attacked by the East German secret service police, marking the start of the Communist regime's demise.

Today, the square is surrounded by beautiful restored buildings, housing many pavement restaurants, cafés and quaint little shops. Only a few steps away is Kollwitzplatz (p132), a welcoming, leafy square with an atmosphere reminiscent of Paris. Nearby Kollwitzstrasse is home to an organic farmers' market on Saturdays.

12

Zeiss-Gross-planetarium

🅰 Prenzlauer Allee 80 (Ernst-Thälmann-Park)
Ⓢ Prenzlauer Allee, then 🚌 156 🚊 M2 🕐 9am–5pm Tue, 9am–8pm Wed & Thu, 9am–9:30pm Fri, 1–9:30pm Sat, 11:30am–6:30pm Sun
🅦 planetarium.berlin

The silvery dome visible from afar is a huge planetarium built in the grounds of a park dedicated to the memory of the interwar Communist leader Ernst Thälmann, who died at Buchenwald concentration camp. The foyer houses an exhibition of optical equipment and various accessories produced by the renowned factory of Carl-Zeiss-Jena.

> **The Protestant community of Gethsemanekirche is proud to have pioneered civil rights movements, and hosted anti-Nazi rallies from 1933 to 1945.**

Mauerpark

🏠 Mauerpark, Gleimstrasse
Ⓤ Bernauer Strasse,
Eberswalder Strasse
🚋 M10

Formerly part of the Berlin Wall (hence the name "Wall Park"), this largely treeless expanse of lawn in Prenzlauer Berg is a magnet for young locals and tourists alike. Although it can be a little claustrophobic on warm days, it is a great spot for people-watching.

Children love the park and an artificial rock can be climbed under professional supervision. From around 3pm on Sundays, aspiring pop stars can attempt karaoke at the amphitheatre and perform to a packed audience. The giant eclectic flea market held next to the park from 10am to 6pm on Sundays attracts huge crowds of mostly 20-somethings on the lookout for a special bargain, be it junk or vintage. Vegan burgers and cold beers complete the experience, which can be a welcome restorative treat after a visit to the haunting Wall Memorial nearby *(p122)*.

The Mauerweg, a shared walking and bicycle path, follows the path of the old Wall right across Mauerpark.

Schloss Schönhausen

🏠 Tschaikowskistrasse 1
Ⓢ & Ⓤ Pankow 🚌 150, 250
🚋 M1 🕐 Jan–Mar: 10am–4pm Sat, Sun & hols;
Apr–Oct: 10am–5:30pm Tue–Sun; Nov & Dec: 10am–5pm Sat, Sun & hols
🌐 spsg.de

This palace, located in an extensive park, belonged to the von Dohna family during the 17th century. Ownership of the estate passed to the Elector Friedrich III in 1691, for whom Johann Arnold Nering designed the palace. In 1704, it was extended to a design by Johann Friedrich Eosander von Göthe, who added side wings. The palace was home to Queen Elisabeth Christine, estranged wife of Frederick

↑ Catching some free entertainment at Mauerpark

the Great, between 1740 and 1797. In 1763, further extensive refurbishment was undertaken by architect Johann Boumann. The property remained in the hands of the Prussian royal family for the next hundred years. Among those who resided here were Princess Auguste von Liegnitz, following the death of her husband, King Friedrich Wilhelm III.

After World War II, the rebuilt palace was occupied by the president of the German Democratic Republic, Wilhelm Pieck. In 1990, after many discussions here, the treaty to reunify Germany was signed on 3 October.

Make time for a stroll through the vast park, which has kept the pleasant

Did You Know?

Peter Joseph Lenné also designed the Tiergarten and Park Sanssouci.

character bestowed on it by Peter Joseph Lenné *(p171)* in the 1820s.

Jüdischer Friedhof Weissensee

🏠 Herbert-Baum-Strasse 45 🄢 Greifswalder Strasse, then 🚋 12, M4, M13 🚌 156, 200 🕐 Hours vary, check website 🌐 jg-berlin. org/judentum/friedhoefe/ weissensee.html

This extensive Jewish cemetery, established in 1880 according to a design by Hugo Licht, is the final resting place of more than 115,000 Berliners, many of whom were victims of Nazi persecution. It is chilling to note that many surnames listed on gravestones simply no longer exist in Germany, due to whole families being eradicated or driven out of the country.

By the main entrance is a place of remembrance for the victims of the Holocaust, with plaques bearing the names of the concentration camps. Buried here are

renowned figures from Berlin's Jewish cultural and commercial past. Among others, here rest the publisher Samuel Fischer and the restaurateur Berthold Kempinski.

Some tombstones are outstanding works of art, such as that of the Panowsky family, designed by Ludwig Hoffmann, or the Cubist tombstone of Albert Mendel, designed by Walter Gropius. Some family graves are adorned with temple-like structures. The Nazis left this burial ground largely unharmed, but in 1999 the cemetery was desecrated in an act of anti-Semitic vandalism. More than 100 headstones were kicked over and some were smeared with swastikas.

Still in use today, most of the new graves in this plot belong to Jewish immigrants from the former Soviet Union, who outnumber the German-born Jewish people in Berlin.

Entrance hall to the Jüdischer Friedhof ↓ Weissensee

NORTHWEST OF THE CENTRE

Haus des Rundfunks

Masurenallee 8-14
Messe Nord/ICC
Theodor-Heuss-Platz
104, 218, X34, X49

This building's depressing, flat, brick-covered façade hides an interior of startling beauty. The huge edifice was constructed as a radio station between 1929 and 1931 to a design by Hans Poelzig. The building has a triangular shape, with three studio wings radiating from the central five-storey hall. The impressive Art Deco interiors, which are spectacularly lit from above, are enhanced by geometrically patterned rows of balconies and large, pendulous, octagonal lamps. They represent one of the finest architectural achievements of this era in Berlin.

From the studio concert hall, concerts are often broadcast on the RBB radio station (Rundfunk Berlin-Brandenburg).

AEG-Turbinenhalle

Huttenstrasse 12-19
Turmstrasse, then
M27

This building is one of the most important textbook examples of modern architecture, dating from the beginning of the 20th century. It was commissioned by the electronics company AEG in 1909 and designed by Peter Behrens in conjunction with Karl Bernhardt. While Berlin's previous industrial buildings were mostly red-brick and fortress-like, the Turbinenhalle was among the earliest structures not to incorporate any element, decorative or otherwise, that reflected previous architectural styles.

A huge hangar of a building, it has enormous windows and stretches 123 m (400 ft) down Berlichingenstrasse. The principal design imperative was to maintain a streamlined profile, while making no effort to disguise the construction materials. Today, the building is part of the Siemens company and is still used as a factory.

Wedding

& Wedding, Gesundbrunnen Seestrasse, Osloer Strasse 133, 222, 224, then a 15-minute walk

Wedding is an interesting, up-and-coming area. Artists are taking over abandoned industrial buildings, a lively theatre and gallery scene is developing and the area is becoming more attractive to renters and buyers. Volkspark Rehberge, a beautiful park, is a hidden gem.

Gedenkstätte Plötzensee

Hüttigpfad Beuselstrasse, then 123 Mar-Oct: 9am-5pm daily; Nov-Feb: 9am-4pm daily
gedenkstaette-ploetzensee.de

A narrow street leads from Saatwinkler Damm to the Plötzensee Memorial, marking the site where nearly 2,500 people convicted of crimes against the Third Reich were hanged. It is a simple memorial in a brick hut, which still has the iron hooks from which the victims were suspended. While the main figures in the unsuccessful assassination attempt on Hitler, on 20 July 1944, were executed in the Bendlerblock (p170), the rest of the conspirators were killed here. Count Helmuth James von Moltke, one of the leaders of the German resistance movement, was also executed here. The count organized the Kreisauer Kreis – a political movement that united German opposition to Hitler.

Villa Borsig

Reiherwerder Alt-Tegel 133, 222, 224, then a 15-minute walk

This villa sits on a peninsula that cuts into the Tegeler See, reminiscent of Schloss Sanssouci in Potsdam (p254). It was built much later, however, between 1911 and 1913. It was designed by Alfred Salinger and Eugen Schmohl for the Borsigs, one

↑ Urban landscape in the formerly industrial district of Wedding

↑ Schloss Tegel, designed by Karl Friedrich Schinkel

Did You Know?

Alexander von Humboldt referred to Schloss Tegel as Schloss Langweil, or "Boredom Palace", as it was far from Berlin.

of the wealthiest industrialist families in Berlin. This villa is particularly picturesque when seen from the lake, so it is worth looking out for it from a boat cruise.

 21

Le Corbusier Haus

🏠 Flatowallee 16
Ⓢ Olympiastadion 🚌 149, 218 🌐 corbusierhaus-berlin.org

This apartment building by Le Corbusier, on a hill near the site of the Olympiastadion (p239), was the architect's entry to the 1957 Internationale Bauausstellung. His innovative design for what he called a *Unité d'Habitation* was an attempt to create fully self-sufficient housing estates in answer to a Europe-wide housing shortage. He built three of these complexes, the most famous being in Marseilles. For his Berlin design, Le Corbusier wanted to build over 500 two-storey apartments with integral services, such as a post office, shops, a sports hall and nursery school. Financial pressures prevented all of Le Corbusier's aspirations from being fulfilled; nevertheless, the monolithic building was a milestone for West Berlin's postwar architecture. For some, it will always be the "*Wohnmaschine*" (dwelling machine) and they criticize the jail-like hallways, called "streets" by the architect. Others praise the Bauhaus-inspired clear lines, airy, light-filled apartments and the architectural departure from ornamental features.

The apartments are mostly privately owned, but you can see the interior on tours that take place on Saturdays; check the website for details.

 22

Schloss Tegel

🏠 Adelheidallee 19–21
📞 886 71 50 Ⓤ Alt-Tegel
🚌 133, 222 🕐 May–Sep: 10am, 11am, 3pm & 4pm Mon 🕐 Oct–Apr

Schloss Tegel is one of the most interesting palace complexes in Berlin. In the 16th century there was already a manor house on this site, which in the second half of the 17th century was rebuilt into a hunting lodge for the Elector Friedrich Wilhelm (p215). In 1766, the ownership of the property passed to the Humboldt family, and, from 1820 to 1824, Karl Friedrich Schinkel (p29) thoroughly rebuilt the palace, giving it its current style.

There are tiled bas-reliefs decorating the elevations on the top floor of the towers. These were designed by Christian Daniel Rauch and depict the ancient wind gods. Some of Schinkel's marvellous interiors have survived, along with several items from what was once a large collection of antique sculptures. The palace is still privately owned by descendants of the Humboldt family, but guided tours are offered at 10am, 11am, 3pm and 4pm on Mondays from May to September. It is also worth visiting the park. On its western limits lies the Humboldt family tomb, designed by Schinkel and decorated with a copy of a splendid sculpture by Bertel Thorwaldsen; the original piece stands inside the palace.

The Georg-Kolbe-Museum, with its collection of 20th-century sculpture

 23

Messegelände

⚑ Hammarskjöldplatz
Ⓢ Messe Nord/ICC
Ⓤ Kaiserdamm 🚌 104, 139, 349, X49

The pavilions of these vast exhibition and trade halls cover more than 160,000 sq m (1,700,000 sq ft). Many of the international events organized here are among the largest events of their kind in Europe.

The original exhibition halls on this site were built before World War I, but nothing of those buildings remains. The oldest part is the Funkturm and the group of pavilions which surround it. The huge building at the front – Ehrenhalle – was built in 1936 to a design by Richard Ermisch, and is one of the few surviving buildings in Berlin designed in a Fascist architectural style.

The straight motorway that lies at the rear of the halls, in the direction of Nikolassee, is the famous Avus, the first German Autobahn, built in 1921. It was adapted for motor racing and became Germany's first car-racing track. It was here that the world speed record was broken before World War II. Now it forms part of the Autobahn system.

 24

Funkturm

⚑ Hammarskjöldplatz
Ⓢ Messe Nord/ICC
Ⓤ Kaiserdamm 🚌 104, 218, 349, X34 🕐 Hours vary, check website
🌐 funkturm-messeberlin.de

This radio tower, which resembles Paris's Eiffel Tower, has become one of Berlin's most recognizable landmarks. Built in 1924 to a design by Heinrich Straumer, it rises 150 m (500 ft) into the air. It now operates as both an air-traffic control tower and radio mast. Visitors can enjoy views on the observation terrace at 125 m (400 ft), or dine at the Funkturm's lofty restaurant at 55 m (180 ft). The terrace may close for safety in bad weather.

25

Georg-Kolbe-Museum

⚑ Sensburger Allee 25
Ⓢ Heerstrasse 🚌 218, X34, X49 🕐 10am–6pm Wed–Mon
🌐 georg-kolbe-museum.de

One of the most well-known German sculptors, Georg Kolbe (1877–1947) bequeathed the house in which he lived and worked for almost his entire life to the city of Berlin. Trained as a painter and draughtsman, Kolbe became famous for his expressive works that came to symbolize the early freedoms of the Weimar era *(p57)*.

Kolbe also left the city 180 of his sculptures and his art collection, which includes works by the Expressionist painter Ernst Ludwig Kirchner and the sculptor Wilhelm Lehmbruck. The museum has expanded its collection to include many more sculptures by Kolbe's peers. Visiting here is not only a rare chance to get to know Kolbe's works but also an opportunity to see his house and workshop, which displays tools and various devices for lifting a heavy sculpture.

26

Spandau

Ⓤ Altstadt Spandau, Zitadelle 🚌 X33

Spandau is one of the oldest towns in the Greater Berlin area. Evidence of the earliest settlement dates back to the 8th century, although the town of Spandau was only granted a charter in 1232.

The area was spared the worst of the World War II bombing, so the town has managed to retain a distinctive, historical character. The heart of the town is a network of medieval streets with a picturesque market square and a number of original timber-framed houses. In the north of Spandau, sections of the 15th-century town wall still stand, and in the centre of town is the magnificent Gothic St-Nikolai-Kirche, dating from the 14th century.

A castle was first built on the site of the **Zitadelle Spandau** (Spandau citadel) in the 12th century, but today only the 36-m (120-ft) Juliusturm (Julius tower) remains. The current fortress was built between 1560 and 1590, to a design by Francesco Chiaramella da Gandino. Though the citadel had a jail, Rudolf Hess, Spandau's most infamous resident, was incarcerated a short distance away in a military prison after the 1946 Nuremberg trials.

Today, the Zitadelle is home to a number of exhibitions, including one covering the history of the castle itself. The most unusual exhibit, however, is a collection of controversial monuments and statues, including busts of militaristic Prussian rulers and a huge granite head of Vladimir Lenin. The exhibit is

The Olympiastadion, built for the historic 1936 Berlin Olympics ↑

intended to foster discussion on difficult aspects of the city's past. A fascinating place to explore, it also hosts a popular music festival in summer.

Zitadelle Spandau

 Am Juliusturm 64 ◷ 10am–5pm daily Ⓦ zitadelle-berlin.de

㉗ Ⓜ️

Olympiastadion

🏠 Olympischer Platz
Ⓢ & Ⓤ Olympiastadion
🚌 218, M49 ◷ Hours vary, check website
Ⓦ olympiastadion.berlin

The plans for this stadium were conceived in 1933, when Adolf Hitler ordered the construction of a grandiose sporting complex for the 1936 Olympic Games in Berlin. It was designed by Werner March in the Nazi architectural style and was inspired by the architecture of ancient Rome.

To the west of the stadium lie the Maifeld and the Waldbühne. The Maifeld is an enormous assembly ground fronted by the Glockenturm, a 77-m (250-ft) bell tower with a viewing platform. The bell inside the tower is a replica of the original, which was damaged during World War II and is now on display outside the stadium. The Waldbühne is an open-air amphitheatre with a design inspired by the ancient theatre of Epidaurus in Greece.

Following a €236-million refurbishment, the stadium reopened in 2004 as a high-tech arena. The Deutsches Sportmuseum next to the stadium also hosts concerts and shows.

▌ **ZITADELLE SPANDAU**

This magnificent, perfectly proportioned 16th-century citadel stands where the Spree and Havel rivers meet. Both the main citadel and its 19th-century additions are still in excellent condition. It holds museums of local history and an observation terrace on the Juliusturm.

Key

① Bastion Kronprinz
② Bastion Brandenburg
③ Palace
④ Main gate
⑤ Bastion König
⑥ Bastion Königin
⑦ Juliusturm
⑧ Ravelin Schweinekopf

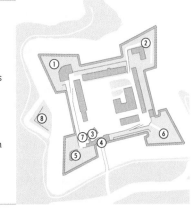

SOUTHWEST OF THE CENTRE

 28

Strandbad Wannsee

 Wannseebadweg 2s
📞 30 22 19 00 11
Ⓢ Nikolassee 🚌 218

The vast, picturesque lake of Wannsee, situated on the edge of the Grunewald forest, is a principal destination for Berliners who are looking for recreation. Here you can take part in watersports, enjoy a

---

EAT

In summer, the sparkling Wannsee lake is a favoured destination for locals and visitors alike, so there are plenty of great dining options here for those who want a day trip out from the city centre.

Bootshaus Bolle
📍 Am Grossen Wannsee 60
🕐 Noon-8pm daily
🌐 bootshaus-bolle.de

€€€

Wannseeterrassen
📍 Wannseebadweg 35
🕐 Noon-10pm daily
🌐 wannseeterrassen. berlin

€€€

Clubrestaurant am Wannsee im MYCvD
📍 Scabellstrasse 10-11 🕐 3-10pm Wed-Fri, 1-10pm Sat & Sun 🚫 Mon & Tue
🌐 restaurant-wannsee.de

€€€

---

lake cruise, bathe or simply relax on the shore.

Near S-Bahn Wannsee there are yachting marinas and harbours, while further north is one of the largest inland beaches in Europe – Strandbad Wannsee. It has been in use since the beginning of the 20th century, and was developed between 1929 and 1930 with the construction of a complex of changing rooms, shops, and cafés on top of artificial terraces.

On sunny summer days, sun-worshippers completely cover the sandy shore, while the lake is filled with yachts and windsurfers. It is also quite pleasant to take a walk around Schwanenwerder island. It has many elegant villas, one of which, Inselstrasse No. 24/26, was built for Axel Springer, the German newspaper publisher.

 29

Königskolonnaden (Kleistkolonnaden)

📍 Potsdamer Strasse
Ⓤ Kleistpark
🚌 106, 204, M46

A short walk north of U-Bahn Kleistpark, the unremarkable architecture of Potsdamer Strasse suddenly transforms dramatically. Leading to the park, the elegant sandstone Königskolonnaden (Royal Colonnade) captivates the passer-by with its Baroque ornamental sculptures. Designed by Carl von Gontard and built between 1777 and 1780, it once graced the route from Königsstrasse to Alexanderplatz *(p106)*. In 1910, to protect it from traffic, it was moved to this new site.

The huge Kammergericht at the far boundary of the park was built between 1909

→
Strandbad Wannsee, ideal for taking a break from city life

and 1913 to a design by Carl Vohl, Rudolf Mönnich and Paul Thömer. The site of the notorious Nazi Volksgericht or "People's Court", it was also used to try members of the failed July 1944 bomb plot against Hitler. From 1945 to 1958 it was the official seat of the Allied Control Council, and is now the Supreme Court of the state of Berlin.

Rathaus Schöneberg

🏛 John-F-Kennedy-Platz 1
Ⓤ Rathaus Schöneberg
🚌 104, M46

The gigantic building with a tower dominating the Schöneberg district's main square is its town hall, built in 1914. From 1948 to 1990 it was used as the main town hall of West Berlin. It was here, on 26 June 1963, that US President John F Kennedy gave his famous speech. More than 300,000 Berliners

HIDDEN GEM
Grunewaldturm

For those who don't like heights, the Grunewald Tower is still worth a visit, not only for the ground-floor restaurant but also the mosaic decorating the ceiling of the memorial hall. The Neo-Byzantine design was created by August Oetken (1868-1951), a German painter and mosaic artist.

assembled to hear the young president say, *"Ich bin ein Berliner"* – "I am a Berliner" – as an expression of solidarity from the democratic world to a city defending its right to freedom. (An urban myth has since claimed that the phrase actually means "I am a small doughnut", but this is incorrect – although there is, indeed, a small doughnut in Germany known as a *Berliner*.)

↑ Statue of Kaiser Wilhelm in the Grunewaldturm

31 🍽

Grunewaldturm

🏛 Havelchaussee 61 🚌 218
🕙 10am-10pm daily

The Neo-Gothic tower built on a hill at the edge of the Havel river is one of the most prominent features of the area. This type of tower became popular in Germany during the 19th century as a way of commemorating important events or people. The Grunewaldturm was built in 1899 on the centenary of the birth of Wilhelm I. After 1871 he was the first Emperor of the Second Reich and the tower was initially named "Kaiser-Wilhelm-Turm". The 56-m (185-ft) tower was designed by Franz Schwechten and is made of red brick with plaster details. The tower is made all the more striking by the green background provided by the surrounding leafy trees. The view from the top of this structure is well worth climbing the 204 steps for.

The pristine Havel river at dusk

32 Haus der Wannsee-Konferenz

🏛 Am Grossen Wannsee 56/58 🚊 Wannsee, then 🚌 114 🕐 10am–6pm daily 🌐 ghwk.de

This is one of the most beautiful of the luxury holiday villas on the shores of Lake Wannsee, and yet because of its past, it is also the most abhorrent. Built in 1915 to a design by Paul Baumgarten, it is in the style of a small Neo-Baroque palace with an elegant portico. In 1940 the villa was sold to the Nazi SS. On 20 January 1942, a meeting took place here between Reinhard Heydrich and 14 other officers from the secret service and the SS, among them Adolf Eichmann. It was then that the decision was taken about "the final solution on the question of Jews". Their plans for the outright extermination of 11 million Jewish people embraced the whole of Europe, including Great Britain and neutral countries.

Since 1992, this has been a museum and place of remembrance. An exhibition depicts the history of the Holocaust with some shocking documents and photographs from the ghettos and extermination camps. For security reasons, the gate to the villa is always locked,

and to enter the park you have to announce yourself through the intercom.

↑ The gravestone of Heinrich von Kleist and Henriette Vogel

33 Grabstätte von Heinrich von Kleist

🏛 Bismarckstrasse (near No. 3) 🚊 Wannsee 🚌 114, 316, 318

A narrow street running from Königstrasse at the viaduct of the S-Bahn Wannsee leads to the gravesite of the playwright Heinrich von Kleist. It is the spot where he committed murder and then died by suicide; on 21 November 1811 he shot his companion Henriette Vogel and then turned the pistol on himself. They are both buried here. Modest stones mark their grave, on which flowers are left by well-wishers.

34 Museumsdorf Düppel

🏛 Clauertstrasse 11 🚊 Mexikoplatz or Ⓤ Krumme Lanke, then 🚌 118, 622 🕐 Late Mar–early Oct: 10am–6pm Sat, Sun & public hols 🌐 dueppel.de

This reconstruction of a medieval village has been made on the site of a 13th-century settlement. It is a living village surrounded by still-cultivated gardens and fields, where traditional breeds of pig and sheep are raised in pigsties and sheds.

On Sundays, the village puts on displays of traditional crafts. Here you can see how primitive saucepans and tools were fashioned; how wool was spun, dyed and woven and how baskets were made.

↑ Max-Lieberman Villa, part of Wannsee's Villenkolonie Alsen

 35 🖼️ 🖼️

Villenkolonie Alsen

📍 Am Grossen Wannsee
🚉 Wannsee, then 🚌114

This clutch of villas on Lake Wannsee forms a delightful holiday resort – the oldest of its kind in Berlin. The villas are thought to be the most beautiful in the district, not just because of their scenic lakeside location, but also because of the quality of their architecture.

Strolling along Am Grossen Wannsee, it is worth looking at the villa at No. 39/41, known as Haus Springer. It was designed by the architect Alfred Messel in 1901 and is covered with shingles, a reflection of contemporary American designs.

Another must-see is the **Max-Liebermann Villa** at No. 42, designed by Paul Baumgarten in 1909 for the painter Max Liebermann (1847–1935). Liebermann spent many summers here painting in the garden on the lake shore. The villa is now a museum and houses around 40 of Liebermann's paintings.

Max-Lieberman Villa

🖼️ 🖼️ 🖼️ 🕐Hours vary, check website
🌐 liebermann-villa.de

MAX LIEBERMANN (1847–1935)

One of the most famed German painters, Max Liebermann was also one of the most interesting and controversial figures of Berlin's elite circles at the start of the 20th century. A sensitive observer as well as an outstanding portraitist, Liebermann was famously stubborn – he could stand up even to the Kaiser himself. From 1920 he was president of the Akademie der Künste (Academy of Arts; *p73*), but in view of his Jewish origin he was removed from office in 1933. He died just two years later, alone, and his wife died by suicide to escape being sent to a concentration camp.

↑ Sculpture by Bernhard Heiliger in the gardens of Kunsthaus Dahlem

36

DAHLEM

Ⓢ Botanischer Garten, Rathaus Steglitz Ⓤ Onkel Toms Hütte, Oskar-Helene-Heim, Freie Universität (Thielplatz), Dahlem Dorf, Podbielskiallee, Breitenbachplatz 🚌 115, 110, M2, M48, M85, X10, X11, X83

First referenced in documents from the 13th century, Dahlem is one of the most interesting suburbs in Steglitz-Zehlendorf, a borough southwest of central Berlin. An affluent and tranquil city suburb, the district was confirmed as a major cultural and educational centre after World War II with the establishment of a university and a museum complex.

①

Brücke-Museum

🏠 Bussardsteig 9 🚌 115 🕐 11am–5pm Wed–Mon 🌐 bruecke-museum.de

One of the more interesting museums dedicated to 20th-century art is hidden away on a leafy, tranquil street lined with attractive villas, in an elegant Functionalist building designed by architect Werner Düttmann. The museum houses a collection of German Expressionist paintings linked to the artistic group known as

Die Brücke (p30), which originated in Dresden in 1905 and was based in Berlin from 1910. The members of this group included Karl Schmidt-Rottluff, Emil Nolde, Max Pechstein, Ernst Ludwig Kirchner and Erich Heckel.

The collection is based on almost 80 works by Schmidt-Rottluff, bequeathed to the town in 1964. The collection quickly grew, thanks to donations and acquisitions. In addition to displaying other works of art contemporary to *Die Brücke* (which was disbanded in 1913), there are

also some paintings from the later creative periods of these artists, and works by other closely associated figures.

Nearby, at Käuzchensteig No. 8, lie the foundation's headquarters, established in the former studio of the sculptor Bernhard Heiliger. The garden, which borders the Brücke-Museum, has a display of his metal sculptures.

---

②

Kunsthaus Dahlem

🏠 Käuzchensteig 8 🚌 115, X10 🕐 11am–5pm Wed–Mon 🌐 kunsthaus-dahlem.de

This exhibition venue was built between 1939 and 1942 as a studio for the sculptor Arno Breker, one of the most prolific sculptors of the Third Reich, on grounds provided by the government.

In 1949, renowned sculptor Bernhard Heiliger, who was a student of Breker, moved into the east wing of the building and lived and worked in the complex until his death in 1995. In the garden adjacent to the Kunsthaus, more than 20 of his striking

> The Onkel-Tom-Siedlung project in Zehlendorf was the realization of the English concept of garden cities.

sculptures are exhibited. During Heiliger's time at the site, different parts of the complex were leased to other prominent artists from around the world.

Since 2015, the building has served as an exhibition space for postwar German Modernist art from both East and West Germany, and also promotes contemporary art.

---

③
Onkel-Tom-Siedlung

🏠 Riemeister Strasse/
Argentinische Allee
🚇 Onkel Toms Hütte

This housing estate, known as "Uncle Tom's Estate", represents one of the most interesting urban architectural achievements of the Weimar Republic *(p57)*. It was built from 1926 to 1932, to a design

→
Colourful houses on the Onkel-Tom-Siedlung estate

by Bruno Taut, Hugo Häring and Otto Rudolf Salvisberg. Their primary intention was to solve the city's housing shortage by building large developments that were both pleasant to live in and fairly inexpensive. The Onkel-Tom-Siedlung project in Zehlendorf was the realization of the English concept of garden cities.

The result is an enormous housing estate comprising single- and multiple-family houses. Set in lush greenery on the borders of Grunewald, it accommodates nearly 15,000 people.

DRINK

Alter Krug

This classic German wood-panelled pub-restaurant offers a smart interior, traditional menu and a beer garden large enough to seat 500 people.

🏠 Königin-Luise-Strasse 52 ⏰ 11am-11pm Mon-Sat, 10am-11pm Sun 🌐 alter-krug-berlin.de

---

④

Domäne Dahlem

🏠 Königin-Luise-Strasse 49 🚇 Dahlem Dorf 🚌 110, X11, X83 ⏰ Hours vary, check website 🌐 domaene-dahlem.de

Domäne Dahlem, a city-farm that combines a manor house and farming estate, is a rare oasis of country life in the Berlin suburbs. The Baroque house was built for Cuno Johann von Wilmersdorff around 1680 and still retains its original character. Part of the Stadtmuseum Berlin (Berlin City Museum), it has period interiors, while the 19th-century farm buildings hold a collection of agricultural tools and a large and varied collection of beehives.

Domäne Dahlem is a working farm as well as a museum, with gardens, workshops and farm animals. There is a small charge to enter the museum; the grounds are free. Festivals and markets held here demonstrate rural crafts and skills, and there is plenty for children to see and do. There is a farm shop selling local, sustainable foods, including the farm's produce, and an organic food market on Saturday mornings.

---

⑤

Museum Europäischer Kulturen

🏠 Arnimallee 25 🚇 Dahlem Dorf 🚌 110, X11, X83 ⏰ 10am-5pm Tue-Fri, 11am-6pm Sat & Sun 🌐 smb.museum

The Museum of European Cultures is an ethnographic museum that specializes in European folk art and culture, and documents the daily life of its inhabitants. It hosts long-running exhibitions, often in conjunction with museums from other European countries. Among the exhibits on display are earthenware items, costumes, jewellery, toys and tools.

---

⑥

Freie Universität

🏠 Henry-Ford-Bau, Garystrasse 35-9 🚇 Freie Universität 🚌 110 🌐 fu-berlin.de

The Free University was established on 4 December 1948 on the initiative of a group of academics and activists, led by Ernst Reuter. This was a reaction to the restrictions introduced at the Humboldt Universität in the Soviet sector, and further evidence of the competition between the two halves of the city. The university was initially located in rented buildings. It was only thanks to the American Ford Foundation that the Henry-Ford-Bau, housing the rector's office, the auditorium and the library, was built. Designed by Franz-Heinrich Sobotka and Gustav Müller and completed in 1954, the building is distinguished by its fine proportions.

Another architectural highlight is the Humanities and Social Science building, designed by Norman Foster and finished in 2005. It has a glass-domed centrepiece

housing the Philological Library, which is nicknamed the "Berlin Brain" due to its cranial shape.

---

⑦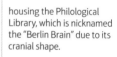

Botanischer Garten

🏠 Unter den Eichen 5-10 & Königin-Luise-Strasse 6-8 ⓢ Botanischer Garten 🚇 Dahlem-Dorf 🚌 M48, X83 ⏰ 9am-8pm daily 🌐 bgbm.org

The Botanical Garden was created towards the end of the 19th century and has a romantic character, dotted with gentle hills and scenic lakes. Of particular interest is the 19th-century palm house, designed by Alfred Koerner. The huge greenhouses were constructed in 1984–87 to a design by Engelbert Kremser. The most popular plants are the tropical species such

↑ The magnificent Palm House and Chinese pavilion *(inset)* in the Botanischer Garten

as the orchids and cacti. There is also the Botanisches Museum (Botanical Museum), home to an excellent collection of plant specimens.

---

 ⑧

Wrangel-Schlösschen (Gusthaus Steglitz)

🏠 Schlossstrasse 48
📞 902 99 39 24 Ⓤ Rathaus Steglitz 🚍 M2, M48, M85

This compact Neo-Classical palace derives its name from Field Marshal Wrangel, the building's mid-19th-century owner. However, the house was built much earlier, in 1804. The simplicity and clarity of its details make it a prime example of early Neo-Classical architecture. It currently houses the cultural centre for the district of Steglitz.

---

⑨

Alliiertenmuseum

🏠 Clayallee 135 Ⓤ Oskar-Helene-Heim 🕙 10am-6pm Thu-Tue 🌐 alliierten museum.de

In the heart of the former US military sector of Berlin is the Allied Museum, which combines exhibition space with open-air grounds.

A fascinating exhibition of everyday objects, military memorabilia, photographs and films explains life during the Cold War and the story of Berlin and its inhabitants between 1945 and 1994. Tours are by appointment.

---

 ⑩

St-Annen-Kirche

🏠 Königin-Luise-Strasse 55
📞 831 38 13 Ⓤ Dahlem Dorf 🚍 110, X11, X83 🕙 11am-1pm Sat & Sun

At the centre of a small leafy cemetery stands the Gothic 14th-century St-Annen-Kirche. The church was built initially with a plain roof. The chancel was completed in the 15th century, the vaulting in the 17th century and the tower was added in the 18th century.

Inside, 14th-century wall paintings depict scenes from the life of St Anna, alongside items of ecclesiastical furnishings. These include a 15th-century painting of the Crucifixion and 11 late Gothic figures of saints.

The cemetery, which dates back to the 13th century, is also worth exploring. It has a 1996 monument dedicated to the victims of Nazi tyranny. During the war, the pastor here was Martin Niemöller, a founder of the Confessing Church, a Protestant movement that resisted the Nazification of churches. He was sent to a concentration camp in 1938, but he survived his imprisonment.

COUNTRY CHURCHES

The establishment of Greater Berlin in 1920 swallowed up nearly 60 villages, some of which were older than the city itself. Now they have evolved into large residential estates, and more than 50 of the parish churches have survived. The most treasured, dating from the 13th century, are in the south of Berlin, for instance in Britz by Backbergstrasse, Buckow (Alt-Buckow), Mariendorf (Alt-Mariendorf) and Marienfelde (Alt-Marienfelde).

37

POTSDAM

 & Potsdam Hauptbahnhof Park Sanssouci, Charlottenhof 605, 606, 610, 631, N14, X5, X15 91, 94, 98 Luisenplatz 3; 9:30am-6pm Mon-Sat, 10am-4pm Sun & hols; potsdamtourismus.de

Southwest of Berlin lies Potsdam, the capital of Brandenburg and one of the most interesting cities in Germany. Tourists flock here to see the royal Park Sanssouci, where an eclectic and lovely mix of buildings seem to bloom along with the plants and flowers in beautifully landscaped gardens.

①

Park Sanssouci

 Schopenhauerstrasse/ Zur Historischen Mühle 612, 614, 695

This vast park (whose name means "without worries" in French), covers some 3 sq km (1 sq mile). It was established in 1725 on the site of an orchard; however, it was only transformed into an enormous landscaped park when construction work began on Schloss Sanssouci (p254). Today, the park is made up of smaller gardens dating from different eras, each of which has been maintained in the original style. At the foot of Schloss Sanssouci is the oldest section, containing the Dutch garden, a number of fountains and the French-style Lustgarten (pleasure garden), with a symmetrical layout and lovely rose beds.

The eastern part of the park is called the Rehgarten, a beautifully landscaped park in the English style designed by Peter Joseph Lenné. This park extends right up to the Neues Palais (p252). To the south, surrounding the small palace, extends the Charlottenhof Park, also designed by Lenné. In the northern section of the park, next to the Orangerie (p257), is the Nordischer Garten and the Paradiesgarten.

The range of different garden styles makes a simple stroll through this park particularly pleasant. There are also a large number of sculptures, columns, obelisks and grottoes for the visitor to explore. The vistas and perspectives that suddenly open up across the park and the picturesque groupings of trees are also beautiful.

②

Communs

 Am Neuen Palais 605, 695

This area of Park Sanssouci consists of a pair of two-storey

Vineyards leading up to one of the palaces in Park Sanssouci

pavilions linked by a semicircular colonnade. They are unusually elegant buildings considering they were used for servants' quarters and the palace kitchens. However, they also served to screen from view the cultivated fields that extended past the park from the palace.

The Communs were completed in 1769 by Carl von Gontard, to a design by Jean-Laurent Le Geay. The buildings are enclosed by an elegant courtyard. The kitchen was in the south pavilion, linked to the palace by an underground passageway, and the north pavilion

The Communs, tucked away behind the Neues Palais

accommodated the servants of the king's guests. Today, the rectors' offices and part of the medicine department of the University of Potsdam are located in the Communs.

③ 🖍 🅼 🍴 🍽 🛍

NEUES PALAIS

📍 Am Neuen Palais 🚌 605, 606, 695 🕐 Apr-Oct: 10am-6pm Wed-Mon; Nov-Mar: 10am-5pm Wed-Mon 🌐 spsg.de

The stunning New Palace was designed to be an impressive display of Prussia's glory and power after its victory in the Seven Years' War.

This imposing Baroque palace, on the main avenue in Park Sanssouci, was built at the request of Frederick the Great. The initial plans were prepared in 1750 by Georg Wenzeslaus von Knobelsdorff. However, construction only began in 1763, after the Seven Years' War (1756–63), to a design by Johann Gottfried Büring, Jean Laurent Le Geay and Carl von Gontard. The result was a vast two-storey building, decorated with hundreds of sculptures and more than 200 richly adorned rooms, which together make up one of Germany's most beautiful palaces.

↑ The entrance to the Neues Palais is through the gate on the western façade

Did You Know?

The palace was rarely used as a royal residence, but instead hosted guests for celebrations.

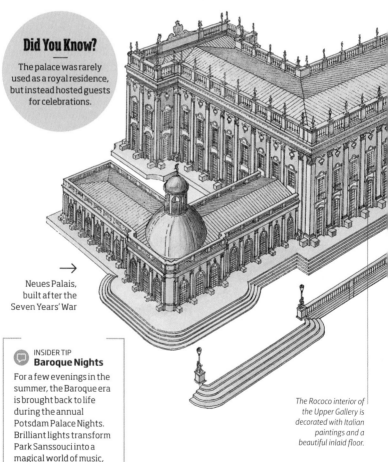

→ Neues Palais, built after the Seven Years' War

💬 INSIDER TIP
Baroque Nights

For a few evenings in the summer, the Baroque era is brought back to life during the annual Potsdam Palace Nights. Brilliant lights transform Park Sanssouci into a magical world of music, theatre and history.

The Rococo interior of the Upper Gallery is decorated with Italian paintings and a beautiful inlaid floor.

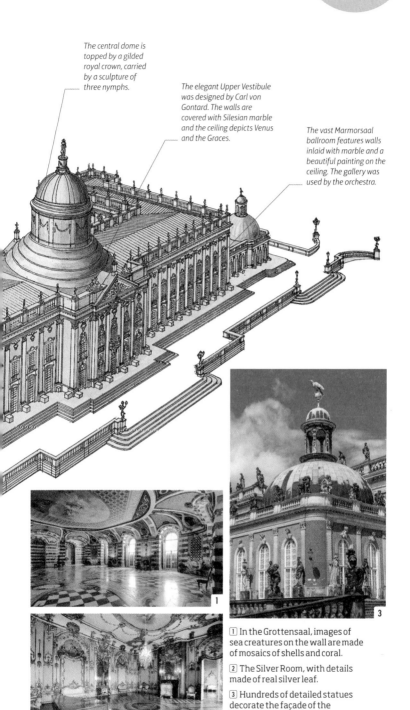

The central dome is topped by a gilded royal crown, carried by a sculpture of three nymphs.

The elegant Upper Vestibule was designed by Carl von Gontard. The walls are covered with Silesian marble and the ceiling depicts Venus and the Graces.

The vast Marmorsaal ballroom features walls inlaid with marble and a beautiful painting on the ceiling. The gallery was used by the orchestra.

1 In the Grottensaal, images of sea creatures on the wall are made of mosaics of shells and coral.

2 The Silver Room, with details made of real silver leaf.

3 Hundreds of detailed statues decorate the façade of the Neues Palais, as well as the grounds and the palace interior.

④ 🚲 📷 🏛

SCHLOSS SANSSOUCI

📍 Park Sanssouci 🚌 612, 614, 650, 695 🚊 91, 94, X8 🕐 Apr–Oct: 10am–5:30pm Tue–Sun; Nov–Mar: 10am–4:30pm Tue–Sun 🌐 spsg.de

A terraced vineyard creates a peaceful approach to Sanssouci Palace, the oldest building in the Park Sanssouci complex. Designed as an intimate royal hideaway, this miniature Rococo palace has captivated visitors for centuries.

The name Sanssouci is French for "without a care" and gives a good indication of the flamboyant character of this enchanting Rococo palace, built in 1745. The original sketches, made by Friedrich II (Frederick the Great) himself, were finalized by Georg Wenzeslaus von Knobelsdorff. The glorious interiors were designed by Knobelsdorff and Johann August Nahl. The king clearly loved this palace, as his final wishes were that he should be buried here, near the tomb of his Italian greyhounds. He was actually interred in the Garnisonkirche, Potsdam, but his wishes were eventually carried out in 1991.

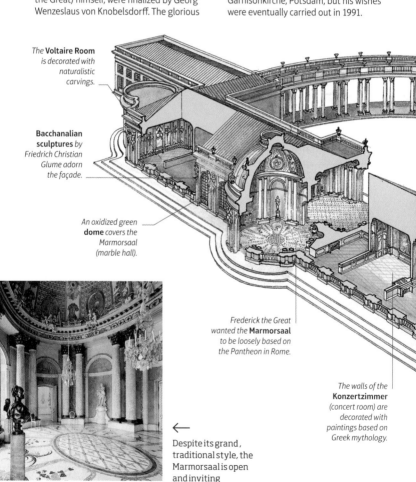

The **Voltaire Room** is decorated with naturalistic carvings.

Bacchanalian sculptures by Friedrich Christian Glume adorn the façade.

An oxidized green **dome** covers the Marmorsaal (marble hall).

Frederick the Great wanted the **Marmorsaal** to be loosely based on the Pantheon in Rome.

The walls of the **Konzertzimmer** (concert room) are decorated with paintings based on Greek mythology.

← Despite its grand, traditional style, the Marmorsaal is open and inviting

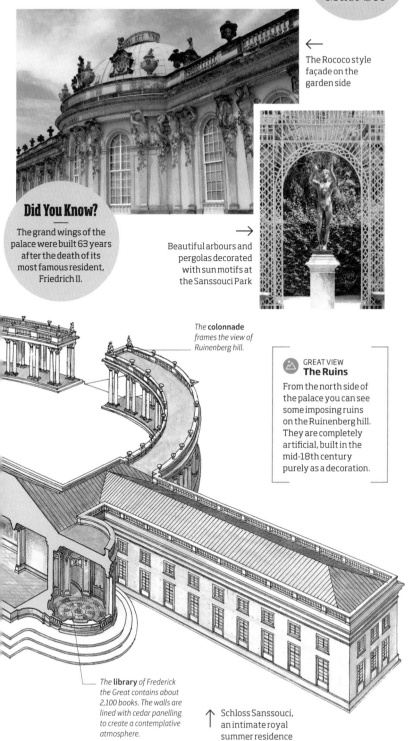

← The Rococo style façade on the garden side

Did You Know?

The grand wings of the palace were built 63 years after the death of its most famous resident, Friedrich II.

→ Beautiful arbours and pergolas decorated with sun motifs at the Sanssouci Park

*The **colonnade** frames the view of Ruinenberg hill.*

GREAT VIEW
The Ruins

From the north side of the palace you can see some imposing ruins on the Ruinenberg hill. They are completely artificial, built in the mid-18th century purely as a decoration.

*The **library** of Frederick the Great contains about 2,100 books. The walls are lined with cedar panelling to create a contemplative atmosphere.*

↑ Schloss Sanssouci, an intimate royal summer residence

EXPERIENCE MORE

Neue Kammern

🏠 Zur Historischen Mühle (Lustgarten) 📞 0331 969 42 00 🚌 695 🕐 Apr–Oct: 10am–5:30pm Tue–Sun

The New Chambers is a Rococo pavilion containing residential apartments. It is the mirror image of the Bildergalerie (p258) and was originally built as an orangery in 1747 to a design by Georg Wenzeslaus von Knobelsdorff. In 1777,

---

POTSDAM TOWN GATES

The city of Potsdam was enclosed by a wall in 1722. This wall did not serve a defensive purpose – it was supposed to contain criminals and prevent soldiers from deserting. When the borders of the town were extended in 1733, new districts were also enclosed by the wall. There was a total of five city gates, of which three remain. One of these is the Jägertor, which has survived in its original condition and dates from 1733.

JÄGERTOR

Frederick the Great (Friedrich II) ordered the building to be remodelled as guest accommodation. The architect, Georg Christian Unger, left the elegant Baroque exterior of the orangery largely untouched and instead concentrated on converting the interior. As well as the sumptuous guest suites, the new design included four elegant halls. The best of these is the Ovidsaal, with its rich reliefs and marble floors.

---

⑥

Schloss Charlottenhof

🏠 Geschwister-Scholl-Strasse 34a (Park Charlottenhof) 🚌 605, 606 🚊 91, 94 🕐 1 May–31 Oct: 10am–5pm Tue–Sun 🌐 spsg.de

The small Neo-Classical Charlottenhof Palace is located in the southern extension of Park Sanssouci, Park Charlottenhof. It was designed by Karl Friedrich Schinkel (p29) in 1829 for the heir to the throne, later King Friedrich Wilhelm IV. This small one-storey building was built in the style of a Roman villa. The rear of the palace has a portico that opens out onto the garden terrace. Some of the wall paintings designed by Schinkel, which were made in the so-called Pompeiian style, are still in place. The most interesting part of the interior is the blue-and-white-striped Humboldt Room, also called the Tent Room due to its resemblance to a tent. The palace is surrounded by a picturesque landscaped park which was designed by Peter Joseph Lenné.

↑ Italianate styling at the Römische Bäder, or Roman baths

⑦

Römische Bäder

🏠 Lenné-Strasse (Park Charlottenhof) 🚌 605, 606 🚊 91, 94, 98 🕐 May–Oct: 10am–5:30pm Tue–Sun 🌐 spsg.de

An attractive group of pavilions, situated by the edge of a lake, forms the "Roman Baths", which actually served as accommodation for the king's guests. It was designed by Karl Friedrich Schinkel, with the involvement of Ludwig Persius, between 1829 and 1840. At the front is the gardener's house, which is adjacent to an asymmetrical low tower in the style of an Italian Renaissance villa. In the background, to the left, extends the former bathing pavilion, which is currently used for temporary art exhibitions. All of the pavilions are arranged around an internal garden planted with a multicoloured carpet of shrubs. A closer

> **The small Neo-Classical Charlottenhof Palace is located in the southern extension of Park Sanssouci, Park Charlottenhof.**

↑ Gilded figures *(inset)* eating, drinking and making music surround the Chinese House

look will reveal that many of these colourful plants are actually vegetables.

⑧ Chinesisches Haus

🏠 Ökonomieweg (Rehgarten) 🚌 606, 695 🚋 91, 94 🕐 May-Oct: 10am-5:30pm Tue-Sun 🌐 spsg.de

The lustrous, gilded pavilion that can be seen glistening from a distance is the Chinese House. Chinese art was popular during the Rococo period – people wore Chinese silk, rooms were wallpapered with Chinese designs, furniture was lacquered, drinks were served in Chinese porcelain and Chinese pavilions were built in gardens.

The Chinesisches Haus was built in Park Sanssouci between 1754 and 1756 to a design by Johann Gottfried Büring. It is circular in shape, with a centrally located main hall surrounded by three studies. Between each of these are pretty *trompe l'oeil* porticoes. Ornaments, together with gilded figures of Chinese gentlemen and ladies, surround the pavilion. Originally the Chinesisches Haus served as a tearoom and a summer dining room. Today, it houses a collection of porcelain and has beautiful interior decoration featuring gilding and ceiling paintings.

⑨
Orangerie

🏠 Maulbeerallee (Nordischer Garten) 🚌 695 🔒 For renovations 🌐 spsg.de

Towering above the park is the Orangerie, designed in the Italian Renaissance style and crowned by a colonnade. The Orangerie was built to house guests, not plants. It was constructed between 1851 and 1860 by Friedrich August Stüler on the initiative and direction of Friedrich Wilhelm IV. The final design was partly based on the plans of Ludwig Persius. It served as a guest residence for the king's sister and her husband, Tsar Nicholas I. The rooms were grouped around the Raphael Hall, which was based on the Sala Regia in the Vatican and decorated with copies of the works of Italian artist Raphael. It is worth climbing up to the observation terrace for the view over Potsdam. The Orangerie is temporarily closed for renovations.

↑ The Bildergalerie, the first gallery built to house a ruler's art collection in Germany

Historische Mühle

🏠 Maulbeerallee 5
🚌 695 ⏰ Apr-Oct: 10am-6pm daily; Nov & Jan-Mar: 10am-4pm Sat & Sun
🚫 Dec 🌐 historische-muehle-potsdam.de

A mill has been located here since the early 18th century, although this is actually a reconstruction, dating from 1993. According to local legend, the original windmill was so noisy that Frederick the Great ordered it to be dismantled. However, a court upheld the miller's cause and the mill stayed. In 1790 a new windmill was built in its place, which lasted until 1945. The mill currently houses a museum of mechanical windmills.

Bildergalerie

🏠 Zur Historischen Mühle
📞 0331 969 42 00 🚌 695
⏰ May-Oct: 10am-5:30pm Tue-Sun

The Picture Gallery, housed in the building adjacent to Schloss Sanssouci was the first purpose-built gallery in Germany. It was constructed in 1764 to a design by J G Büring. The façade facing the garden is ornamented with an allegorical tableau representing Art, Education and Crafts, while busts of renowned artists have been placed in the windows.

The gallery contains an exhibition of Baroque paintings once owned by Frederick the Great, although part of the collection can be found in the Gemäldegalerie (p158). Highlights include Caravaggio's *Doubting Thomas* and Guido Reni's *Death of Cleopatra*, as well as a number of canvases by Rubens and van Dyck. The stunning interior has a floor inlaid with yellow marble, complementing the gilded ceiling.

Friedenskirche

🏠 Am Grünen Gitter 🚌 695
🚊 91, 94 ⏰ Nov-Mar: 11am-4pm 🌐 spsg.de

Close to Schloss Sanssouci (p254) is Friedenskirche, or the Church of Peace. The foundation stone was laid by King Friedrich Wilhelm IV in 1845 and the church was completed in 1848. Designed by Ludwig Persius, Friedrich August Stüler and Ludwig Hesse, the church is based on San Clemente in Rome.

Inside, the vaulted ceiling of the apse is covered by a 12th-century mosaic that depicts the figure of Christ as a judge. This Byzantine mosaic was originally located in the church of San Capriano on the island of Murano in Venice. Next to the church is a mausoleum containing the tombs of Friedrich Wilhelm I, Friedrich Wilhelm IV and Kaiser Friedrich III.

Surrounding Friedenskirche is the Marlygarten, created in the mid-19th century. The garden was also designed by royal architect Ludwig Persius.

Did You Know?

—

Friedenskirche's mosaic was rescued from a Venetian church and brought to Potsdam by Friedrich Wilhelm IV.

⑬

Nikolaikirche

🏠 Am Alten Markt 🚌 604, 605, 609, 610, 695 🚋 91, 92, 93, 94, 96, 99, X98 🕐 10am–7pm Mon–Sat, 11:30am–7pm Sun 🌐 nikolai-potsdam.de

This imposing church, built in a late Neo-Classical style, is the most beautiful church in Potsdam. It was designed in 1830 by Karl Friedrich Schinkel (p29) and the building work was overseen by Ludwig Persius. The main body of the church is based on a square cross, with a semicircular presbytery.

It was decided only in the 1840s to crown the church with a vast dome, supported on a colonnaded tambour (a wall that supports a dome). Schinkel had envisaged this from the beginning, but it was not part of the king's orders. It was first thought that the dome would be supported by a wooden structure, though ultimately it was built using iron, between 1843 and 1848, according to a design by Persius and Friedrich

August Stüler. The interiors and the ecclesiastical furnishings of the church date back to the 1850s, and in the main area of the church they were based on the earlier interior designs by Schinkel.

In front of the church is an obelisk built between 1753 and 1755 to a design by Prussian architect Georg Wenzeslaus von Knobelsdorff. It was decorated by medallions with the portraits of Prussian rulers, but during restorations carried out after World War II, they were replaced with portraits of renowned Prussian architects.

---

⑭

Marmorpalais

🏠 Am Ufer des Heiligen Sees (Neuer Garten) 🚌 692, 695 🕐 Nov–Mar: 10am–4pm Sat, Sun & hols; Apr: 10am–5:30pm Sat, Sun & hols; May–Oct: 10am–7:30pm Tue–Sun 🌐 spsg.de

The Marble Palace is situated on the edge of the lake in

Neuer Garten (p267), a park northeast of the centre of Potsdam. This small palace is a beautiful example of early Neo-Classical architecture and owes its name to its façade, which is clad in Silesian marble.

The square main body of the palace was the initiative of King Friedrich Wilhelm II. The original building was completed in 1791, but it turned out to be too small, and in 1797 it was extended. An extra floor and two wings were added, which gave the Marmorpalais the character of a Palladian villa.

The main part of the palace contains Neo-Classical furnishings from the late 18th century, including furniture from the workshops of Roentgen and porcelain from the English firm Wedgwood. The interiors of the wings date from slightly later, from the 1840s. The concert hall in the right-hand wing is particularly beautiful. King Friedrich Wilhelm II died in this palace in 1797.

← The Italianate campanile, or bell tower, visible from the tranquil cloister of Friedenskirche

Schloss Cecilienhof, scene of the Potsdam Conference

⑮ Schloss Cecilienhof

⌂ Am Neuen Garten
☎ 0331 969 42 00 🚌 692
⏰ For renovations

Completed in 1917, the Cecilienhof Palace was the last palace built by the House of Hohenzollern that ruled the Kingdom of Prussia and the German Empire until the end of World War I. Designed by Paul Schultze-Naumburg in the style of an English country manor, the palace is a sprawling, asymmetrical building with wooden beams that make a pretty herringbone pattern on its exterior walls.

Schloss Cecilienhof remained the Hohenzollern family residence after they lost the crown; the family remained in Potsdam until February 1945, when it played a brief but important role in European history: it was here that the 1945 Potsdam Conference took place. Today, it functions as a first-class hotel and restaurant, where visitors can relax amid carefully tended shrubbery. Most of the historic furnishings used during the famous Potsdam conference are on display. The Cecilienhof Palace is closed for building and restoration work until 2027.

THE POTSDAM CONFERENCE OF 1945

On 17 July 1945, the heads of government of Great Britain, the United States and the Soviet Union met in Schloss Cecilienhof to confirm the decisions made earlier that year at Yalta. The aim of both conferences was to resolve the problems arising at the end of World War II. They decided to abolish the Nazi Party, to limit the size of the German military and monitor it indefinitely, and also to punish war criminals and establish reparations. The conference played a major part in establishing a political balance of power in Europe.

Stalin Truman Churchill

⑯ Holländisches Viertel

⌂ Friedrich-Ebert-/ Kurfürsten-/Hebbel-/ Gutenbergstrasse 🚌 604, 609, 692 🚃 91, 92, 94, 96

Just as amazing as the Russian district of Alexandrowka (p266) is Potsdam's charming Dutch Quarter. The area is home to numerous independent shops and boutiques, galleries, cafés and beer cellars, especially along the central Mittelstrasse, all of

> The palace is a sprawling, asymmetrical building with wooden beams making a pretty herringbone pattern on its exterior walls.

which draw tourists and day trippers visiting from Berlin.

The area was first established when Dutch workers, invited by Friedrich Wilhelm I, arrived in Potsdam at the beginning of the 18th century. Between 1733 and 1742, a settlement was built for them, comprising 134 gabled houses arranged in four groups, according to plans by Johann Boumann the Elder. They were built from small red bricks and finished with stone and plaster details. These houses are typically three-storey, with picturesque roofs and gables.

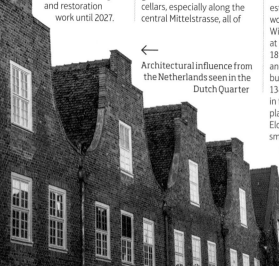
← Architectural influence from the Netherlands seen in the Dutch Quarter

↑ The graceful tower of the church of St Peter and St Paul

Restaurant Juliette

Francophile spot Juliette is one of Potsdam's most popular dining spots thanks to its interesting range of dishes (from couscous to steak and *foie gras*) and great wine list.

🏠 Jägerstrasse 39
⏰ 5-10pm Wed-Fri, noon-2:30pm & 5-10pm Sat & Sun 🌐 restaurant-juliette.de

€€€

Biosphäre

🏠 Georg-Hermann-Allee 99 🚌 604, 609, 638, 697 🚊 96 ⏰ 9am-6pm Mon-Fri, 10am-7pm Sat, Sun & hols 🌐 biosphaere-potsdam.de

This large glass-and-steel heated greenhouse was built to create a tropical rainforest environment that is now home to 20,000 different plants and animals (including a butterfly house), waterfalls and more. Follow the various jungle pathways across mangrove swamps and up to the tree canopy, while learning about the various flora and fauna. The tropically themed café is a decent spot for a drink and a snack; book ahead if you want to have breakfast.

Französische Kirche

🏠 Bassinplatz 📞 0331 29 12 19 🚌 604, 609, 612 🚊 93, 94, 99 ⏰ Late Mar-Oct: 1:30-5pm daily

The French Church, which is reminiscent of the Pantheon in Rome, was built especially for the Huguenots in 1752. Following their expulsion from France, they were given the option of settling in Prussia in 1685. Those who settled in Potsdam initially benefited from the hospitality of other churches, then eventually the Französische Kirche was built for them. It was designed by Johann Boumann the Elder in the shape of an ellipse. The front elevation is supported by a grand columned portico. The side niches, which are the entrances of the church, are decorated with the allegorical figures of Faith and Knowledge. The interior dates from the 1830s and is based on designs by Karl Friedrich Schinkel.

Peter und Paul Kirche

🏠 Bassinplatz 📞 0331 230 79 90 🚌 604, 609, 612 🚊 91, 92, 94, 96 ⏰ Mon-Sat; hours vary, call ahead

This 19th-century church was the first large Catholic church built in Potsdam, at the initiative of Friedrich Wilhelm IV. The work of Wilhelm Salzenberg, it was built in 1870, in the shape of a Neo-Romanesque cross. Its slender tower is a copy of the campanile of San Zeno Maggiore in Verona, Italy. Inside are three beautiful paintings by French painter Antoine Pesne.

↑ The Marstall, a former stables and now a film museum

⑳ Neuer Landtag

🏛 Alter Markt 1 🕐 Hours vary, check website
🌐 landtag.brandenburg.de

Although this building now houses the parliament of the federal state of Brandenburg, its elaborate façade is a replica of the Potsdam Royal Palace that once stood here. Originally built in 1662, over time the palace was greatly enlarged and modernized to become a massive two-storey building with three wings, an elegant courtyard and a superb gateway crowned by a tower. A bombing raid in 1945 left the palace in ruins and it was finally demolished in 1960.

At the start of the 21st century, it was decided to construct a replica of the former palace façade, along with a modern interior. The works were finished in 2013 and the building now houses the Brandenburg parliament. Visitors are free to enter the inner courtyard through the entrance gate, the Fortuna Portal, as well as the entrance hall, with its famous Knobelsdorff staircase. There is also a roof terrace, a canteen and exhibition space.

㉑ Marstall (Filmmuseum)

🏛 Breite Strasse 1A 🚌 605, 695 🚊 91, 92, 96, 98
🕐 10am–6pm Tue–Sun
🌐 filmmuseum-potsdam.de

This Baroque pavilion, once used as a royal stables, is the only remaining building of a former royal residence. It was first established in 1714 by refashioning an orangery built by Johann Nering in 1685. In 1746 it was extended and refashioned once more. It suffered extensive damage in World War II, and in 1977, after major restoration, it was converted into a film museum. As well as mounting temporary exhibitions, the museum documents the history and work of the Babelsberg studios, Germany's earliest film studios. Exhibits include old projectors, cameras and other equipment as well as props used in some of the most famous German films.

㉒ Telegrafenberg

🏛 Albert-Einstein-Strasse
🚉 Potsdam Hauptbahnhof

The buildings on the Telegrafenberg hill are considered to be some of the best 20th-century structures in the world and attract many admirers of

---

EARLY GERMAN CINEMA

German cinema gained international prominence with the rise of Expressionism. The UFA film studios in Babelsberg became the heart of the film industry and rivalled Hollywood as a centre for innovation. Many famous films were produced here, including the Expressionist masterpiece *The Cabinet of Dr Caligari* (1920) by Robert Wiene, *Nosferatu* (1922) by Friedrich Murnau and Fritz Lang's futuristic *Metropolis* (1927). After Hitler came to power, many directors and actors left Germany.

modern architecture. The hill received its current name in 1832, when an optical telegraph station linking Berlin and Koblenz was built here. In the late 19th century, various educational institutes were located here, including the Institute of Astrophysics, for which the complex of buildings in yellow brick was built.

The meandering avenues lead to a picturesque clearing where the small Einsteinturm (Einstein's Tower) breaks through the surrounding trees. Specially designed to observe the solar system, the tower was intended to provide information that would support Einstein's Theory of Relativity. It was built in 1920 by Erich Mendelsohn and is regarded as one of the finest architectural examples of German Expressionism. Its fantastical appearance was intended to show what could be achieved with reinforced concrete. However, due to cost, everything above the first storey is

→

The Wasserwerk Sanssouci, with its decorative dome and Moorish brickwork

brickwork covered in plaster. The building is open from May to October for guided tours only, which must be pre-booked (call 0331 749 94 69).

Filmpark Babelsberg

📍 August-Bebel Strasse 26-53 (enter at Grossbeeren Strasse) 🚇 Griebnitzsee 🚌 601, 619, 690 🕐 Hours vary, check website ❌ Nov–Feb 🌐 filmpark-babelsberg.de

This amazing theme park was established on the site of the film studios where Germany's first films were produced in 1912. From 1917, the studio belonged to Universum Film AG (UFA), which produced some of the most renowned films of the silent era, such as *Metropolis*. Nazi propaganda films were also made here.

The studio is still operational today, although part of the complex is open to visitors. There are plenty of sets from old films to explore, as well as behind-the-scenes professionals who demonstrate their skills to visitors – from set-building and makeup to handling animal stars. Older children can enjoy an explosive stunt show, 4D cinema, an interactive XD gaming arena and a spooky "submarine of horror"; for younger children there are gentler rides and activities, many featuring much-loved German children's characters.

Wasserwerk Sanssouci

📍 Breite Strasse 28 📞 0331 969 42 25 🚌 605, 606 🚋 91, 94, X98 🕐 May–Oct: 10am–5:30pm Sat, Sun & hols

Designed by Ludwig Persius in 1842, the Sanssouci Waterworks were built to resemble a mosque. The building actually contains a special steam pump that serviced the fountains in Park Sanssouci *(p250)*. Inside you can see the preserved steam-powered machinery made by the Borsig company.

Altes Rathaus

⌂ Am Alten Markt 9 ☏ 0331 2896868 🚌 603, 605, 609, 631, 638, 639, 695 🚋 91, 92, 93, 96, 98, 99 ⌚ 10am–5pm Tue, Wed & Fri, 10am–7pm Thu, 10am–6pm Sat & Sun

The Old Town Hall is an elegant, colonnaded building, constructed in 1753 on the eastern side of Alter Markt. The uppermost storey, which features an ornamental attic roof, is decorated with the crest of Potsdam and allegorical sculptures. A glass passageway links the building to a neighbouring mid-18th-century building housing the Potsdam Museum. The museum's rich collection of artifacts tells the story of Potsdam's development. A nearby branch of the museum, Memorial Lindenstrasse 54/55, is a former prison and interrogation centre used by both the Nazi and East German regimes.

Alexandrowka

⌂ Russische Kolonie Allee/ Puschkinallee 🚌 604, 609, 692, 697 🚋 92, 96 ⌚ Hours vary, check website ⓦ alexandrowka.de

A trip to Alexandrowka takes the visitor into the world of Pushkin's stories. Wooden houses decorated with carved motifs and set in their own gardens create a very pretty residential estate. Although they appear to be traditional Russian houses, they were constructed in 1826 under the direction of a German military architect for the singers of a Russian choir. The choir was set up in 1812 to entertain the troops and was recruited from

↑ *Dacha*-style wooden house in former Russian estate of Alexandrowka

Russian prisoners of war who had fought with Napoleon. In 1815, when the Prussians and the Russians joined forces, the choir was retained by Friedrich Wilhelm III.

Peter Joseph Lenné was responsible for the overall appearance of the estate, and it was named Alexandrowka after Tsar Alexander I. It is

based on the shape of the cross of St Andrew inscribed within an oval. In all, 12 houses were built here, as well as an outhouse that now has a small museum on the choir. Some of the dwellings are still owned by the descendants of the choir. To the north of this estate stands the Russian Orthodox church of Alexander Nevski.

Peter Joseph Lenné was responsible for the overall appearance of the estate, and it was named Alexandrowka after Tsar Alexander I.

(27)

Museum Barberini

⌂ Humboldtstrasse 5-6
Ⓢ Potsdam Hauptbahnhof
🚌 603, 605, 606, 609, 614, 631, 638, 650 🚊 91, 92, 93, 96, 98, 99 ⏱ 10am-7pm Wed-Mon 🌐 museum-barberini.com

This museum is located inside a stunning replica of Frederick the Great's 18th-century Barberini Palace. The exhibits on permanent display were built from a collection of French Impressionist landscape paintings donated by the museum's founder, philanthropist Hasso Plattner. On display are 100 Impressionist and Modern paintings, with more than 30 by Monet. These works form Europe's largest collection of 19th- and 20th-century French paintings outside Paris.

(28)

Neuer Garten

⌂ Am Neuen Garten 🚌 692

Running along the edge of Heiliger See lake, on what was once the site of palace vineyards, is the New Garden, a park laid out between 1787 and 1791. It was landscaped originally by Johann August Eyserbeck following the instructions of Friedrich Wilhelm II, while the current layout was created by Peter Joseph Lenné *(p171)* in 1816.

It is a Romantic park ornamented with numerous pavilions and sculptures. The charming Marmorpalais stands beside the lake, while the northern section contains the early 20th-century Schloss Cecilienhof *(p262)*. Elsewhere you can see the red and green gardeners' houses, the pyramid-shaped ice-house and a Neo-Gothic library pavilion completed in 1794.

View over the Neuer Garten from Italianate Belvedere Pfingstberg

NEED TO KNOW

A train crossing the Oberbaumbrücke

BEFORE
YOU GO

Things change, so plan ahead to make the most of your trip. Be prepared for all eventualities by considering the following points before you travel.

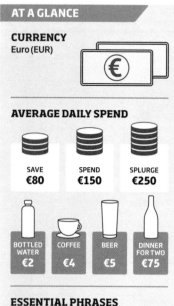

CURRENCY
Euro (EUR)

AVERAGE DAILY SPEND

SAVE	SPEND	SPLURGE
€80	€150	€250

BOTTLED WATER	COFFEE	BEER	DINNER FOR TWO
€2	€4	€5	€75

ESSENTIAL PHRASES

Hello	Guten Tag
Goodbye	Auf Wiedersehen
Please	Bitte
Thank you	Danke
Do you speak English?	Sprechen Sie Englisch?
I don't understand	Ich verstehe nicht

ELECTRICITY SUPPLY

Power sockets are type F, fitting two-pronged plugs. Standard voltage is 230 volts.

Passports and Visas

For entry requirements, including visas, consult your nearest German embassy or check the **German Federal Foreign Office** website. Citizens of the UK, US, Canada, Australia and New Zealand do not need visas for stays of up to three months but in future must apply in advance for the European Travel Information and Authorization System (**ETIAS**). Visitors from other countries may also require an ETIAS, so check before travelling. EU nationals do not need a visa or an ETIAS.
German Federal Foreign Office
🆆 auswaertiges-amt.de
European Travel Information and Authorization System (ETIAS)
🆆 travel-europe.europa.eu/etias_en

Government Advice

Now more than ever, it is important to consult both your and the German government's advice before travelling. The **UK Foreign, Commonwealth & Development Office (FCDO)**, the **US Department of State**, the **Australian Department of Foreign Affairs and Trade** and the **German Federal Foreign Office** offer the latest information on security, health and local regulations.
Australian Department of Foreign Affairs and Trade
🆆 smartraveller.gov.au
German Federal Foreign Office
🆆 auswaertiges-amt.de
UK Foreign, Commonwealth & Development Office (FCDO)
🆆 gov.uk/foreign-travel-advice
US Department of State
🆆 travel.state.gov

Customs Information

You can find information on the laws relating to goods and currency taken in or out of Germany from the **Zoll** (Federal Customs Service) website.
Zoll
🆆 zoll.de

Insurance

We recommend taking out a comprehensive insurance policy covering theft, loss of belongings, medical care, cancellations and delays, and read the small print carefully.

EU citizens are eligible for free emergency medical care in Germany provided they have a valid **EHIC** (European Health Insurance Card). UK citizens are also eligible, but will need a valid **GHIC** (Global Health Insurance Card).

EHIC
🔳 ec.europa.eu
GHIC
🔳 gov.uk/global-health-insurance-card

Vaccinations

No inoculations are needed for Germany.

Booking Accommodation

Berlin offers a huge variety of accommodation to suit any budget, ranging from luxury five-star hotels to family run B&Bs and budget hostels. Lodgings can fill up during the busy summer months and prices are inflated during peak seasons, so it's worth booking in advance.

A comprehensive list of accommodation to suit all needs can be found on **Visit Berlin**, the city's official tourism website (p276).

Money

Major credit, debit and prepaid currency cards are accepted in most shops and establishments. Contactless payments have become the norm since the COVID-19 pandemic, though it is still not used on public transport. Carry cash, as some smaller businesses don't accept card.

Travellers with Specific Requirements

Berlin's wide streets and open spaces make it a wheelchair-friendly city. Pavements are sloped at junctions and most public buildings are fitted with lifts and ramps. Wheelchairs can be hired from the **German Red Cross** (DRK).

Not all S- and U-Bahn stations are equipped with lifts. If you are in the U-Bahn, wait at the head of the platform and the driver will put up a ramp. In the S-Bahn, speak to the station manager to have a ramp set up. BVG maps show all of the accessible stations. Buses with a wheelchair symbol have a ramp. Download the free **accessBerlin** app (p276) for details of the most accessible routes around the city.

Berlin's charitable association for the blind and sight-impaired, the **Allgemeiner Blinden- und Sehbehindertenverein**, offers practical advice and useful information.

Allgemeiner Blinden-und Sehbehindertenverein
🔳 absv.de
German Red Cross
🔳 drk-berlin.de/reservierung.html

Language

German is the official language, but Berlin is an international city, and English is almost as prevalent as German.

Opening Hours

Situations can change quickly and unexpectedly. Always check before visiting attractions and hospitality venues for up-to-date opening hours and booking requirements.

Monday Many museums and some major tourist attractions are closed for the day.
Sunday Most shops and some small businesses close early or for the entire day.
Public holidays Schools, post offices and banks are closed for the entire day.

PUBLIC HOLIDAYS	
1 Jan	New Year's Day
Apr/Mar	Good Friday
Apr/Mar	Easter Monday
1 May	Labour Day
End May	Ascension Day
May/Jun	Whit Monday
3 Oct	Day of German Unity
25 Dec	Christmas Day
26 Dec	St Stephen's Day

GETTING
AROUND

Once divided between East and West, Berlin is now connected by an excellent public transport system that crisscrosses the city and beyond.

AT A GLANCE

PUBLIC TRANSPORT COSTS
Tickets are valid on all forms of public transport in Berlin.

SINGLE

€3.80

(zones A–B)

DAY TICKET

€9.90

(zones A–B)

7-DAY TICKET

€41.30

(zones A–B)

SPEED LIMIT

MOTORWAY

130 km/h (80 mph)

REGIONAL ROADS

100 km/h (60 mph)

RURAL ROADS

70 km/h (40 mph)

URBAN AREAS

50 km/h (30 mph)

Arriving by Air

Berlin's two international airports, Tegel (TXL) and Schönefeld (SXF), were replaced in October 2020 by a new regional hub, the long-awaited **Berlin-Brandenburg (BER)**. Situated some 18 km (11 miles) southeast of the city, Berlin-Brandenburg is extremely well connected and receives regular flights from Europe, North America and Asia. Schönefeld now operates as Brandenburg's fifth terminal.

The fastest ways to and from the airport are the S-Bahn lines S9 and S45, the commuter trains RE8, RB22, RB23 and RB14 or the FEX Airport Express, direct to Berlin Hauptbahnhof in 30 minutes. Regular buses link the airport to the U-Bahn network.
Berlin-Brandenburg (BER)
W berlin-airport.de

International Train Travel

International high-speed trains connect Berlin to other European cities. Reservations are essential.

You can buy tickets and passes for multiple international train journeys from **Eurail** or **Interrail**. You may need to pay an additional reservation fee depending on which service you travel with. Always check that your pass is valid on the service you wish to travel with before boarding.

Eurostar runs a regular service from London to Brussels via the Channel Tunnel, where you can change for Berlin. **Deutsche Bahn** also runs a regular high-speed service to and from many other European destinations.

Students and those under the age of 26 can benefit from discounted rail travel both to and within the country. For more information on discounted tickets and passes, visit the **Eurail** or **Interrail** website.
Deutsche Bahn
W bahn.de
Eurail
W eurail.com
Eurostar
W eurostar.com
Interrail
W interrail.eu

GETTING TO AND FROM BERLIN BRANDENBURG

Transport to city centre	Journey time	Price
Airport Express (FEX)	25 mins	€3.80
RE7	30 mins	€3.80
RB14	30 mins	€3.80
S-Bahn (S9/S45)	50 mins	€3.80
Taxi	40 mins	€60

Long-Distance Bus Travel

Eurolines offers a variety of coach routes to Berlin from other European cities. Fares start from £19, with additional discounts for students, children and seniors. Other services include **FlixBus**, **Student Agency Bus** and **Ecolines**.

Berlin's central bus station, the **Zentraler Omnibusbahnhof (ZOB)**, is the city's largest long-distance bus station with connections to other towns and cities all over Germany and throughout the rest of Europe. Check online for the latest timetables and ticket prices.

Ecolines
W ecolines.net
Eurolines
W eurolines.eu
FlixBus
W flixbus.de
Student Agency Bus
W studentagencybus.com
Zentraler Omnibusbahnhof (ZOB)
W zob.berlin

Public Transport

The **Berliner Verkehrsbetriebe (BVG)** is Berlin's main public transport authority and service provider. Safety and hygiene measures, time-tables, ticket information, transport maps and more can be found online.
Berliner Verkehrsbetriebe (BVG)
W bvg.de

Tickets

Berlin is divided into three zones: A, B and C. Zone A covers the city centre, Zone B covers the outskirts of town and Zone C includes Berlin's suburban areas, Potsdam and its environs, as well as Berlin-Brandenburg airport. Tickets are available for each combination of zones and are valid on all forms of public transport, including regional and local trains, S-Bahn, U-Bahn and ferries, for two hours, with unlimited changes.

Ticket machines at train stations and on board trams accept cash only. Newer trains also accept debit cards (German only). Exact change is required on buses. Tickets are validated in the red or yellow time-stamping machine. If caught without a valid ticket you may face a €60 fine.

Travel is only valid in one direction, so a second ticket is required for the return journey. Short-trip (*Kurzstrecke*) tickets are cheaper, but can only be used for three stops on trains and six stops on buses and trams. Daily (*Tageskarte*) and seven-day tickets (*7-Tageskarte*), costing €8.80 and €36 respectively for zones A–B, are better value if you are making multiple journeys. Seven-day tickets also allow you to travel with one extra adult or up to three children for free after 8pm, on weekends, and on public holidays.

Discounted tickets are available with some tourist cards that combine public transport with museum entry (*p277*).

Regional and Local Train Travel

Germany's railways are operated by Deutsche Bahn (DB). The Regional Bahn and Regional Express (RB and RE) trains service the wider Berlin-Brandenburg region and beyond. Use this service for day trips to Potsdam and other smaller towns near Berlin.

Tickets can be bought from automatic machines on station platforms or from ticket offices. Special offers include a five-person ticket that is valid for one day. Berlin's universal ticketing system means that tickets for RB and RE services are also valid on the S-Bahn and U-Bahn, as well as on other public transport services in Berlin.

U-Bahn

Don't let the name confuse you; Berlin's "underground" trains also run on elevated tracks above ground. There are ten U-Bahn lines in total, each connecting with S-Bahn and other U-Bahn lines at various points across the city.

The service usually closes down between 12:30am and 4am. On weekends all lines are open 24 hours except the U4 and U55.

U-Bahn stations are marked by a rectangular blue sign, featuring a large, white letter U.

S-Bahn

The S-Bahn is faster than the U-Bahn, and its stations are further apart from one another. Berlin has 16 S-Bahn lines in total, running well beyond the confines of the city. Trains run every 10 or 20 minutes, or more frequently during peak travel times.

S-Bahn stations are marked by a round, green sign, featuring a large, white letter S.

Buses

Several bus services operate in Berlin, and conveniently they all use the same ticket tariffs.

Regular buses are marked by three-digit route codes and operate every 20 minutes between 5am and midnight. Important routes are serviced by Metro buses (marked by a letter "M" before the route number), operating 24 hours a day, and running every 10 to 20 minutes, while express buses (marked by a letter "X") run every 5 to 20 minutes.

The night bus service operates every half an hour from midnight until 4am when the U-Bahn service resumes. Regular tickets are not valid on this service. Night bus tickets can be bought directly from the driver (cash only).

All bus routes have a detailed timetable on display at each stop, and inner-city bus stops are equipped with digital screens indicating waiting times. Consult the BVG website (p273) for specific route information, safety and hygiene measures, or temporary changes to services.

Trams

Despite only servicing the eastern parts of the city, trams (Strassenbahnen) are a popular way to get around for locals and visitors to the city, particularly if you are travelling from Mitte to any part of Prenzlauer Berg.

Important routes are serviced by Metro trams running every 10 or 20 minutes, 24 hours a day. Some run a reduced service on weekends. Other tram services run every 20 minutes between 5 or 6 am and midnight.

Berlin's integrated transport system allows the use of tram tickets on buses, S- and U-Bahn train services, and vice versa. Tickets can be purchased at the usual vending points, or by using machines (coin only) on board.

Public Ferries

Visitors to Berlin may be surprised to discover that Berlin has miles of tranquil waterways. In fact, an extensive system of canals and lakes links Berlin's city centre with neighbouring Potsdam, Spandau, Charlottenburg and the area of Müggelsee, making boating in the city a fun and viable way to get around.

Six ferry lines operate in Berlin as part of the integrated public transport system. Marked by a letter F, they provide cross-river connections in locations to the east where there are no bridges. The F10 provides a particularly charming trip from Wannsee (near Potsdam) to the beautiful lakeside village of Alt-Kladow.

Taxis

Official Berlin taxis are cream, have a "Taxi" sign on the roof and have a meter on the driver's dashboard. Taxi apps such as Uber and Lyft operate in Berlin. Also popular is **BVG Mulva**, an on-demand ride sharing service.

Taxis can be hailed on the street, picked up at an official taxi rank (Würfelfunk), or booked in advance online or over the phone from firms such as **Taxi Funk Berlin** or **Würfelfunk**.

If you are travelling 2 km (1 mile) or less, ask for a short trip (Kurzstrecke) for €5 – this can only be done in taxis you have hailed from the street.

BVG Mulva
w bvg.de/en/connections/bvg-muva
Taxi Funk Berlin
w funk-taxi-berlin.de
Würfelfunk
w wuerfelfunk.de

Driving

Driving licences issued by any of the European Union member states are valid throughout the EU. If visiting from outside the EU, you may need to apply for an International Driving Permit. Check with your local automobile association before you travel.

Driving to Berlin

Berlin is connected to other major European cities via E-roads, which form the International European Road Network.

Germany's regional roads (Landesstrassen) are marked with yellow road signs. Motorways (Autobahnen) are marked with blue road signs. Some stretches of motorway have variable speed limits depending on weather and road conditions; others have no enforced speed limit at all. German drivers therefore tend to zoom along at speeds of up to 200 km/h (125 mph).

Berlin is surrounded by a circular motorway called the Berliner Ring, which has numerous clearly signposted exits into the city centre.

Drivers must carry their passport and insurance documentation with them at all times if driving a foreign-registered vehicle in Germany.

Contact **ADAC Auto Assistance** in the event of a vehicle breakdown, accident, or if you need assistance on the road.

ADAC Auto Assistance
🔲 adac.de

Car Rental

You must be 21 or over and have held a valid driver's licence for at least a year to rent a car in Germany. By law, drivers aged 21–2 must purchase a Collision Damage Waiver (CDW). Drivers under the age of 25 may incur a young-driver surcharge.

Driving in Berlin

The city is relatively straightforward to navigate by car; road layouts are clear and streets are well signposted. Parking is also relatively cheap when compared to other major European cities.

If you are flying to Berlin and staying within the metro area, the most efficient way to travel is by public transport. There are also park-and-ride facilities on the outskirts of the city, which are a lot cheaper than inner-city parking.

When driving in the city, beware of cyclists and trams. Trams take precedence; take care when turning; and allow cyclists right of way.

Rules of the Road

Drive on the right. Unless otherwise signposted, vehicles coming from the right have priority.

At all times, drivers must carry a valid driver's licence, registration and insurance documents. Seatbelts are compulsory in a hired car, lights must be used in tunnels and the use of a mobile phone while driving is prohibited, with the exception of a hands-free system. The drink-drive limit (p277) is strictly enforced.

All drivers must have third-party insurance (*Haftpflichtversicherung*) – it is the minimum insurance requirement in Germany. Also compulsory is an environmental badge for vehicles driving within environmental green zones known as **Umweltzonen**. The majority of downtown Berlin is classified as an *Umweltzone*. Certification can be purchased online.

Umweltzonen
🔲 umwelt-plakette.de

Cycling

Berlin is generally considered a bike-friendly city, with many designated cycle lanes and traffic lights at intersections.

Should you get tired of pedalling, bicycles can be taken on the U-Bahn, S-Bahn and trams, but they are prohibited on buses, except night buses, which can carry up to two at the driver's discretion. For all public transport an additional bicycle (*Fahrrad*) ticket is required.

Bicycle Hire

Deutsche Bahn operates an excellent public bicycle system called **Call a Bike**. Bikes can be picked up from train stations and major intersections. They can be dropped off at any of the Call a Bike stations conveniently dotted throughout the city.

To rent a Call a Bike, you must register by providing your credit card details. On the basic tariff, a €1 unlock fee is applied to each ride. The first 15 minutes cost €1 and a maximum fee of €9 is charged per day. Additional fees are applied if bikes are not returned to train stations.

You can also hire bikes at many cycling shops for similar or cheaper rates; one of the most reliable is **Fahrradstation**. Be aware that drink-drive limits (*p277*) also apply to cyclists.

Fahrradstation
🔲 fahrradstation.com
Call a Bike
🔲 callabike.de

Bicycle Safety

Cyclists should always ride on the right. If you are unsure or unsteady, it is a good idea to practise in one of the many inner-city parks before taking to the city roads. If in doubt, dismount and walk with your bicycle: many cyclists prefer to cross busy junctions on foot; if you do so, switch to the pedestrian section of the crossing. Beware of tram tracks; always try to cross them at an angle to avoid slipping or getting the bicycle wheels stuck.

For your own safety, do not walk with your bike in a bike lane or cycle on pavements, on the left side of the road, in pedestrian zones or in the dark without lights. The locals usually don't bother, but wearing a helmet is recommended.

Walking

Berlin is one of the largest cities in Europe. Despite covering such a vast area, visitors will be pleasantly surprised to find that most of the major sights are located within a relatively small, mostly walkable area.

Organized walking tours are a popular option for those looking to explore the city by foot. **Sandemans New Europe** provide free daily walking tours of the city's highlights, taking in major sights such as the Holocaust Memorial, Museumsinsel, Checkpoint Charlie, the Berlin Wall and the Brandenburg Gate. It is encouraged to tip the tour guide once the tour is over. Many other tour providers offer tours on specific themes, from LGBTQ+ history to street art.

Sandemans New Europe
🔲 neweuropetours.eu

PRACTICAL
INFORMATION

A little local know-how goes a long way in Berlin. Here you will find all the essential advice and information you will need during your stay.

AT A GLANCE

EMERGENCY NUMBERS

GENERAL EMERGENCY

112

POLICE

110

TIME ZONE
CET/CEST
Central European
Summer Time (CEST)
is observed Mar–Oct.

TAP WATER
Unless otherwise
stated, tap water
in Germany is safe
to drink.

WEBSITES AND APPS
Visit Berlin
    The city's official tourist information
    website contains a wealth of
    information (visitberlin.de)
accessBerlin
    A free app detailing the most accessible
    routes around the city
BVG FahrInfo Plus
    Live departures and travel updates from
    the city's local transport operator BVG
Berlin Wall Art
    This free app reconstructs the Iron
    Curtain with the last and most complete
    photo collection of the Berlin Wall.

Personal Security

Berlin is a relatively safe city, but as in most cities, use common sense. Pick-pocketing is common, particularly on crowded buses and in popular tourist areas. Contact your embassy if your passport has been stolen, or in the event of a serious crime or accident.

Germans, and Berliners in particular, are generally accepting of all people, regardless of their race, gender or sexuality. Homosexuality was officially legalized in Germany in 1994. Despite all the freedoms that the LGBTQ+ community enjoy in Berlin, acceptance is not always a given. If you do at any point feel unsafe, the **Safe Space Alliance** pinpoints your nearest place of refuge. The **Maneo** emergency hotline run by **Mann-O-Meter** supports victims of homophobic behaviour. **Lesbenberatung** is a lesbian safe space that offers help, advice and counselling for women, girls and transgender people.
Lesbenberatung
W esbenberatung-berlin.de
Maneo
C (030) 216 33 36
W maneo.de
Mann-O-Meter
W mann-o-meter.de
Safe Space Alliance
W safespacealliance.com

Health

Berlin is known for its world-class health service. EU and UK citizens can receive emergency medical treatment in Germany free of charge (p271), but you may have to pay upfront for medical treatment and reclaim on your insurance later. For other visitors, payment of medical expenses is the patient's responsibility. It is therefore important to arrange comprehensive medical insurance before travelling (p271).

For minor ailments go to a pharmacy (Apotheke). Details of the nearest 24-hour service (Notdienst) are posted in all pharmacy windows and on the **Apothekerkammer** website.
Apothekerkammer
W akberlin.de

Smoking, Alcohol and Drugs

Germany has a smoking ban in all public places, including bars, cafés, restaurants and hotels. Many establishments circumvent these laws by naming themselves a *Raucherkneipe*, or smoking pub. Since 2024, the possession of up to 25 grams of cannabis is legal for adults but it remains illegal to purchase or sell cannabis. The possession of other narcotics is strictly prohibited and could result in prosecution and a prison sentence.

Unless stated otherwise, it is permitted to drink alcohol on the streets and in public parks and gardens. Germany has a strict limit of 0.05 per cent BAC (blood alcohol content) for drivers.

ID

There is no requirement for visitors to carry ID, but in the event of a routine check you may be asked to show your passport. If you don't have it with you, the police may escort you to wherever your passport is being kept.

Local Customs

Germany has strict laws on hate speech and symbols linked to Adolf Hitler and Nazism. Disrespectful behaviour in public places can warrant a fine, or even lead to prosecution. Be respectful when visiting Berlin's historical sights and monuments. Pay attention to signage indicating when photos aren't allowed.

Visiting Places of Worship

Dress respectfully: cover your torso, upper arms and knees.

Responsible Tourism

The climate crisis is having an impact on Berlin with rising temperatures and extreme weather more and more frequent. Do your bit by using a reusable water bottle and recycling other bottles through the nation-wide Pfand (deposit return) system. Enjoy park barbecues in designated areas and check signage during warmer months, when droughts are common and the risk of forest fires increases. Failure to observe smoking and fire bans can result in fines up to €50,000.

Mobile Phones and Wi-Fi

Free Wi-Fi hotspots are widely available in Berlin's city centre. Cafés and restaurants are usually happy to permit the use of their Wi-Fi on the condition that you make a purchase.

Visitors travelling to Berlin with EU tariffs will be able to use their devices abroad without being affected by data roaming charges. This means that you pay the same rates as you would at home.

Post

German post offices and post boxes are usually fairly easy to spot with their distinctive yellow *Deutsche Post* signs.

Stamps (*Briefmarken*) can be bought in post offices, newsagents, tobacconists and most major supermarkets. There are usually self-service stamp machines conveniently placed outside post offices.

Taxes and Refunds

VAT is 19% in Germany. Non-EU residents are entitled to a tax refund subject to certain conditions. In order to do this, you must request a tax receipt and export papers (*Ausfuhrbescheinigung*) when you purchase your goods. When leaving the country, present these papers, along with the receipt and your ID, at customs to receive your refund.

Discount Cards

The **Berlin Welcome Card** offers free entry to 30 major tourist attractions and discounted entry for nearly 200 more. It also includes unlimited use of public transport during your trip.

With the **Berlin Pass**, visitors get free entry to over 60 attractions, tours and museums and the option of an integrated travel card.

Save up to 30% on the city's top 10 tourist attractions and enjoy unlimited free travel on public transport with the **Berlin City Tour Card**.

Berlin City Tour Card
W citytourcard.com
Berlin Pass
W berlinpass.com
Berlin Welcome Card
W berlin-welcomecard.de

INDEX

Index

PHRASE BOOK

IN AN EMERGENCY

Where is the telephone?	Wo ist das telefon?	voh ist duss tele-fon?
Help!	Hilfe!	hilf-uh
Please call a doctor	Bitte rufen Sie einen Arzt	bitt-uh roof'n zee ine-en artst
Please call the police	Bitte rufen Sie die Polizei	bitt-uh roof'n zee dee poli-tsy
Please call the fire brigade	Bitte rufen Sie die Feuerwehr	bitt-uh roof'n zee dee foyer-vayr
Stop!	Halt!	hult

COMMUNICATION ESSENTIALS

Yes	Ja	yah
No	Nein	nine
Please	Bitte	bitt-uh
Thank you	Danke	dunk-uh
Excuse me	Verzeihung	fair-tsy-hoong
Hello (good day)	Guten Tag	goot-en tahk
Goodbye	Auf Wiedersehen	owf-veed-er-zay-ern
Good evening	Guten Abend	goot'n ah b'nt
Good night	Gute Nacht	goot-uh nukht
Until tomorrow	Bis morgen	biss morg'n
See you	Tschüss	chooss
What is that?	Was ist das?	voss ist duss
Why?	Warum?	var-room
Where?	Wo?	voh
When?	Wann?	vunn
today	heute	hoyt-uh
tomorrow	morgen	morg'n
month	Monat	mohn-aht
night	Nacht	nukht
afternoon	Nachmittag	nahkh-mit-tahk
morning	Morgen	morg'n
year	Jahr	yar
there	dort	dort
here	hier	hear
week	Woche	vokh-uh
yesterday	gestern	gest'n
evening	Abend	ah b'nt

USEFUL PHRASES

How are you? (informal)	Wie geht's?	vee gayts
Fine, thanks	Danke, es geht mir gut	dunk-uh, es gayt meer goot
Until later	Bis später	biss shpay-ter
Where is/are?	Wo ist/sind...?	voh ist/sind
How far is it to...?	Wie weit ist es...?	vee vite ist ess
Do you speak English?	Sprechen Sie Englisch?	shpresh'n zee eng-glish
I don't understand	Ich verstehe nicht	ish fair-shtay-uh nisht
Could you speak more slowly?	Könnten Sie langsamer sprechen?	kurnt-en zee lung-zam-er shpresh'n

USEFUL WORDS

large	gross	grohss
small	klein	kline
hot	heiss	hyce
cold	kalt	kult
good	gut	goot
bad	böse/schlecht	burss-uh/shlesht
open	geöffnet	g'urff-nett
closed	geschlossen	g'shloss'n
left	links	links
right	rechts	reshts
straight ahead	geradeaus	g'rah-der-owss

MAKING A TELEPHONE CALL

I would like to make a phone call	Ich möchte telefonieren	ish mer-shtuh tel-e-fon-eer'n
I'll try again later	Ich versuche es später noch einmal	ish fair-zookh-uh es shpay-ter nokh ine-mull
Can I leave a message?	Kann ich eine Nachricht hinterlassen?	kan ish ine-uh nakh-risht hint-er-lahss-en
answer phone	Anrufbeantworter	an-roof-be-ahnt-vort-er
telephone card	Telefonkarte	tel-e-fohn-kart-uh
receiver	Hörer	hur-er
mobile	Handy	han-dee
engaged (busy)	besetzt	b'zetst
wrong number	Falsche Verbindung	falsh-uh fair-bin-doong

SIGHTSEEING

library	Bibliothek	bib-leo-tek
entrance ticket	Eintrittskarte	ine-tritz-kart-uh
cemetery	Friedhof	freed-hofe
train station	Bahnhof	barn-hofe
gallery	Galerie	gall-er-ree
information	Auskunft	owss-koonft
church	Kirche	keersh-uh
garden	Garten	gart'n
palace/castle	Palast/Schloss	pallast/shloss
place (square)	Platz	plats
bus stop	Haltestelle	hal-te-shtel-uh
national holiday	Nationalfeiertag	nats-yon-ahl-fire-tahk
theatre	Theater	tay-aht-er
free admission	Eintritt frei	ine-tritt fry

SHOPPING

Do you have/ Is there...?	Gibt es...?	geept ess
How much does it cost?	Was kostet das?	voss kost't duss
When do you open/ close?	Wann öffnen Sie? schliessen Sie?	vunn off'n zee shlees'n zee
this	das	duss
expensive	teuer	toy-er
cheap	preiswert	price-vurt
size	Grösse	gruhs-uh
number	Nummer	noom-er
colour	Farbe	farb-uh
brown	braun	brown
black	schwarz	shvarts
red	rot	roht
blue	blau	blau
green	grün	groon
yellow	gelb	gelp

TYPES OF SHOP

antique shop	Antiquariat	antik-var-yat
chemist (pharmacy)	Apotheke	appo-tay-kuh
bank	Bank	bunk
market	Markt	markt
travel agency	Reisebüro	rye-zer-boo-roe
department store	Warenhaus	vahr'n-hows
chemist's/ drugstore	Drogerie	droog-er-ree
hairdresser	Friseur	freezz-er
newspaper kiosk	Zeitungskiosk	tsytoongs-kee-osk
bookshop	Buchhandlung	bookh-hant-loong
bakery	Bäckerei	beck-er-eye
post office	Post	posst
shop/store	Geschäft/Laden	gush-eft/lard'n

film processing shop	Fotogeschäft	fo-to-gush-**eft**
self-service shop	**Selbstbedienungs-laden**	selpst-bed-**ee**-nungs-lard'n
shoe shop	**Schuhladen**	shoo-**lard**'n
clothes shop	**Kleiderladen/Boutique**	klyder-lard'n boo-**teek**-uh
food shop	**Lebensmittel-geschäft**	**lay**-bens-mittel-gush-eft
glass, porcelain	**Glas, Porzellan**	glars, port-sell-ahn

STAYING IN A HOTEL

Do you have any vacancies?	**Haben Sie noch Zimmer frei?**	harb'n zee nokh tsimm-er-fry
with twin beds?	**mit zwei Betten?**	mitt tsvy bett'n
with a double bed?	**mit einem Doppelbett?**	mitt ine'm dopp'l-bet
with a bath?	**mit Bad?**	mitt bart
with a shower?	**mit Dusche?**	mitt doosh-uh
I have a reservation	**Ich habe eine Reservierung**	ish harb-uh ine-uh rez-er-**veer**-oong
key	**Schlüssel**	shlooss'l
porter	**Pförtner**	pfert-ner

EATING OUT

Do you have a table for...?	**Haben Sie einen Tisch für...?**	harb'n zee tish foor
I would like to reserve a table	**Ich möchte eine Reservierung machen**	ish **mer**-shtuh ine-uh rezer-**veer**-oong makh'n
I'm a vegetarian	**Ich bin Vegetarier**	ish bin vegg-er-**tah**-ree-er
Waiter!	**Herr Ober!**	hair **oh**-bare!
The bill (check), please	**Die Rechnung, bitte**	dee **resh**-noong bitt-uh
breakfast	**Frühstück**	froo-shtock
lunch	**Mittagessen**	mit-targ-ess'n
dinner	**Abendessen**	arb'nt-ess'n
bottle	**Flasche**	flush-uh
dish of the day	**Tagesgericht**	tahg-es-gur-isht
main dish	**Hauptgericht**	howpt-gur-isht
dessert	**Nachtisch**	nahkh-tish
cup	**Tasse**	tass-uh
wine list	**Weinkarte**	vine-kart-uh
tankard	**Krug**	khroog
glass	**Glas**	glars
spoon	**Löffel**	lerff'l
teaspoon	**Teelöffel**	tay-lerff'l
tip	**Trinkgeld**	trink-gelt
knife	**Messer**	mess-er
starter (appetizer)	**Vorspeise**	for-shpize-uh
the bill	**Rechnung**	resh-noong
plate	**Teller**	tell-er
fork	**Gabel**	gahb'l

MENU DECODER

Aal	**arl**	eel
Apfel	**upf'l**	apple
Apfelschorle	**upf'l-shoorl-uh**	apple juice with sparkling mineral water
Apfelsine	**upf'l-seen-uh**	orange
Aprikose	**upri-kawz-uh**	apricot
Artischocke	**arti-shokh-uh-**	artichoke
Aubergine (eggplant)	**or-ber-jeen-uh**	aubergine
Banane	**bar-narn-uh**	banana
Beefsteak	**beef-stayk**	steak
Bier	**beer**	beer
Bockwurst	**bokh-voorst**	a type of sausage
Bohnensuppe	**burn-en-zoop-uh**	bean soup

Branntwein	brant-vine	spirits
Bratkartoffeln	brat-kar-toff'ln	fried potatoes
Bratwurst	brat-voorst	fried sausage
Brot	brot	bread
Brötchen	bret-tchen	bread roll
Brühe	bruh-uh	broth
Butter	**boot**-ter	butter
Champignon	**shum**-pin-yong	mushroom
Currywurst	kha-ree-voorst	sausage with curry sauce
Dill	**dill**	dill
Ei	**eye**	egg
Eis	**ice**	ice/ice cream
Ente	**ent**-uh	duck
Erdbeeren	ayrt-**beer**'n	strawberries
Fisch	**fish**	fish
Forelle	for-**ell**-uh	trout
Frikadelle	Frika-dayl-uh	rissole/hamburger
Gans	ganns	goose
Garnele	**gar**-nayl-uh	prawn/shrimp
gebraten	g'**braat**'n	fried
gegrillt	g'**grilt**	grilled
gekocht	g'**kokht**	boiled
geräuchert	g'**rowk**-ert	smoked
Geflügel	g'**floog**'l	poultry
Gemüse	g'**mooz**-uh	vegetables
Grütze	**grurt**-ser	groats, gruel
Gulasch	**goo**-lush	goulash
Gurke	**goork**-uh	gherkin
Hammelbraten	hamm'l-**braat**'n	roast mutton
Hähnchen	**haynsh**'n	chicken
Hering	**hair**-ing	herring
Himbeeren	him-beer'n	raspberries
Honig	**hoe**-nikh	honey
Kaffee	kaf-**fay**	coffee
Kalbfleisch	kalp-flysh	veal
Kaninchen	ka-**neensh**'n	rabbit
Karpfen	**karpf**'n	carp
Kartoffelpüree	kar-toff'l-poor-ay	mashed potatoes
Käse	**kayz**-uh	cheese
Kaviar	**kar**-vee-ar	caviar
Knoblauch	k'nob-lowkh	garlic
Knödel	k'**nerd**'l	noodle
Kohl	**koal**	cabbage
Kopfsalat	**kopf**-zal-aat	lettuce
Krebs	**krayps**	crab
Kuchen	**kookh**'n	cake
Lachs	**lahkhs**	salmon
Leber	**lay**-ber	liver
mariniert	mari-neert	marinated
Marmelade	marmer-**lard**-uh	marmalade, jam
Meerrettich	may-re-tish	horseradish
Milch	**milsh**	milk
Mineralwasser	minn-er-**arl**-vuss-er	mineral water
Möhre	**mer**-uh	carrot
Nuss	**nooss**	nut
Öl	**erl**	oil
Olive	o-**leev**-uh	olive
Petersilie	payt-er-**zee**-li-uh	parsley
Pfeffer	**pfeff**-er	pepper
Pfirsich	**pfir**-zish	peach
Pflaumen	**pflow**-men	plum
Pommes frites	pomm-**fritt**	chips/French fries
Quark	kvark	soft cheese
Radieschen	ra-**deesh**'n	radish
Rinderbraten	**rind**-er-brat'n	joint of beef
Rinderroulade	**rind**-er-roo-lard-uh	beef olive
Rindfleisch	**rint**-flysh	beef
Rippchen	**rip**-sh'n	cured pork rib
Rotkohl	roht-koal	red cabbage
Rüben	rhoob'n	turnip
Rührei	**rhoo**-er-eye	scrambled eggs

Saft	**zuft**	*juice*
Salat	*zal-aat*	*salad*
Salz	**zults**	*salt*
Salzkartoffeln	*zults-kar-toff'l*	*boiled potatoes*
Sauerkirschen	*zow-er-**keersh'n***	*cherries*
Sauerkraut	*zow-er-krowt*	*sauerkraut*
Sekt	**zekt**	*sparkling wine*
Senf	**zenf**	*mustard*
scharf	*sharf*	*spicy*
Schaschlik	*shash-lik*	*kebab*
Schlagsahne	*shlahgg-zarn-uh*	*whipped cream*
Schnittlauch	*shnit-lowhkh*	*chives*
Schnitzel	**shnitz'l**	*veal or pork cutlet*
Schweinefleisch	**shvine**-*flysh*	*pork*
Spargel	**sparg'l**	*asparagus*
Spiegelei	*shpeeg'l-eye*	*fried egg*
Spinat	*shpin-art*	*spinach*
Tee	*tay*	*tea*
Tomate	*tom-art-uh*	*tomato*
Wassermelone	*vuss-er-me-lohn-uh*	*watermelon*
Wein	*vine*	*wine*
Weintrauben	*vine-trowb'n*	*grapes*
Wiener Würstchen	*veen-er voorst-sh'n*	*frankfurter*
Zander	*tsan-der*	*pike-perch*
Zitrone	*tsi-trohn-uh*	*lemon*
Zucker	**tsook-**er	*sugar*
Zwieback	*tsvee-bak*	*rusk*
Zwiebel	**tsvee**b'l	*onion*

NUMBERS

0	**null**	*nool*
1	**eins**	*eye'ns*
2	**zwei**	*tsvy*
3	**drei**	*dry*
4	**vier**	*feer*
5	**fünf**	*foonf*
6	**sechs**	*zex*
7	**sieben**	*zeeb'n*
8	**acht**	*uhkht*
9	**neun**	*noyn*
10	**zehn**	*tsayn*
11	**elf**	*elf*
12	**zwölf**	*tserlf*
13	**dreizehn**	*dry-tsayn*
14	**vierzehn**	*feer-tsayn*
15	**fünfzehn**	*foonf-tsayn*
16	**sechzehn**	*zex-tsayn*
17	**siebzehn**	*zeep-tsayn*
18	**achtzehn**	*uhkht-tsayn*
19	**neunzehn**	*noyn-tsayn*
20	**zwanzig**	*tsvunn-tsig*
21	**einundzwanzig**	*ine-oont-tsvunn-tsig*
30	**dreissig**	*dry-sig*
40	**vierzig**	*feer-sig*
50	**fünfzig**	*foonf-tsig*
60	**sechzig**	*zex-tsig*
70	**siebzig**	*zeep-tsig*
80	**achtzig**	*uhkht-tsig*
90	**neunzig**	*noyn-tsig*
100	**hundert**	*hoond't*
1,000	**tausend**	*towz'nt*
1,000,000	**eine Million**	*ine-uh mill-yon*

TIME

one minute	**eine Minute**	*ine-uh min-oot-uh*
one hour	**eine Stunde**	*ine-uh shtoond-uh*
half an hour	**eine halbe Stunde**	*ine-uh hullb-uh shtoond-uh*
Monday	**Montag**	*mohn-targ*
Tuesday	**Dienstag**	*deens-targ*
Wednesday	**Mittwoch**	*mitt-vokh*
Thursday	**Donnerstag**	*donn-ers-targ*
Friday	**Freitag**	*fry-targ*
Saturday	**Samstag/ Sonnabend**	*zums-targ / zonn-ah-bent*
Sunday	**Sonntag**	*zon-targ*
January	**Januar**	*yan-ooar*
February	**Februar**	*fay-brooar*
March	**März**	*mairts*
April	**April**	*april*
May	**Mai**	*my*
June	**Juni**	*yoo-ni*
July	**Juli**	*yoo-lee*
August	**August**	*ow-**goost***
September	**September**	*zep-**tem-**ber*
October	**Oktober**	*ok-toh-ber*
November	**November**	*no-**vem**-ber*
December	**Dezember**	*day-**tsem**-ber*
spring	**Frühling**	*froo-ling*
summer	**Sommer**	*zomm-er*
autumn (fall)	**Herbst**	*hairpst*
winter	**Winter**	*vint-er*

ACKNOWLEDGMENTS

DK would like to thank the following for their contribution to the previous edition: Małgorzata Omilanowska, Zoe Ross, Paul Sullivan

The publisher would like to thank the following for their kind permission to reproduce their photographs:

Key: a-above; b-below/bottom; c-centre; f-far; l-left; r-right; t-top

123RF.com: Shanti Hesse 13cr; iloveotto 10-1b, 31tr, 150-1t; Anton Ivanov 260-1; lauradibias 19t, 142-3; marina99 220-1; Jaroslav Moravcik 195tl; Karl-Heinz Spremberg 12-3b, 240-1b; Lothar Steine 44tl; Anibal Trejo 132-3t; T.W. van Urk 202t; Velislava Yovcheva 257cra;

akg-images: Album / Prisma / Antonin Mercie *Gloria Victis* (1874) 67cra, Brazalete de bronce. Siglo III d. 86crb.

Alamy Stock Photo: 500px 60-1; Adam Eastland Art + Architecture 125tl; Adam Eastland 90–91, 93b; A Media Press 86clb; zAF Archive 264br; Agencja Fotograficzna Caro 58-9t, / Andreas Teich 32bl, / Muhs 97br; Artexplorer 158br; Berlin-Zeitgeist 182cla; Walter Bibikow 122; Bildagentur-online / Schoening 193bl, 264t; bilwissedition Ltd. & Co. KG 245br; Eden Breitz 40b, 41tl, 47tl, 140bl, 184cra, 237t; Bridgeman Images 58tl; Chronicle 57bc, 157bc; Peter Delius 227tr; Digital-Fotofusion Gallery 37cl; dpa picture alliance 32-3t, 45tr, 58br, 147tr, / Britta Pedersen 47cl, / Bernd Settnik 253bl; CTK / Martin Weiser 169t; Eva Agata Draze 33cl; Adam Eastland 34-5b, 159, 161t, 182-3b, 226cra, 226-7b, 244-5tc, Eddy Galeotti 157cr; Eden Breitz 98, 135br; Edward Krupa 173clb; EyeEm / Oliver Byunggyu Woo 36-7t; Alexandre Fagundes 250t; Falkensteinfoto 55tr; frantic 12t; Stephane Gautier 106bl; Scott Goodno 109tl; hanohikirf 184br; Andrew Hasson 189tl; hemis.fr / Eric Planchard 26bl, René Mattes 158clb; Juergen Henkelmann 244bl; Historical image collection by Bildagentur-online 54t; Peter Horree 56bc, 92bl, 125cra, 164-5t; 59bl; 183tl, / Helmut Baar 228bl; INTERFOTO 56cr; Masterpics 30tl, 160br; Iain Masterton 38-9t, 137t, 166b, 183tr, 185, 192t, 248cra, / Karl Schmidt-Rottluff © DACS 2018 30-1b, / Bernhard Heiliger © DACS 2018 *Tor der Kugel* at Kunsthaus Dahlem 246t; imageBROKER / Karl-Heinz Spremberg 8clb, imageBROKER / Siegfried Grassegger 35br; Image Professionals GmbH / Spörl, Lukas 20cb, 196-7; Imago 46tl; Ingo Jezierski 230cla; Juergen Henkelmann Photography 90cb; Lothar Steiner 96-97t; mauritius images GmbH / Torsten Elger 115br; Michael Brooks 157br; Niday Picture Library 54br; PAINTING 158cb; Paul Brown 173b; Pictorial Press Ltd 262cra; Prisma Archivo 90cra; Ricardo Ribas 213; Sergi Reboredo 141tl; Tetiana Tuchyk 190-91; TravelCollection / Inga Wandinger 216bl; travelpix 149tr; travelstock44.de / Juergen Held 8cl, 20tl, 38-9b, 178-9, 188b; United Archives 55tl; Urbanmyth 174-75t; UtCon Collection 160tl; Lucas Vallecillos 28-9t, 48-9t; Scott Wilson 35cla; Julie g Woodhouse 29crb, 67bl, 158cra, 177br; World History Archive 56-7, 58bc, 157clb.

AWL Images: Sabine Lubenow 4, 17tl, 82-3.

Berliner Ensemble: Lovis Ostenrick 129br.

Berliner Fernsehturm: Marco Wendt 24t.

BerlinerFestspiele: Camille Blake 47br; Mutesouvenir / Kai Bienert 46b; MaerzMusik / Camille Blake 53tl.

Berlinische Galerie / BG Gebäude: © Foto: Nina Straßgütl 190cla.

Bridgeman Images: Berlinische Galerie / Otto Dix © DACS 2018 *The Poet Iwar von Lücken* (1926) 31br.

C/O Berlin: 205t.

DDR Museum: 24br.

Depositphotos Inc: chrissi 225cb; claudiodivizia 247crb; Elnur 29cla; Konrad Kerker 21, 208-9; S Kohl 212br; philipus 217t; whatslove 262b.

Dorling Kindersley: Dorota and Mariusz Jarymowicz 127tr, 130bc, 215br.

Dreamstime.com: 22tomtom 108bl; Andersastphoto 73br; Andreykr 239tr; Andrey Andronov 253crb; Anticiclo 111tl; Anyaivanova 53br; Axel Lauer 52cl; Michal Bednarek 75t; Blitzkoenig 265br; Vladimir Bondarenco 12clb; Boris Breytman 109cr, 251tr; Carolannefreeling 110b; Cbechinie 42bl; Claudiodivizia 22bl, 86cr, 124–5b; Creativeimpression 170cb; Dedi57 256bl; Delstudio 146cra; Demerzel21 81cra, 133br; Draghicich 232b; Eddygaleotti 76-7t, 123ca; Eldadcarin 234tl; Elenaburn 117tl; Elenasfotos 263tl, 266tr; Alexandre Fagundes De Fagundes 86cra, 212cla; Alessandro Flore 89br; Franz1212 191br; Gekaskr 16, 62-3; Guadapad 45cla; Hanohiki 172tr; Ixuskmitl 106tr; Jdm512 28-9b; Marek Jelinek 230t; Antonios Karvelas 219br; Katatonia82 167tr, 214t; Sergey Kelin 50-51b; Vassiliy Kochetkov 229t; Patryk Kosmider 218cla; Oleksandr Kovalenko 26cr; Ivan Kravtsov 253clb; Anna Krivitskaia 86bc; Laudibi 256tr; Markwaters 53al, 139tr, 148tr, 241tr; Vasilii Maslak 114tr; Meinzahn 18, 24cr, 118-9, 266-7b; Merlindo 68br; Mijeshots 69t; Minnystock 6-7b, 107, 170-1b; Jaroslav Moravcik 89cr, 93tr, 187b; Moskwa 258tl; Oanap24 147cla; Sean Pavone 234-5t; Oleksandr Prykhodko 49br; Sergey Kohl 52bl; Plotnikov 257t, 258-9b; Radiokafka 224c; Rphstock 225tl; Rumifaz 70bl; Jozef Sedmak 109br; 200cra; Snake81 255tl; Stefan Baum 204bl; Tomas1111 94t, 112tl; Tupungato 78tl, 134-5t; T.w. Van Urk 101tl; Noppasin Wongchum 100b; Yorgy67 212clb; Velislava Yovcheva 255cra; Yuryz 236bl.

Festival of Lights: Frank Hermann 89tr, Morten Carlsson 52br.

Gedenkstätte Berlin-Hohenschönhausen: Thomas Weber 231b.

Georg Kolbe Museum; Berlin: Enric Duch 238t.

Getty Images: age fotostock / Reiner Elsen 149cra; Alinari Archives 55bc; Jon Arnold 8-9b; Adam Berry 26crb; Estate of Emil Bieber / Klaus Niermann 56tl; Bloomberg / Jochen Eckel 37crb; Corbis Documentary / Ruggero Vanni 31cla; Christian Marquardt 32br; DEA / Biblioteca Ambrosiana 57bl; Sean Gallup 43b; Benjamin Matthijs Lichtwerk 252tr; The LIFE Picture Collection / Hugo Jaeger 58cla; Moment Open / Federica Gentile 146-7b; Popperfoto / James Jarche 58cr; ullstein bild 55cra, 56br, 57tr, / Heilke Heller 123bc, / Koch 254bl; ullstein bild / Rolf Schulten 156br; Universal History Archive 54bc.

Getty Images / iStock: _ultraforma_ 51cl; Antonistock 24clb; benedek 51tr; Lutz Berlemont-Bernard 242-3; bluejayphoto 163bl; E+ / mbbirdy 19bl, 152-3; German Select / Franziska Krug 42-43t; Giflishtih 138-9b; golero 13t; holgs 33bc, 52cr, 200bl, 201; hsvrs 48bl; kavunchik 72t; Jonny Kristoffersson 40tl; jotily 268-69; JJFarquitectos 22t; lechatnoir 11br, 41br; lesart777 116bl; lucamato 194bl; MarioGuti 41cl, 164bl; matthewleesdixon 156-57t; Maxlevoyou 192br; Max Ozerov 52cra; mije_shots 17cb, 102; mikkelwilliam 59br; Mlenny 13br; Nikada 22cr, 59tr, 78-9b, 130-1t, 163tr; Leonardo Patrizi 43cla; querbeet 44-5b, 99bl; RomanBabakin 35t; Terroa 39cla; typo-graphics 49crb; VFKA 22crb; Ziutograf 90cl.

Jewish Museum Berlin: Yves Sucksdroff 50tl.

Museum fur Kommunikation Berlin: Michael Ehrhart 34tl.

Museum fur Naturkunde: Carola Radk 126b.

Courtesy Peres Projects; Berlin: Matthias Kolb 148b.

Pierre Boulez Salle: Volker Kreidler 70-1.

Robert Harding Picture Library: Stefan Huwiler 74br; Yadid Levy 10cla.

Salt n Bone: 39crb.

Sammlung Boros: Installationsansicht mit Arbeiten von Michel Majerus / © NOSHE 128-9t
.
Science Center Spectrum Stiftung Deutsches Technikmuseum Berlin: Clemens Kirchner 186tr.

MIX
Paper | Supporting responsible forestry
FSC™ C018179
www.fsc.org

A NOTE FROM DK

The rate at which the world is changing is constantly keeping the DK travel team on our toes. While we've worked hard to ensure that this edition of Berlin is accurate and up-to-date, we know that opening hours alter, standards shift, prices fluctuate, places close and new ones pop up in their stead. So, if you notice we've got something wrong or left something out, we want to hear about it. Please get in touch at travelguides@dk.com

---

Penguin Random House

This edition updated by
Contributors Petra Falkenberg, Alexander Rennie
Senior Editors Dipika Dasgupta, Keith Drew
Senior Designers Laura O'Brien, Stuti Tiwari
Project Editor Sarah Allen
Assistant Art Editor Divyanshi Shreyaskar
Proofreader Stephanie Smith
Indexer Helen Peters
Assistant Picture Research Administrator Manpreet Kaur
Senior Picture Researcher Nishwan Rasool
Deputy Manager, Picture Research Virien Chopra
Publishing Assistant Simona Velikova
Jacket Designers Laura O'Brien, Divyanshi Shreyaskar
Senior Cartographer Mohammad Hassan
Cartography Manager Suresh Kumar
DTP Designer Rohit Rojal
Production Controller Kariss Ainsworth
Deputy Managing Editor Dharini Ganesh
Managing Editors Beverly Smart, Hollie Teague
Managing Art Editor Gemma Doyle
Senior Managing Art Editor Priyanka Thakur
Art Director Maxine Pedliham
Publishing Director Georgina Dee

First edition 2000

Published in Great Britain by
Dorling Kindersley Limited,
20 Vauxhall Bridge Road,
London SW1V 2SA

The authorised representative in the EEA is
Dorling Kindersley Verlag GmbH. Arnulfstr.
124, 80636 Munich, Germany

Published in the United States by DK Publishing,
1745 Broadway, 20th Floor, New York, NY 10019, USA

Copyright © 2000, 2025 Dorling Kindersley Limited
A Penguin Random House Company
24 25 26 27 10 9 8 7 6 5 4 3 2 1

A CIP catalogue record for this book
is available from the British Library.

A catalogue record for this book is available
from the Library of Congress.

ISSN: 1544 1554
ISBN: 978 0 2417 1063 0

Printed and bound in China

www.dk.com